SUA SPONTE

SUA SPONTE

The Forging of a Modern American Ranger

DICK COUCH

BERKLEY CALIBER, NEW YORK

3?/6399

BERKLEY BOOKS
Published by the Penguin Group
Penguin Group (USA) Inc.
375 Hudson Street, New York, New York 10014, USA
Penguin Group (Canada), 90 Eglinton Avenue East, Suite 700, Toronto, Ontario M4P 2Y3, Canada
(a division of Pearson Penguin Canada Inc.) • Penguin Books Ltd., 80 Strand, London WC2R 0RL,
England • Penguin Group Ireland, 25 St. Stephen's Green, Dublin 2, Ireland (a division of Penguin
Books Ltd.) • Penguin Group (Australia), 250 Camberwell Road, Camberwell, Victoria 3124, Australia
(a division of Pearson Australia Group Pty. Ltd.) • Penguin Books India Pvt. Ltd., 11 Community
Centre, Panchsheel Park, New Delhi—110 017, India • Penguin Group (NZ), 67 Apollo Drive,
Rosedale, Auckland 0632, New Zealand (a division of Pearson New Zealand Ltd.) • Penguin Books
(South Africa) (Pty.) Ltd., 24 Sturdee Avenue, Rosebank, Johannesburg 2196, South Africa

Penguin Books Ltd., Registered Offices: 80 Strand, London WC2R 0RL, England

This book is an original publication of The Berkley Publishing Group.

The publisher does not have any control over and does not assume any responsibility
for author or third-party websites or their content.

FIRST EDITION: July 2012

Library of Congress Cataloging-in-Publication Data

Couch, Dick, date.
Sua sponte : the forging of a modern American Ranger / Dick Couch.—1st ed.
p. cm.
ISBN 978-0-425-24758-7
1. United States. Army. Ranger Regiment, 75th. 2. United States. Army. Ranger Regiment,
75th—Recruiting, enlistment, etc. 3. United States. Army—Commando troops—Training of.
4. Special forces (Military science)—United States. I. Title. II. Title:
Forging of a modern American Ranger.
UA34.R36C68 2012
356'.16750973—dc23
2011038693

PRINTED IN THE UNITED STATES OF AMERICA

10 9 8 7 6 5 4 3 2 1

This book is dedicated to all special operations training cadres—the veterans who take time from their operational units to cycle back through the training commands and pass along their experience, their wisdom, their culture, and their values to the next generation of special operators. Through their dedication and professionalism, each generation of these special warriors prepares for the mission a little better, gets to the fight a little quicker, and executes on target just a little more skillfully.

ACKNOWLEDGMENTS

A writer, even a former special operator turned writer, does not easily enter the closed and private world of a Special Operations Forces (SOF) component's selection and assessment. Modern special operators have a very formatted and tradition-bound approach to choosing who will and will not become one of their own. So it is with those who will and will not soldier with the 75th Ranger Regiment. For allowing me free and unprecedented access to their selection and training venues, I'd like to thank the Regimental Commanding Officers and Regimental Command Sergeant Majors who allowed this to take place during their tenure of command: Colonel Richard Clarke and Command Sergeant Major Chris Hardy; Colonel Eric Krilla and Command Sergeant Major Richard Merritt. And my thanks to the Regimental Deputy, Colonel Bill Ostlund, who served both of those commanders and was most helpful to me. I'd be remiss if I neglected to mention their boss, Lieutenant General Frank Mulholland, Commander, U.S. Army Special Operations Command. For my time with the Ranger Training Brigade, I'd like to thank Command Sergeant Major Dennis Smith. For my time with the 1st Ranger Battalion, I'm indebted to Lieutenant Colonel Mike Foster and Command Sergeant Major Nicholas Bielich, who made me most welcome at 1/75. And for all the many cadre noncommissioned officers in charge (NCOICs), cadre sergeants, company commanders, company first sergeants, platoon leaders, platoon sergeants, squad leaders, fire-team leaders, and individual Rangers; thank you all for so graciously making time for me as you trained the warriors and as you yourselves prepared for war. You held me to standard and taught me of the high standard that is a way of life for those who serve in the 75th Ranger Regiment.

Rangers Lead the Way!

SUA SPONTE.

Latin for "of their own accord."

Describes an action taken on one's own initiative and without formal permission from or the approval of higher authority. Also the motto of the 75th Ranger Regiment.

FOREWORD

How does an organization recruit, train, educate, develop, and motivate professional Soldiers the caliber of Sergeant First Class Leroy Petry? Sergeant Petry was recently awarded the Medal of Honor. He was also a member of the 75th Ranger Regiment, one of the most prestigious special operations units in the U.S. military. Sergeant Petry remains on active duty as a Regimental Ranger, even though he lost his right hand in the action for which he was awarded the medal. Sergeant Petry's Regiment has been in continuous combat since November 2001, with approximately one-third of the Regiment deployed overseas at any given period. Yet despite this arduous deployment cycle and the rigorous physical and mental standards for selection, this Regiment does not lack for volunteers. Nor does it lack for experience. It has one of the highest reenlistment rates in the U.S. Army.

Sua Sponte is a must-read—for the military historian, for the young man considering volunteering for the Regiment, or for anyone wanting to understand what it is to soldier with the 75th Rangers. For those "scrolled Rangers," past and present, it will bring back memories of what forged their foundation as one of America's premier warrior-leaders. Dick Couch, a renowned former Navy SEAL with an enviable combat record, was granted unprecedented access to the regimental selection process and training venues. As an embed with the 1st Ranger Battalion during its prerotation work-up, he was able to document how Rangers prepare for modern combat deployment. His chronicle of the rigorous training that develops a young Soldier into a young, apprentice Ranger is detailed, accurate, and captivating without compromising issues the Regiment wishes not to divulge for security reasons. Dick expands his account to address the selection process for new and returning officers and noncommissioned officers who wish to serve as leaders in the 75th Ranger Regiment. There are no double standards in the Regiment when it comes to physical and tactical skill requirements for senior leader; the selection process differs from that of the junior Soldiers, especially during the leadership- and psychological-assessment phases.

Without question, Dick Couch drew upon the physical stamina and mental toughness he developed as a SEAL as he went into the field for his research on this book. There is a saying in the Rangers that "you have to live hard to be hard." The reader will fully appreciate the meaning of that saying and the ordeal that Dick went through to capture the training regimen of the Ranger Assessment and Selection Program and Ranger predeployment training. This is a fascinating book to read, even for the seasoned SOF operator. It is both factual and fast paced, and accompanied by numerous vignettes that make the reader feel he or she is there witnessing the training. Having had several tours with the Regiment, including one as the Regimental Commander, I felt a flood of memories while I read the book and reflected back on the most special time in my military career.

Sua Sponte rekindled the pride I knew in serving with the very special patriots who make up the Regiment.

I have personally witnessed these magnificent warriors in combat. They are men of character and values, committed foremost to the mission but also to each other. Their training is both hard and realistic, and instills in them the confidence and the competence to succeed under the most stressful conditions. There is a standard for everything they do, and they hold themselves to that standard, never leaving a task until every member of the team has met it. This builds pride, cohesion, and professionalism. Discipline is demanded, and a Ranger takes personal pride in displaying that in all aspects of his duties. In holding themselves to this rigid standard, there is little room for compromise; minor infractions can result in relief from the Regiment. The national mission currently assigned to the Regiment demands discipline, obedience, ingenuity, and resourcefulness in addition to precise combat skills.

But, as Dick Couch's book reveals, simply having the desire and physical attributes to be a Ranger are not enough to make it through selection. The Regiment wants not only Rangers who are professional operators and future leaders, but also intelligent team members with sound judgment and a moral foundation. The Regiment demands a quiet professional who will be an integral part of a cohesive team. As conditions change and evolve on the battlefield, mission requirements may exceed the orders given on the eve of the mission tasking. A Ranger must then understand the commander's intent and use his initiative and intellect to accomplish the mission within the rules of engagement and the laws of war. Character, intellect, and emotional stability are as important as physical and tactical prowess during the assessment of a Ranger candidate.

As the Honorary Colonel of the Regiment, I am indebted to Dick Couch for capturing the physical, mental, and emotional commitment of those who serve in the Regiment. I applaud the selfless dedication of the young soldiers who volunteer to be Rangers. And as a retired Ranger, I envy them their journey. They will live the Ranger Creed. They will be courageous and victorious on the battlefield. They will join a Band of Brothers who represent all that is noble and honorable in the warrior profession.

W. F. "Buck" Kernan
General, USA (Ret.)

PREFACE

When people talk about the "Modern Rangers," they are most often referring to the period of time since 1974, when the Ranger battalions were re-formed for the first time since World War II. General Creighton Abrams, then chief of staff of the Army, activated the Ranger battalions not to become an elite strike force, but rather to serve as a role model for what the Army *should* be. General Abrams envisioned that these new Ranger battalions, now the 75th Ranger Regiment, would train leaders that would return to the conventional Army to pass on their experience and expertise. They were activated to create change in the Army and to give leaders a professional example of what the Army could become. They have done that and more. The things that can be directly traced to the Ranger Regiment range from the universal use of the word *HOOAH*, to the concept "Training to Standard," to family support groups, and even to the Soldier's Creed. The Army's current marksmanship, physical training combatives programs, and combat tactics all bear the mark of the 75th Rangers.

More than anything, the Rangers have produced leaders, leaders who continue to change the Army from bottom up, as evidenced by the number of command sergeant majors produced by the Regiment. At one time, unit leaders told former Regimental Ranger noncommissioned officers (NCOs), "This ain't no Ranger Battalion, Sergeant, we can't do that here," because they didn't think they could ask their soldiers to perform to Ranger standards. Over time, the Ranger standards became the Army standards as more Ranger leaders entered the force. The Army now realizes that competent leaders can ask for, and get, a higher professional standard.

All Rangers are leaders. Yet even among Ranger leaders, respect is earned, not given, no matter what the rank. That said, Ranger noncommissioned officers lead the way in the Regiment as perhaps nowhere else in the Army. Officer leaders rotate in and they rotate out, but the NCOs are always there. But NCO leadership has a price: meeting and exceeding the standard, year in and year out with no exceptions. Today in the Regiment, leadership means combat leadership. Few E-7 platoon sergeants in the 75th Ranger Regiment have less than *twelve combat rotations*. For these veteran combat leaders, the Ranger motto, "Rangers Lead the Way," is more than just a saying. In addition to serving as a leadership laboratory, the Ranger Regiment became an elite strike force. It has been involved in every ground combat operation since the Vietnam War. It was one of the first units deployed in the Global War on Terrorism, going into action on October 19, 2001. The 75th Ranger Regiment has been continuously deployed ever since.

This work has special meaning to me as I am a Ranger to my core. I was with the 1st Ranger Battalion for sixteen years, beginning as a private soldier and moving up through the ranks to company first sergeant. I served four years as the Regimental Command Sergeant Major and eight more years as the Command Sergeant Major of the

Ranger Regiment's operational and administrative higher headquarters. My last assignment was as the senior enlisted adviser for the International Security Assistance Force in Afghanistan. In 2010, just a few weeks before I retired, I had the privilege of accompanying the Rangers from the 2nd Ranger Battalion on an air assault mission to capture a high-value target. That final mission made me think how the Rangers had changed from what I knew as a young private in 1976. The uniforms, weapons, equipment, tactics, and mission sets were all drastically different. But one thing remained constant, unchanged: A Ranger is a Ranger, first and foremost, no matter his rank, military occupational specialty, or duty position. There is something that is unique about a Ranger. I can still pick one out of any crowd, day or night.

There is a saying in the Rangers: "It's easy to make it into the Regiment, but the hard part is maintaining the standard *every* single day." Dick Couch captures this, and why it is unique in this organization. *Sua Sponte* begins with recruiting the right men, training them to standard, and then insisting that they live up to that standard in garrison and in their personal lives. This is important; the assessment of a Ranger in the Regiment is never over and is never taken for granted.

There are no big secrets in the life of a regimental Ranger—no formula locked away in some vault to which only a select few have access. The standards haven't changed significantly since 1974. It matters not if you are the Regimental Commander, a Command Sergeant Major, a chaplain's assistant, a rifle-platoon sergeant, a cook, or a new infantry private. All are bound by the Ranger standard. Many soldiers do not make it through the initial assessment process, and many more are released for failing to maintain a Ranger standard. The attrition rate is high, as it has been since Major William O. Darby ran the first "selection and assessment" for the World War II Rangers. There's another saying in the Regiment: "You earn your [Ranger] Scroll every day." The Scroll of the 75th Ranger Regiment, as you will see in this book, is difficult to earn. Once earned, it is also difficult to live up to, but the standards of those who soldier with the 75th Ranger Regiment are both exacting and inflexible.

Dick begins his text with a history of the Rangers. Our history is extremely important to us. Our roots are deep and dated; they precede the founding of our nation. Yet even before the chapter on Ranger history, there is the Ranger Creed. For a Ranger, these are sacred words. The Ranger Creed was not intended to be just a poem to memorize for recitation; it is a way of life. It's how Rangers live; it's who they are and who they will be for the rest of their lives. During the battle for the Haditha Dam in Iraq in late March 2003, a Republican Guard counterattack left a 3rd Battalion Ranger severely wounded. On reaching the wounded man where he had fallen, his Command Sergeant Major found that he had a large piece of fragmentation protruding from the side of his head. In spite of the severity of his condition, he was quietly reciting the Ranger Creed to keep calm. I can think of no more forceful commentary on the strength and courage of a young Ranger, nor of the power of the Ranger Creed.

Rangers are individuals—as people, as soldiers, and as warriors. They have individual strengths, weaknesses, and, yes, egos. Yet their enduring quality is to merge these personal traits into a collective standard of excellence. Rangers let their actions speak for themselves, and perhaps at no point in their modern history have they spoken so eloquently as with their ongoing combat rotations into the active theaters. We may not be a nation at war, but the 75th Rangers are a regiment at war. It was my honor and privilege to serve with the 75th Ranger Regiment. And thank you, Dick Couch, for your fine work in telling our story.

Michael Hall
Command Sergeant Major, USA (Ret.)

THE RANGER CREED

Recognizing that I volunteered as a Ranger, fully knowing the hazards of my profession, I will always endeavor to uphold the prestige, honor, and high esprit de corps of my Ranger Regiment.

Acknowledging the fact that a Ranger is a more elite soldier, who arrives at the cutting edge of a battle by land, sea or air, I accept the fact that as a Ranger, my country expects me to move further, faster, and fight harder than any other soldier.

Never shall I ever fail my comrades. I will always keep myself mentally alert, physically strong, and morally straight, and I will shoulder more than my share of the task, whatever it may be, one hundred percent and then some.

Gallantly will I show the world that I am a specially selected and well trained soldier. My courtesy to superiors, my neatness of dress, and my care of my equipment shall set the example for others to follow.

Energetically will I meet the enemies of my country. I shall defeat them on the field of battle for I am better trained and will fight them with all my might. Surrender is not a Ranger word. I will never leave a fallen comrade to fall into the hands of the enemy and under no circumstances will I ever embarrass my country.

Readily will I display the intestinal fortitude required to fight on to the Ranger objective and complete the mission, though I be the lone survivor.

AN INTRODUCTION

Kaihan huddled close to the small fire with his father, two of his uncles, and one of his many brothers. This was the first time he had been allowed to accompany the older men of the family who were all seasoned fighters. They had just harvested the poppies that were well on their journey to becoming heroin to satisfy the addictions of the nonbelievers in the West. It was now time for jihad, and Kaihan took no small amount of pride to be an apprentice warrior in the service of Islam. Next month he would be fifteen. He and the others had been three weeks on their pilgrimage from their fields to the south, having left their village shortly after the devastating attacks on America. Kaihan now sat as an equal with the others, wearing a threadbare *chapan* coat, a castoff from a cousin who had died in the fighting, and a *pakol* hat that was too big, but could be pulled down to cover the tops of his ears for warmth. He tugged self-consciously at his sparse beard, hoping that it would soon grow long and thick like those of his elders. The only thing about Kaihan that was clean was his Kalashnikov rifle that had been wiped so often that much of the blueing had been rubbed away. He squatted close to the fire with the weapon between his knees, gripping the polished forestock. All the men kept their weapons close at hand, and Kaihan especially so. This rifle, with its curved thirty-round magazine and distinctive over-the-barrel gas piston tube, was a symbol of Kaihan's commitment to Allah and his manhood.

Their duty was to help provide security for the imam's compound located just west of Kandahar. They had never entered the compound itself, but each day one of the women brought food out for them. The men camped a few hundred yards from the compound by night and took shelter in a nearby wadi during the day. The imam was the spiritual leader of the Taliban, and it was a great honor that their family had been tasked to help with security. Their sector was to the north of the walled structure, where they now huddled around the small fire. Kaihan's job during the day was to gather sticks and brush, enough for a small fire to keep the tea hot throughout the night and a little warmth for the cold hours just before dawn.

They talked about the attacks on America that had taken place a little more than a month earlier. How would the Americans respond? How long would it take them to recover from the blow? Would they ever recover, or had the brave martyrs who had perished in the attacks mortally wounded that decadent nation? Only time would tell, but surely anything the Americans could do would take a while. Had the damage to their great cities been unprecedented? Were the Americans not on the other side of the world, across great oceans? Seated around the fire, they also talked of the assassination of Ahmad Shah Massoud, the leader of the Northern Alliance. He had been slain the day before the attacks on America. Praise be to Allah and to his servant Osama who had orchestrated these crushing defeats on their enemies. *Am I not fortunate*, Kaihan thought, *to be a soldier in the Army of God at such an exciting time?*

Uncle Faheem heard it first, cocking his head to one side and raising a hand for silence. It was a murmur, then a soft growl but growing louder. It seemed to be coming from the east and getting nearer at a fast pace. Without a sound, Kaihan's father kicked dirt over the small fire and the five rose as one to listen.

"There," said Uncle Jawid, pointing to the sky east of the compound. It was a dark night, but they could make out three—now four—shapes coming over the horizon. They were evenly spaced and quite low—low enough for the shapes to begin sprouting wings as they drew closer. They were large aircraft. Then Kaihan saw small dark forms begin to blossom from the rear of each.

"Parachutists," his father said. "Parsa, take your brother to the rally point and wait for us there. Now!"

Parsa, two years older than Kaihan and a veteran fighter, grabbed Kaihan by the cuff of his coat and pulled him away. Kaihan followed without protest; their father's commands were to be obeyed without question. Like all good Pashtun fighters, their father had designated a safe place for them to meet should they be separated in battle. This place was a sheltered, shallow rocky rise a half mile from the compound. Kaihan glanced over his shoulder and saw his father and uncles, now just dark forms, moving in a line abreast toward the compound. He wished he were with them, knowing that if there was to be fighting, they would be a part of it and he would not. Yet there was little time to think as Parsa drew him away from the compound. Kaihan would never see his father or uncles alive again.

Throughout the night, Kaihan and Parsa heard the rattle of machine-gun fire and an occasional explosion. Off to the north and west, they heard the sounds of jet aircraft and the distant *krump* of bombs. As dawn broke, they each in turn surveyed the compound through Parsa's binoculars. They were Russian binoculars and one of his brother's prized possessions. As Kaihan looked down from their hiding site, he could see armed men in security positions around the compound and others patrolling near the walls. On a short pole atop one building in the compound a flag was flying. It had not been there the previous day. In the growing light, Kaihan was able to make out the stripes and cluster of stars of an American flag, their hated symbol. *So it was the Americans*, Kaihan marveled to himself. *How did they get here so swiftly? How could they come so far and at night, without warning, and parachute onto the compound of their leader?*

Kaihan and Parsa watched throughout the day. They watched as the Americans moved freely throughout the compound. They watched later that afternoon as the large transports landed and took the soldiers back aboard and left. Just before dark, the two boys made their way down to the deserted compound. They found the bodies of their father and uncles, but their weapons were gone. They had been laid out with some reverence and covered with blankets. After burying them, the two brothers made their way back to their village with the sad news. The grief of the extended family was intense but brief—such was their way of life. Within the year, both Kaihan and Parsa would be dead. Parsa would be killed by Northern Alliance fighters outside Kandahar as they and their Army Special Forces allies swept down from Turkmenistan. Kaihan would die from a 105-millimeter cannon round fired from a special operations AC-130 gunship while he and several others slept in what they thought was a safe building. They, too, would be buried in hasty, shallow graves by their younger brothers and cousins, who would then take up the fight. One of them would have the Kalashnikov rifle Kaihan kept so clean; another, Parsa's Russian binoculars. They would be brave and fight well, yet most would die in the struggle.

The above account is, of course, fictional. The fact that the American response to the attacks of 9/11 was swift and highly professional is not. On the night of October 19, 2001, scarcely a month after the attacks on the World Trade Center and the Pentagon, the U.S. Special Operations Command conducted a bold raid on the compound of the Taliban leader Mullah Mohammed Omar, near Kandahar in Afghanistan. The centerpiece of this action was a night parachute drop of close to two hundred Rangers from the 3rd Battalion of the 75th Ranger Regiment—the first boots on the ground, in force, in what we now call the Global War on Terrorism. These Rangers flew halfway around the world to make this combat drop from a Special Operations MC-130 Combat Talon aircraft at eight hundred feet— quite an undertaking. That it took so much time—five weeks—for America to respond after the attacks of 9/11 had to do with intelligence, targeting, and political considerations. The Rangers of the 3rd Battalion, in accordance with their standing orders, were ready to make that combat drop eighteen hours after the first plane hit the towers in New York. A single company of the 3rd Battalion was on a nine-hour standby. As America's premier light-infantry force, the 75th Ranger Regiment keeps one of its three rifle battalions on this kind of alert status 24/7. It was true then as it is today. This on-call requirement is in addition to their keeping a full battalion or a full battalion plus deployed in the active theater and in harm's way. Their mantra, "Rangers Lead the Way," is not just a slogan; it is a way of life.

On one hand, the raid on Mullah Omar's compound accomplished little. The imam was not in residence and there was very little of significant intelligence value retrieved from the compound. A few Taliban fighters in the area were killed and a few Rangers injured in the night parachute operation. Yet the message sent to the Taliban and al-Qaeda leadership was quite clear; anytime, anywhere, and under any conditions, you may be visited by tough and capable American warriors. Most likely, they will come at night in inclement weather. If you are unfortunate enough to be present when they arrive, you will be captured or killed. Most likely those warriors will be American special operators, and there is a good probability those special operators will be Rangers—anytime, anywhere, day or night, and under any conditions.

All military organizations are cultures. The Army, Navy, Air Force, and Marine Corps are separate and distinct cultures, as is the U.S. Special Operations Command. Within the SPECOPs Command reside the minicultures of the service-centric components that make up America's special operations forces, or SOF. Those primary SOF elements engaged in ground combat are the Green Berets, the SEALs, the Marine Special Operations Regiment, and the Rangers, along with the highly classified special mission units of the Joint Special Operations Command. This work is focused on the story of the Rangers: where they come from, their storied past, their current deployment posture, their rigorous training, and, above all, their culture—part brotherhood, part family, and all warrior.

There is a good deal of misunderstanding about the individual roles of our SOF ground-combat components and their mission sets. What are their primary and secondary missions, and when, if ever, do these missions overlap? And what are they doing today now that the active combat rotations have shifted from Iraq to Afghanistan? Let's first talk about Army Special Forces—the Green Berets. They have broad military training and can serve as raiders in a direct-action role, but their *primary* role is that of a counterinsurgent and unconventional-warfare force. Special Forces were the ones who helped to mobilize the Northern Alliance that took Afghanistan in a matter of months—something the Russians failed to do in a decade of fighting. The seizing of all Afghanistan by Afghan tribal fighters, under the standard of the Northern Alliance, assisted by Army Special Forces and a generous dose of American air power, is considered a classic unconventional-warfare operation. These same Green Berets were the ones who helped to train the Iraqis to deal with insurgents during the long aftermath following the fall of Saddam Hussein. This counterinsurgency role is also called foreign internal defense. Theirs is a "by, with, and through" discipline that demands language and cross-cultural skill sets. Special Forces have to work well with others. In my book *Chosen Soldier*, I describe the Army Special Forces soldier as the most valuable individual on the battlefield. In today's insurgent battlespace, I stand by that statement. It takes a special individual to be a Green Beret—and it takes a long time to train one. Special Forces training, along with language and medical or specialty training, can take from eighteen to thirty-six months. Unconventional-warfare and counterinsurgency operations are difficult and nuanced, and the warriors who practice this vital and demanding work are among our most skilled special operators.

Also on the ground in the current fight are the Navy SEALs. The acronym SEAL stands for sea-air-land, and SEALs are trained to move and fight in all three mediums. While they are the primary maritime proponents of the U.S. Special Operations Command, they have a broad skill set and do quite well on land. SEALs, like their brother special operators, have been deployed continuously in Iraq and Afghanistan. They are a versatile force and able to conduct the full range of special operations, including direct-action raids, special reconnaissance, unconventional warfare, and counterinsurgency. They are at home high in the Hindu Kush, just as they are in the water. While they are capable generalists, their specialty is direct action and special reconnaissance in littoral or maritime environments. Due to this broad, versatile skill set and their lengthy maritime-centric training, it takes thirty-six months to make a U.S. Navy SEAL out of a U.S. Navy sailor, and to prepare him for combat deployment. Both SEALs and Special Forces, by the nature of their specialty training and mission taskings, are long lead-time items. They are expensive to train, and the attrition rates of their lengthy training pipelines are horrific. Only about one in four make it through SEAL or Special Forces training.

Before moving onto the focus of this book, the Army Rangers, I'll briefly mention the other two SOF ground-combat components. The first is the Marine Special Operations Command, or MARSOC.

The MARSOC is relatively new to the U.S. Special Operations Command force mix in that it was commissioned as a SOCOM component in February 2006. Our MARSOC is currently a regimental-sized force that specializes in direct action, special reconnaissance, and foreign internal defense. The force draws heavily on Marine reconnaissance units and while the MARSOC is unique in much of its training and force projection, its mission set and deployment posture most closely resemble that of Army Special Forces. The core, a seven-month Marine special operations training course, has similarities to the Green Beret's training. The other special operations component or components operating on the ground in the active theaters are the special mission units that collectively train and deploy as elements of the Joint Special Operations Command. The mission set and operational responsibilities of the special mission units are beyond the scope and classification of this work. These secret and highly specialized elements recruit their personnel from veterans of the other SOF ground-combat components.

I would be remiss if I did not mention the SOF aviation components. The Air Force Special Operations Command and the Army's 160th Special Operations Aviation Regiment (Airborne) are well staffed with experienced and talented aviators. They fly fixed and rotary-wing special operations platforms, and support their SOF brothers on the ground as well as conduct special operations missions on their own. They, too, have been on continuous combat rotation into the battlespace since 9/11.

With this brief primer on U.S. special operations ground-combat elements, we now turn our attention to the Rangers—specifically, the 75th Ranger Regiment. The Regiment enjoys a much narrower and more focused mission than its brother SOF combatants. While Rangers may be called on to support other disciplines and mission sets, they are pure raiders. As a primary skill set, they do not train allied soldiers in foreign internal defense, nor do they conduct unconventional-warfare operations. They are not called upon to conduct routine patrols or engage in special reconnaissance. Their coun-terinsurgent duties primarily involve tracking down enemy fighters, and capturing them or killing them. As the Rangers are called on to do little else, they are able to execute their direct-action mission responsibilities very well. During operations in Iraq, and now exclu-sively in Afghanistan, they are usually tasked to conduct raids as small units, but they also train to conduct large-scale raids as well. One of their primary missions is the seizure of enemy airfields, which are often preceded with a company-sized parachute drop, not unlike the one on Mullah Omar's compound. Ongoing requirements in the active theaters have downsized the types of operational raids Rang-ers routinely carry out, but these current operations have not relieved the Regiment of its airfield-capture responsibilities. The on-call Ran-ger battalion must be ready to launch within eighteen hours for enemy-airfield capture—again, anywhere and anytime.

Airfield seizure is more of a large-scale, maneuver-warfare capability—something more suited to the Cold War or as a part of an invasion operation. Yet the 75th Ranger Regiment still makes time in its busy training/deployment schedule to keep this mission skill current. It requires time and a great deal of professionalism to conduct this kind of large-scale raid, for it would most certainly be done at night and in the face of stiff opposition. Operations like this fall into the category of high-risk undertakings. So one might think that given the current focus on small-unit tactics in an insurgent environment, why would the Rangers bother with this kind of mass-parachute operation? There are good reasons. Should the government of Pakistan fall into the hands of extremists and American policy makers not wish the Pakistani nuclear arsenal to be in the hands of those extremists, who would we send on a recovery mission? If we were to need boots-on-the-ground evidence of Iran's nuclear weap-ons development, what unit is best suited to seize, secure, and hold a nuclear bomb factory for a few hours to get that information? And if an American embassy is under siege and the local government is unable to control the mob that threatens Americans in that embassy, what force can we get there in a hurry to save those lives? The 75th Ranger Regiment represents an important light-infantry, on-call response capability that is unique in our military.

Yet, for now, the business currently at hand is counterinsurgency, and that business, primarily in Afghanistan, requires that we win the people to our side. It has been stated many ways and certainly in more complex terms, but the premise of a counterinsurgency campaign is a three-phase undertaking: clear, hold, build. Insurgents must first be cleared from the area. The area must then be held in such a way that the insurgents cannot return and hide amid the local population and exert their control over the people. Basically, there has to be security; the people have to be free of intimidation by the insurgents. And, finally, there's the building process—building schools, building relationships, and building trust in the local government. The clearing process is pretty straightforward; it often means targeting insurgent leaders and fighters, and killing them. Both the holding and the building are difficult, time-consuming, expensive, frustrating, and dangerous work. Holding often involves patrolling the streets and maintaining a visible presence to provide security. It also involves training the local police forces in security operations. Building efforts have to be done in concert with the local leaders and officials on *their* terms—within the context of the local customs and culture. Holding and building are the stock and trade of Army Special Forces. The SEALs have been pressed into this important work, though most SEALs would rather be tasked with direct-action missions than working with local security forces. The Marine Corps, with its small-wars approach to the business of counterinsurgency, prides itself on doing all three—at the same time.

Rangers focus on the clearing process. They are not involved with training the locals or conducting security patrols or building infrastructure. Here again, they are pure raiders, and their work, while dangerous, is rather straightforward. They capture and kill insurgents, and disrupt insurgent operations. This requires neither the language and cross-cultural skills of Special Forces (or SOF Marines) nor the multidimensional/maritime skill set of the SEALs. Theirs is a basic direct-action mission set. In many ways, what the Rangers were asked to do before 9/11 and what they do today has changed little. They train in all forms of airborne and mobile tactical assault. This training focuses on what the Rangers call the Big Five: mobility, marksmanship, medical (first aid), physical fitness, and battle drills. Their art is the raider's art, and they are very good at it.

In speaking to the simplicity of the Rangers' direct-action calling, this does not imply that it does not take a great deal of professionalism and discipline to do it well. A professional football team or a ballet troop moves from competence to excellence with practice and drill. To stay with the sports analogy, there is a certain amount of elegance in a run-oriented offense moving the football down the field. Execution is everything. Even if the defense knows what you're going to do, it cannot stop you. This kind of precision comes from a commitment to precision, individually and as a team, that can only be achieved with drill, repetition, and close attention to detail. It's the same with combat assault.

Perhaps the most startling aspect of Ranger work when compared with that of Army Special Forces and Navy SEALs is the relatively short period of time required to train and deploy a combat-capable Army Ranger. When compared with unconventional warfare and counterinsurgency, the assault business is a simple business. Dangerous and stressful, yes, but again, straightforward. A young man graduating high school in the spring of his senior year may find himself in the middle of a combat tour as an Army Ranger on the one-year anniversary of his high school graduation. For a Green Beret or a SEAL, it may be as long as three years before he enters the fight.

Sua Sponte is the story of how the 75th Ranger Regiment selects, trains, and prepares a young Ranger for this difficult and deadly work. It is a professional process and a cultural transformation that goes to the core of this unique warrior brotherhood. The process first seeks to find those young men who have the heart and the physical capacity to become Rangers. Then these same men are vetted to see if they have the aptitude and personal discipline to play their role on a combat assault team. It is both a screening and a rite of passage.

Before continuing, let me take a minute to clarify an important distinction between a Ranger who serves in the 75th Ranger Regiment and a soldier who is "Ranger Qualified" by way of his completion of Ranger School. Rangers who serve in the 75th Regiment are assessed, selected, and trained in the Regiment's Ranger Assessment and Selection Program, or RASP. A good deal of *Sua Sponte* is about the unique and challenging RASP process. Ranger School is conducted by the U.S. Army Training and Doctrine Command, and is the Army's premier combat-leadership school. It teaches young officers and soldiers that they can fight and lead even though they've had little to eat and have not slept for several days. Ranger School has been called sixty-one days of hell. Those who complete this important and difficult leadership course are awarded the Ranger Tab. While there are few books on regimental Ranger training, a great deal has been written about this school. Only about 45 percent of those who enroll in Ranger School earn the Tab. Since the school began in 1950, twenty-seven soldiers have been killed during this difficult and demanding training.

There has been a great deal of misunderstanding regarding Ranger School and its important role in the regular Army, and the role of the school as it applies to the 75th Ranger Regiment. Few outside the Army really know or understand the difference. Ranger School occupies a unique place in the Army unlike any other school in any other service. For an Army officer, especially for an Infantry Branch or Armor Branch officer, the Tab—that little strip of khaki cloth awarded those who complete Ranger School—is a career maker or a career breaker. Any soldier (or sailor or marine, as SEALs and marines attend Ranger School on a limited basis) who completes the school has earned the right to call himself a Ranger. There are young privates who proudly wear the Ranger Tab on the shoulder of their uniform; so do most generals in the Army. Most of those who complete Ranger School and are awarded the coveted Ranger School Tab *do not* serve in the 75th Ranger Regiment.

Yet, in many ways, Ranger School is what binds the Regiment to the rest of the U.S. Army. To serve in the Regiment, a soldier must complete RASP; to stay in the Regiment and to be a leader in the Regiment, a Ranger must earn the Ranger Tab. Often, a young soldier will complete RASP and make one or more Ranger deployments *before* he attends Ranger School. Those soldiers who complete RASP are awarded the Tan Beret and the Regimental Scroll. Then there is the Tab that they award to Ranger School graduates. Both are hard to come by, and both define what it is to be a Ranger. There is a saying in the Regiment: "The Tab is the school but the Scroll is a way of life." Yet without the Tab, life in the Regiment ceases.

While a portion of this book will address Ranger School, *Sua Sponte* is the story of the forging of those battle-ready Rangers who will serve in the Regiment. It is about the assessment, selection, and training of our nation's most capable warriors. It tells about the transformation that must take place for a soldier to be a part of the unique culture that is the 75th Ranger Regiment. *Sua Sponte* follows this journey step by step—a journey that only about one in four survive to go on to serve as Rangers in this storied Regiment. As the first writer granted unlimited access to the 75th Ranger Regiment and its training, I am very privileged to have the opportunity to tell its story.

No U.S. military unit can claim a longer or more storied history than the 75th Rangers. In the first chapter, we will learn about this history and the remarkable traditions that our modern Rangers carry with them into the current fight.

CHAPTER ONE

RANGER HISTORY

Life in America during colonial times was hazardous business. In addition to making their way in this harsh and untamed land, there were hostile Indians to deal with. The new settlers farmed and hunted, and they also felled trees to build stockades to protect themselves from Indian attacks. Much of the early life of the white man in America was spent well bunkered behind protective walls. Danger lurked outside the fortifications as Indians, skilled in stalking game and tribal warfare, would often lie in wait for these new colonists. Those tilling the ground, even near the stockade, were targets, as were hunting parties searching for game nearby. A trip to the stream for water could invite attack.

By 1630, scarcely two decades after the founding of Jamestown, established colonists in Maryland and Virginia began to organize and hire groups of men to patrol the perimeters of their holdings as a means of early warning against Indian attack. Many military historians hold that these defensive measures were the first Ranger-type operations conducted in America.

The first offensive ranger operations in the New World, aside from those conducted by the Native Americans themselves, took place in Massachusetts. In 1675, a particularly skilled and aggressive Indian chief named Metacomet of the Wampanoag tribe began savaging the colonists there with lightning-fast hit-and-run raids. To counter these raids, Governor Josiah Winslow of the Plymouth Colony commissioned his principal aide, Benjamin Church, to take action. Church, a carpenter by trade, raised a company of men and began ranging out from the settlements to conduct scouting operations against Metacomet and his war parties. Eventually, with the help of recruited friendly Indians, Captain Church began to attack the Wampanoag villages. In a series of actions known as King Philip's War (Metacomet was known locally as King Philip), Church was able to take the fight to the enemy. These scouting and raiding actions continued for three years, ending with the capture and execution of Metacomet. In describing the scouting and reconnaissance activity of Church's mixed force, there appeared written reports that stated, "Today we ranged out four miles to the west," and the term *Ranger* was born.

It was not until three-quarters of a century later that the first by-name Ranger unit was formed. This took place prior to the French and Indian War (1754–1763) with the forming of His Majesty's First Independent Company of American Rangers in 1747. The French and Indian War was an American extension of the Seven Years' War between England and France. The New World version of this conflict pitted the New England colonists against the French Canadians and their native allies. This first true Ranger company was recruited and formed by a frontiersman named Robert Rogers. After forming the first Ranger company, Rogers went on to form nine additional companies of Rangers that took the fight and the British cause deep into territory claimed by the French. His campaign leadership in those uncertain times is an important part of modern Ranger lore.

These first Rangers were brought to the attention of most Americans in the 1940 film *Northwest Passage*, starring Spencer Tracy and Robert Young. Like other military leaders in the fledgling colonies, Rogers was a compelling and enigmatic figure who stamped his fighters with his own personality; they were his "Rogers' Rangers." An early and perhaps somewhat embellished description of the American Ranger and this first Ranger leader was an account by Joseph B. Walker that appeared in the Massachusetts publication *Bay State Monthly* in 1885:

He was a man of vigorous constitution, inured to the hardships of forest life. He was capable of long marches, day after day, upon scant rations, refreshed by short intervals of sleep while rolled in his blanket upon a pile of boughs, with no other shelter but the sky. He knew the trails of the Indians, as well as their ordinary haunts and likeliest places of ambush. He knew, also, all the courses of the streams and the carrying places between them. He understood Indian wiles and warfare, and was prepared to meet them.

Stand such a man in a pair of stout shoes or moccasins; cover his lower limbs with leggins and coarse small clothes; give him a close-fitting jacket and a warm cap; stick a small hatchet in his belt; and a good-sized powder-horn by his side, and upon his back buckle a blanket and a knapsack stuffed with a moderate supply of bread and raw salt pork; to these furnishings add a good-sized hunting-knife, a trusty musket and a small flask of spirits, and you have an average New Hampshire Ranger of the Seven Year's War, ready for skirmish or pitched battle; or for the more common duty of recon-noitering the enemy's force and movements, of capturing his scouts and provision trains, and getting now and then a prisoner, from whom all information possible would be extorted; and, in short, for annoying the French and Indian foe in every possible way.

If you will add three or four inches to the average height of such a soldier, give him consummate courage, coolness, readiness of

*resource in extremities, together with intuitive knowledge of the ene-
my's wiles, supplemented with a passable knowledge of French and
Indian speech, you will have a tolerable portrait of Captain Robert
Rogers at the beginning of our Seven Year's War.*

Following the French and Indian War and into the American
Revolution, Robert Rogers's life became a series of misfortunes. Rogers was in and out of prison and in and out of favor with both British and American authorities. He served as a British officer for a
short time during the Revolution, and helped to unmask and capture
Nathan Hale, the famous American patriot who was hanged as a
spy. At the time of his death, Nathan Hale was also serving in a
Continental Ranger company. Robert Rogers died penniless and in
obscurity in 1795. One of the factors that propelled him into financial ruin was that during the French and Indian War, he paid his
men out of his own pocket.

Today's modern Rangers can trace their roots and heritage back
to this bold, charismatic, and perhaps tragic figure. In addition to
his contributions to small-unit tactics and an intrepid campaign history, he left us (among other military publications) *Robert Rogers'
28 Rules of Ranging.* He also left us with his Rogers' Rangers Standing Orders, which is quoted in the front of every edition of the *Ranger Handbook,* right after the Ranger Creed, and repeated here.

ROGERS' RANGERS STANDING ORDERS
1. Don't forget nothing.
2. Have your musket clean as a whistle, hatchet scoured, sixty
   rounds of powder and ball, and be ready to move at a minute's
   warning.
3. When you are on the march, act the way you would if you was
   sneaking up on a deer; see the enemy first.
4. Tell the truth about what you see and what you do. There is an
   Army depending on us for correct information. You can lie all

you please when you tell other folks about the Rangers. But never lie to an Officer or Ranger.

5. Don't never take a chance you don't have to.

6. When we're on the march, we march single file, far enough apart so one shot can't go through two men.

7. If we strike swamps, or soft ground, we spread out abreast so it's hard to track us.

8. When we march, we keep moving until dark so as to give the enemy the least possible chance at us.

9. When we camp, half the party stays awake while the other half sleeps.

10. If we take prisoners, we keep 'em separate till we have had time to examine them so they can't cook up a story between 'em.

11. Don't ever march home the same way. Take a different route so you won't be ambushed.

12. No matter whether we travel in big parties or little ones, each party has to keep a scout 20 yards ahead, 20 yards on each flank, and 20 yards in the rear, so the main body can't be surprised and wiped out.

13. Every night you will be told where to meet if surrounded by a superior force.

14. Don't sit down to eat without posting sentries.

15. Don't sleep beyond dawn; dawn's when the French and Indians attack.

16. Don't cross a river by a regular ford.

17. If somebody's trailing you, make a circle, come back onto your own trail, and ambush the folks that aim to ambush you.

18. Don't stand up when the enemy's coming against you. Kneel down, lie down, hide behind a tree.

19. Let the enemy come till he's close enough to touch. Then let him have it and jump out and finish him up with your hatchet.

Major Robert Rogers, 1759

In 1775, the Continental Congress authorized the formation of a number of companies of expert riflemen. George Washington was to later call these companies the Corps of Rangers, but the term *Ranger* was seldom used during the revolution. One might have thought the colonists would have turned to Robert Rogers, a proven leader, when forming such a force. Rogers offered his services, but Washington turned him down. As a former British officer, Washington did not trust him. The general sought leaders who had no ties to the British. Leading one of these new rifle companies was a tough Virginian and former teamster named Daniel Morgan. Morgan was a big man, with a history of drinking and gambling, and a deep-seated dislike for the British army, which once had him flogged to the point of near death. He was poorly educated, but he had a natural flare for unconventional warfare and tactical maneuver. Captain Daniel Morgan led his sharpshooters from Virginia on a forced march to help relieve the colonists in the Siege of Boston. He participated in the Battle of Quebec, during which he was taken prisoner. He was later repatriated, and went on to serve in a prominent role in the Battle of Saratoga. For his service at Saratoga, Morgan was promoted to colonel and given a regimental command in the Continental Army that included a five-hundred-man unit of select marksmen to be used as light infantry. Morgan put them to good use as a reconnaissance force and for harassment and interdiction of British supply lines. During the course of the war, he became adept at using light infantry, irregular forces, and sharpshooters in support of main-force engagements.

We now remember Morgan for his direction of the American victory at the Battle of Cowpens in January 1881, a battle that ended a series of British victories in the southern colonies. His orders were to harass the British, not confront them. In direct violation of those orders, he used his sharpshooters and militia troops to lure a regiment of British infantry onto ground of his choosing. Morgan ordered his irregulars to fire a volley, then fall back. Morgan knew that the

British regiment was commanded by the brash Colonel Banastre Tarleton, who had a low opinion of irregular troops. When the Continental irregulars gave ground, Tarleton, as Morgan anticipated, ordered a charge. As the redcoats charged, Morgan's Virginia sharpshooters raked the leading elements of Tarleton's light infantry, halting their advance. This allowed Morgan to conduct a double envelopment of the British main body with his own light infantry and all but annihilate the British regiment. Tarleton escaped, but of his eleven-hundred-man force, two hundred were killed and more than eight hundred captured, along with the entire British supply train. It was *the* tactical gem of the war, and one of the few times a double envelopment has been employed in modern military warfare.

Following the Revolution, Daniel Morgan was recalled to active service, during which he led the militia in the Whiskey Rebellion and put down the insurrection without firing a shot. He served two terms in the U.S. House of Representatives and died in July 1802. As an interesting historical aside, this early Ranger leader was a relative of the famous privateer and pirate Henry Morgan.

Much of early Ranger lore seems to be tied to noted unconventional and charismatic military leaders, and the person of Colonel Francis Marion is no exception. Marion, widely known as the Swamp Fox, conducted a guerrilla-type campaign in South Carolina during the Revolutionary War. He was born a South Carolinian and grew up in Georgetown, South Carolina, at the time a thriving seaport. Marion was a sickly child, but, encouraged by his parents, he went to sea on a trading schooner at the age of fifteen. The schooner foundered after being struck by a whale and young Marion was adrift in an open boat, without food or water, for six days before making landfall. He began his military career during the French and Indian War as an officer in the South Carolina militia and first saw action in border skirmishes with the Cherokees.

In 1775, Francis Marion, then a member of the South Carolina Provincial Legislature, was commissioned a captain in the South

Carolina 2nd Regiment. He participated in several engagements, but the colonial militias and newly formed regular units proved no match for the British redcoats. Most organized resistance in the southern colonies collapsed after the fall of Charleston in May 1780. At the time, Marion and an irregular unit of several dozen men were the only force opposing the British in South Carolina. Marion joined General Horatio Gates's command in the Continental Army, which re-formed itself in Charlotte, North Carolina. However, Gates had no use for Marion and sent him to take command of the militia forces in northeastern South Carolina. Gates, the hero of Saratoga, was then crushed by Cornwallis in the Battle of Camden, and organized resistance in the southern colonies all but ceased.

Following the setbacks at Charleston and Camden in the summer of 1780, Marion set about his duties as a raider, conducting hit-and-run raids against British outposts and supply lines. He proved to be a capable leader of irregular forces. Marion was able to stay a step ahead of the British because of his intelligence networks among the procolonial local population. He also was quite adept at moving through the swamps of South Carolina. The British put a premium on the catching of Marion, then a lieutenant colonel, and sent the infamous Banastre Tarleton to South Carolina to track him down. Marion proved elusive, prompting Tarleton to say, "That damned fox; the devil himself could not catch him," and the legend of the Swamp Fox was born. While his raiding tactics were a harbinger of modern Ranger operations, Marion's leadership and motivation of local militias in an unconventional-warfare campaign might well be more in keeping with the work of modern Army Special Forces. For his work as a militia organizer and guerrilla leader, Francis Marion was promoted to brigadier general of state troops. Following the war, he served several terms in the South Carolina State Senate before his death in 1795. A few modern historians have taken issue with the career of Francis Marion, suggesting that he approved of the killing of unarmed combatants and the use of torture on prisoners.

Similar charges have been leveled against the likes of Robert Rogers and Daniel Morgan. But these were desperate times in a wild and savage land. All three of these early Rangers cut their teeth fighting Indians, which helped to form their tactical mind-set, and what we today might call an unenlightened approach to dealing with enemy combatants. The structure of military units was very unlike that of today. Soldiers were often not bound by enlistment contracts; they came and went as they pleased. Military leaders were charged with recruiting, training, and leading these irregular forces in battle, and that demanded a charismatic and sometimes heavy-handed commander. Often their duties were almost tribal in nature. With irregular troops, these units often lived off the land, and there was no convenient rear area to hold captured prisoners. It was a different era, and I contend that these frontiersmen turned paramilitary leaders were simply a product of their time.

Each of these leaders contributed to the early Ranger methodology and lore in their own way, but in my opinion, Daniel Morgan, perhaps the least known of the three, stands out. He certainly rises above the others when his battle tactics are compared with those of modern Rangers. Morgan understood the use of irregulars in support of main-force actions. He knew how to use sharpshooters and rifle companies in the role of light infantry. He had also proved himself in both conventional and unconventional battle. And if we in modern times on occasion look at these irregular-force leaders as barbarous or ungentlemanly or even marginal in their contributions, one only has to look at the tactical genius of Morgan at Cowpens. He gave the Continental Army a southern victory when it most desperately needed one.

During America's westward expansion, local rangering operations were a part of the effort to counter attacks by Indians whose land was being taken by the new settlers. This was never more the case than in Texas. Texas was settled by Americans and Europeans with the approval of the Mexican government. Collectively, they were led by Stephen F. Austin. The new settlers had to become Mexican citizens, convert to Catholicism, and speak Spanish. In 1823, in order to protect the settlers from marauding Indians, among them the dreaded Comanche, Austin, under his military powers, created a ranging company to defend against these Indian raids. In 1835, this unit was named the Corps of Rangers by the Texas Colonial Assembly, though it was not formally called the Texas Rangers until well after the Civil War. These Rangers were active during the struggle for Texas independence against Mexico, and remained a small ranging force during the time of the Lone Star Republic. Texas's admission to the Union in 1845 precipitated the Mexican-American War (1846–1848), during which the Rangers in Texas were mustered into the federal forces as scouts.

The Rangers of this era in Texas added another chapter to the history of ranging, which had begun during the Revolutionary era. They were an irregular force at best, used personal firearms and mounts, were highly individual, and were led by a series of charismatic and mercurial leaders. They were a diverse force that counted immigrant Americans and Europeans, Mexicans, and Indians among their number. In keeping with the spirit of the earlier colonial ranging units, the Rangers of Texas carried the Ranger standard into the Civil War.

During the Civil War, there were a host of units that historians cite as Ranger-type elements drawn from local militias or irregulars. Many of these units operated as independent cavalry. On the Union side, there were the Loudoun Rangers, Cole's Maryland Cavalry, the Means Scouts, and the Jesse Scouts, to name a few. These Union forces were tasked with the normal ranging duties of raiding, harassing, and scouting, but most of these units were formed to counter the Southern Ranger-type outfits. In 1862, the Confederacy authorized the formation of partisan Ranger bands to raid and ambush the enemy behind Northern lines. Southern Rangers, led by men like John McNeill, John Morgan, and Turner Ashby, penetrated well into the North. While these Southern raiders ranged much farther into enemy territory and were far more effective than their Northern counterparts, it should be noted that in the Northern states, the war drew Federal troops back from the frontier, and unrest among the Indians soared. Many western states raised Ranger-type units to stay home and deal with the Indians, which made these units unavailable for the eastern engagements of the Civil War.

Before the Civil War, Rangers had fought Indians, the French, and the British. Yet the Civil War often pitted brother against brother, and this was never more the case than in the Ranger units. Since Rangers often operated in and among both partisan and hostile populations, loyalties and allegiances sometimes split whole families. Literally, brother fought against brother.

As with their predecessors, Ranger units on both sides consisted of hard men generally skilled in the use of weapons and characterized by a good measure of personal independence—men suited to small units, informal organization, and living off the land. By the time of the Civil War, the mobility of these units also required that these men be both comfortable on horseback and able to provide their own mount. Also in keeping with early Ranger tradition, these units were usually led by dynamic, charismatic, and unusual men. No Civil War Ranger leader embodied those qualities, nor was more renowned, than the Confederate Ranger leader John S. Mosby.

Mosby, who became known as the Gray Ghost of the Confederacy for his wartime exploits, was the most famous of the Civil War Rangers. In many ways, he was a transitional figure, having more in common with modern Rangers and modern Ranger leaders than those who preceded him. John Mosby was born in Virginia in 1833. He was a frail boy of medium height and was often picked on by other boys. Early on, he developed a combative nature, but with a firm conviction about right and wrong. While not one to shy away from a confrontation, he was often the loser of a fight. He was also highly intelligent and excelled in his early studies and later at the

University of Virginia. John Mosby was both smart and principled. In an altercation with a bully at the university, Mosby produced a gun and shot his tormentor, wounding him seriously. This incident led to his expulsion from school and a year in jail. While incarcerated, Mosby studied law, and after being released, he continued to read the law under the mentorship of the prosecutor who convicted him and sent him to jail. The fact that he schooled himself while in prison speaks to both his intelligence and his desire to succeed.

Mosby was admitted to the bar in Virginia and was practicing law at the outbreak of the Civil War. Though he had spoken out against secession, he enlisted in the Confederate army as a private soldier and participated in the First Battle of Manassas. Mosby gravitated to intelligence gathering and scouting. He soon caught the eye of Jeb Stuart and finally General Robert E. Lee himself, who later often commended Mosby for his service. Mosby moved up through the ranks and in January 1863 was allowed to form and take command of a battalion of partisan Rangers. Over the last 150 years, the exploits of John Mosby have been well documented by historians, from *Mosby and His Men*, by J. Marshall Crawford (1867), to the superb work by James Ramage, *Gray Ghost: The Life of Col. John Singleton Mosby*, (1999). Mosby's exploits were indeed legion, and both Stuart and Lee put a great deal of trust in his scouting reports. While Mosby's operations most certainly fell into the context of the unconventional, even by modern standards, he was hardly an independent agent—a rogue operator doing what he pleased. At all times, he operated under the command of the Confederate army.

What secures Mosby's place in special operations and Ranger history is the man himself. He was no larger-than-life figure, as he stood only five feet eight and weighed 130 pounds. Mosby was not a son of the frontier who brought tracking and woodland skills to his service. He had no formal military training, nor did he come from a military family. Mosby brought only intelligence, a refined sense of right and wrong, and a strong desire to serve. In essence, he was a patriot. He enlisted as a private soldier, and rose through the ranks due to his determination and ability. These are the same qualities that today's special operations forces seek to recruit and retain. Today, these same attributes are found in the commissioned and noncommissioned officer ranks of the 75th Rangers.

On the character of John Mosby, one incident stands out. So effective were Mosby's interdiction of supplies and couriers that General Ulysses S. Grant ordered General Phil Sheridan to hang all captured soldiers who rode for Mosby. In September 1864, seven Confederates who were thought to be Mosby's soldiers were executed. After informing General Lee of his intentions, Mosby selected seven captured Union soldiers, by lottery, for execution. Only three of these soldiers were actually hung. In November of that same year, Mosby wrote a letter to Sheridan asking that both sides forgo these executions. He pointed out that this was in Sheridan's best interest, as he captured far more of General Sheridan's men than Sheridan had taken of his own. Sheridan agreed, and no more prisoners taken on either side for the remainder of the war were formally executed.

Following the Civil War, Rangers all but disappeared from the ranks of the American military. There was Teddy Roosevelt and his Rough Riders in the Spanish-American War in 1898, but no Rangers. There were also no Ranger units in the Great War in Europe. I suspect that those in the patrols of the American Expeditionary Force who left the wire to venture into no-man's-land during World War I (1914–1918) were Ranger-like doughboys, but they were not called such. Rangers, as a part of the American military culture, were not to surface again until World War II, and then in a most remarkable and worthy fashion. If those early Rangers, from Rogers to Mosby, provided history and precedent, the Rangers of World War II gave modern Rangers a generous measure of organization, professionalism, and documented battlefield courage. In a word, the Rangers of the Greatest Generation were magnificent. No study of

today's 75th Ranger Regiment is complete without a careful examination of the Rangers of World War II.

In December 1941, the United States had a peacetime army and
no special units. Six months after Pearl Harbor, Brigadier General
Lucian Truscott, U.S. liaison to the British General Staff, petitioned
the Army's chief of staff, General George C. Marshall, to create an
American unit similar to the British commandos, who were organized in battalion-sized units. Permission was given for a U.S. commando unit to be organized, but not without some reservation by
senior leaders such as generals George Marshall and Dwight D. Eisen-
hower. Understandably, they were consumed with the task of building a national army to confront the German Wehrmacht and the
Imperial Japanese Army, which at the time were having their way
with Allied forces in the field. They needed to create whole divisions
and corps—not mere battalions, however capable. There was also
an issue with small components that were considered "special." Our
senior leaders knew that final victory depended on the larger conventional Army and Marine units. They did not want to undermine
the "specialness" of the rank-and-file GIs and marines on whom the
victory would depend. Nor did they want to create a talent drain
from a young conventional force that needed all the leadership it
could find. So the 1st Ranger Battalion was authorized on the premise that it would train and embed small units of these new Rangers
with British commandos to gain valuable combat experience—
experience they could bring back to the rapidly expanding U.S.
Army.

The term *Ranger* was also a convention of Truscott's. In his words,
"I selected 'Rangers' because few words have a more glamorous con-
notation in American military history . . . (men who) exemplified
such high standards of individual courage, initiative, determination,
and ruggedness." So the modern Ranger battalion came to be as the
United States steeled itself for what was to become its first truly
global war.

During the course of the war, six more battalions of Rangers were to follow the 1st Battalion. They served with distinction in the European and North African campaigns, start to finish, and at the end of the war in the Pacific. Like the early Rangers, the exploits of this war's Rangers can be told through a series of remarkable leaders that trained the Rangers and led them in combat. For the purposes of this work, I will focus on just three: William O. Darby, James Earl Rudder, and Robert Prince.

William Orlando Darby was a staff officer with the U.S. Army's V Corps stationed in Northern Ireland in the spring of 1942. A thirty-one-year-old captain, Darby had graduated from West Point in 1933 and then gone on to become an artillery officer with experience in infantry and amphibious operations. He was also an outgoing and charismatic officer—a leader of men. Darby was promoted to major and tasked with organizing and training the 1st Ranger Battalion. The battalion was stood up on June 19, 1942, and Darby personally interviewed 2,000 volunteers from various V Corps units to select the 575 recruits for the 1st Battalion. The fledgling Rangers then put themselves in the hands of the training cadre at the British Commando Training Center near Achnacarry, Scotland. At Achnacarry, they received training in weapons, hand-to-hand combat, patrolling, small-boat handling, and mountaineering. There were also physical conditioning and long road marches. Training involved live-fire drills that took the life of one recruit and wounded several others. Darby and 472 other officers and men of the 1st Battalion survived this rigorous training to become the first of these new Rangers.

William Darby set the standards for the Ranger organization and training in World War II—standards still practiced in the 75th Ranger Regiment today. First, he carefully recruited the volunteers for his unit, looking for men who were motivated and were physically and mentally tough. Then he sought the best training available. At the time, the corporate Allied knowledge in commando tactics and operations resided with the British. Finally, Darby willingly accepted the attrition that comes from an arduous training regime. He organized his battalion on the model of the British commandos—highly mobile, self-contained, and with great firepower. He led from the front. Darby, his fellow officers, and the noncommissioned officers went through the same training as the private soldiers.

A contingent of these first Rangers participated in the ill-fated Dieppe Raid in August 1942, going ashore with the British Number 3 and Number 4 Commandos. They were the first Americans bloodied in the European theater, gaining experience that would prove itself during the Allied invasion of Normandy. As a unit, the 1st Ranger Battalion would spearhead the Allied landings in North Africa with a bold amphibious assault on the Algerian port of Arzew in November 1942, paving the way for the landing of the 1st Infantry Division. The 1st Battalion later fought to secure key mountain passes in the battle for Tunisia. Based on the success of the 1st Ranger Battalion, Darby was ordered to form two more Ranger battalions. Using veterans from his six Ranger companies, he formed the 3rd and 4th Ranger battalions. Darby remained in command of the 1st Battalion, and overall command of all three, which became the 6615th Ranger Force (Provisional). These three battalions became known as Darby's Rangers as they prepared for the invasion of Sicily and Italy. The 1st, 3rd, and 4th fought throughout the Italian campaign, taking on critical and difficult mission sets, including the landings at Salerno and the assault on the Chiunzi Pass. During the Battle of Cisterna, in January 1944, the three battalions found themselves in the path of a division-sized German counterattack. Half of the Rangers from these battalions were killed, wounded, or captured. After Cisterna, the Rangers in the Mediterranean theater ceased to exist as a stand-alone, independent force.

Darby himself was recalled to Washington after Cisterna, but he was later to return to the Mediterranean theater. While serving as assistant commander of the 10th Mountain Division, he was killed by German artillery in April 1945. At the time of his death, Darby had been recommended for advancement to brigadier general, to which he was posthumously promoted. Sadly, the first of the modern Rangers would not live to see the heroism of his Rangers during the Normandy invasion.

While the 1st, 3rd, and 4th were fighting their way up the supposed "soft under-belly of the Axis," military planners were preparing for the important and dangerous cross-channel invasion of Europe. The massive invasion plan called for deception, an airborne assault, and a massive amphibious operation into the teeth of the most heavily defended coastline in history. The success on the American landings on the beaches designated Omaha and Utah hinged on the taking of the fortifications on Pointe du Hoc, where a battery of six large coastal artillery guns commanded both landing sites. These guns were embedded in bunkers atop a ninety-foot cliff that rose between Utah and Omaha. This critical mission fell to the 2nd Ranger Battalion, led by James Earl Rudder.

Earl Rudder was a Texan, a football player, and a Texas high school and college football coach. He was commissioned a second lieutenant in the Army Reserve in 1932 as an infantry officer. Rudder was recalled to active duty in June 1941. The 2nd Ranger Battalion was commissioned on April 1, 1943, at Fort Camp Nathan Bedford Forrest in Tennessee, some ten months after the formation of the 1st Battalion. Due to the success and notoriety of Darby's Rangers, there was no shortage of volunteers for the new battalion. The 2nd had a small but solid cadre of veterans from the 1st Ranger Battalion, many of whom were recovering from combat wounds. This new Ranger battalion got off to a slow start due to a series of commanders who were either inept or transient, or both. Major Rudder took over the 2nd Battalion on July 1, 1943, and told his soldiers that things were about to change. Rudder announced that those in his command were going to work their butts off and soldier with the best in the Army, or they could put in for a transfer. The new commander quickly gained a reputation as a tough and fair leader with very high standards. He listened to his men, worked to make their living and training conditions better, and always led from the front. He also stressed cross-training discipline; every man had to know the other Rangers' jobs, and every man had to be a leader, from private to company commander. His soldiers gave their all for Rudder and then some. As he weeded men out due to the arduous training, there was an ample supply of stateside volunteers wanting to become Rangers. These volunteers wanted to get to the fight as quickly as possible. James Earl Rudder was one of them.

Rudder's Rangers trained in the United States, then followed in Darby's 1st Battalion footsteps and trained at the British Commando Training Center in Scotland. Along with amphibious training and a steady diet of running and forced road marches, the Rangers practiced extensively on scaling steep cliffs. While the 2nd Battalion trained in Scotland, military planners determined that another Ranger battalion would be needed for the invasion, so the 5th Ranger Battalion was activated on September 1, 1943, at Camp Forrest. Their training paralleled that of the 2nd Battalion in the United States and then in Scotland. In early May 1944, the 2nd and the 5th were joined to form the Provisional Ranger Group for the Normandy invasion. As the senior officer, Rudder, now a lieutenant colonel, commanded the group.

On D-day, four companies of Rangers from the 2nd Battalion stormed ashore with the first waves of Allied troops. The remaining two companies from the 2nd and the 5th Battalion waited offshore to reinforce those on the beach. Three companies of Rangers from the 2nd Battalion plus a headquarters element, led by Lieutenant Colonel Rudder, scaled the cliffs at Pointe du Hoc. A single company from the 2nd Battalion landed on Omaha Beach and scaled the heights at Pointe et Raz de la Percée to link up with Rudder's element at Pointe du Hoc. Much has been made of the heroism of the 2nd Battalion that day, perhaps the single most noted Ranger action of the war. Rudder's Rangers fought as they trained, but they paid a heavy price that day. Half of them were killed or wounded; Rudder himself was wounded twice. In the words of President Ronald Reagan at Omaha Beach on the fortieth anniversary of the D-day invasion, "These are the boys of Pointe du Hoc. These are the men who took the cliffs. These are the champions who helped free a continent. These are the heroes who helped end a war."

A great deal has been written about Rudder and the courage of the Rangers of the 2nd Battalion who scaled those cliffs under fire. If I had to choose one book, I recommend *The Battalion: The Dramatic Story of the 2nd Ranger Battalion in World War II*, by Colonel Robert Black. Colonel Black's fine work also details the hard fighting endured by the 2nd (and 5th) Battalion during the Brittany campaign, the Hürtgen Forest, and the Battle of the Bulge. By many accounts, the fighting in the Hürtgen Forest, specifically Hill 400, was the most difficult and costly Ranger engagement of the war. As for James Earl Rudder, he rose to the rank of major general in the Army Reserve and served as the president of Texas A&M University for eleven years, until his death in 1970.

While the 2nd and 5th battalions fought in Europe and the 1st, 3rd, and 4th in the Mediterranean, the 6th Battalion, which was to serve in the Pacific theater, came to the war by a more circuitous route. The 98th Field Artillery Battalion stationed in Colorado consisted of three batteries of 75-millimeter howitzers, one thousand men, and eight hundred mules. They were slated for duty in the Pacific theater and shipped out in early 1943; they wound up in Port Moresby, New Guinea, as a part of the Sixth Army. They trained there for a year but saw no action. Horse-drawn artillery was deemed obsolete just as command of the 98th fell to an enterprising 1936 West Point graduate by the name of Henry Mucci. Lieutenant Colonel Mucci had run a training camp in Hawaii that employed Ranger tactics and, with permission from the Sixth Army, Mucci set about turning his mule skinners into Rangers. The artillery officers

and veterinarians were swapped for infantry and engineering officers, and the unit was attrited from a thousand-man artillery unit
to a five-hundred-man Ranger battalion. In September 1944, after
a year of hard training, the 98th was commissioned as the 6th Ranger Battalion.

The 6th Rangers first saw action in the Philippine campaign. In
October 1944, the unit took several small islands that guarded the
approaches to the Leyte Gulf landing beaches. With the islands in
Ranger hands, the landings took place without incident and General
MacArthur was able to wade ashore from his landing craft to the
waiting troop of photographers. The first boots on the ground (with
respect to those few Americans and many Filipinos fighting in the
resistance) on the day of the general's famous return to the Philippines were Ranger boots.

The 6th Battalion fought many engagements in the Philippines
and participated in the initial occupation of Japan. However, it will
be forever remembered for its brilliant rescue of the American and
Allied prisoners at the Japanese POW camp in Cabanatuan in late
January 1945. This famous raid has been chronicled in Hampton
Sides's fine book *Ghost Soldiers* (2001) and the feature films *Back to
Bataan* (1945) and *The Great Raid* (2005). In this textbook rescue,
Lieutenant Colonel Mucci led a reinforced company of Rangers
through Japanese lines and marched them thirty miles to a position
near the camp. There, 512 prisoners of war, including some 450 who
were survivors of the Bataan Death March, were facing a possible
mass execution by the retreating Japanese forces. There were 6,000
to 8,000 Japanese troops in the vicinity of the 120-man Ranger force.
The Rangers were aided in their movement behind the lines by Philippine partisan forces and a small contingent of the elite Sixth Army
Alamo Scouts. Mucci delegated "my wonderful captain," Robert
Prince, to plan and lead the final assault on the camp.

Robert Prince was a tall, quiet Stanford graduate who had grown
up in Seattle. He was trusted by Mucci and revered by his enlisted

Rangers. On the eve of the raid, the Rangers had been on the move for two days, sleeping an average of two hours per day. With final but sketchy intelligence from Filipino partisans and the Alamo Scouts, Prince planned his raid. He would attack with two elements of Rangers; one to engage and neutralize the two-hundred-man Japanese guard force and the other to manage the prisoners. Because of the open terrain around the camp, the Rangers had to literally crawl the last fifteen hundred meters on their bellies. The assault force was able to take advantage of an American P-61 night fighter that circled low over the camp to create a diversion. This well-chronicled action went off extraordinarily well. All 512 POWs were freed and escorted back through the lines. Two Rangers were killed and ten wounded in the raid; the Japanese guard force of more than two hundred soldiers was wiped out. An additional three hundred or more Japanese were killed by Filipino partisans and U.S. air strikes as the enemy pursued the Rangers and former prisoners back to the safety of the American lines.

For those who study special actions, this successful raid is a classic—all the more so for the hasty preparation and superb execution on the part of Prince and his weary Rangers. Most actions of this size and complexity demand aerial photography, sand-table terrain models, and multiple rehearsals. Prince drew it up in the dirt. This was like sketching a few musical notes on scrap paper, then handing it to an orchestra and asking it to play a symphony. The Cabanatuan raid was a masterful piece of soldiering.

After the war, the self-effacing Robert Prince played down his own role in the Great Raid. Yet he was always quick to point out the courage of his Rangers. He would talk about the skill of the P-61 pilots, who feigned engine trouble by cutting and restarting one of their engines to simulate an aircraft in peril, allowing the Rangers to crawl up to the camp. Prince praised the critical last-minute intelligence delivered by the Alamo Scouts. And he lauded the partisan Filipinos who served as a blocking force and fought off a Japanese counterattack as the Rangers returned to friendly lines with the former POWs.

"People everywhere thank me," Prince said of the raid in an interview with the *Seattle Post-Intelligencer* in April 1945. "I think the thanks should go the other way. I'll be grateful for the rest of my life that I had a chance in this war to do something that was not destructive. Nothing for me can ever compare with the satisfaction I got from freeing those men." I am also personally blessed to share this sentiment; I, too, on a far smaller scale, led a successful POW rescue raid in Vietnam. It's something that stays with you. The look of men who have just been freed from cages is too poignant to describe.

Robert Prince died quietly in his home in Port Townsend, Washington, on January 2, 2009. He was eighty-nine years old. He was, in the words of his family, "a reserved and humble man." One of his Rangers put it differently: "The Japanese in that camp had their Emperor, but we had a Prince. And that made all the difference."

Leaders like William Darby, James Earl Rudder, and Robert Prince, among many others, serve as superb role models for today's Rangers. These Ranger leaders displayed dedication, determination, initiative, integrity, and both courage and coolness under fire. They were patriotic and humble—men who let their exploits in battle and in garrison define their character. They deflected praise from themselves to the brother Rangers they commanded and those elements that supported them in battle. These Ranger leaders and the Ranger battalions from World War II left a gallant legacy. Few combat units today enjoy such a rich tradition of sacrifice and service. Yet with great respect for the hallowed and honored precedent of the brave combat leaders mentioned above, I personally believe the greatest contribution of the World War II Rangers is the important and underreported service of the enlisted Ranger leaders: the noncommissioned officers.

We know much of Ranger leaders from the commissioned-officer ranks in World War II and going back to colonial times, but little, or not enough, has been written about the steady and often critical leadership that comes from the Ranger ranks. Perhaps no historian has more closely captured the valor and the critical role of our Army's NCOs during World War II than Stephen Ambrose in his *Band of Brothers*—the book and the made-for-TV miniseries. In my reading of Ranger history, perhaps no action serves as a better example of NCO leadership than the story of the "fabulous four."

On September 9, 1944, the 2nd Ranger Battalion was tasked with helping to take the channel port of Brest. Ports like Brest were critical to supply the Allied breakout from the beachheads at Normandy. That morning, First Lieutenant Robert Edlin, Sergeant William Dreher, Sergeant Warren Burmaster, and Sergeant William Courtney were conducting a patrol leader's reconnaissance of a battery of the huge 11-inch coastal guns that protected Brest. A patrol leader's recon is a standard preassault infantry tactic to gather intelligence before attacking a fortified installation. This battery was protected by pillboxes, minefields, and a battalion of German paratroopers. The mission of Edlin's patrol was to bring the information on these defenses back to Lieutenant Colonel Rudder so they could plan their assault on this heavily defended position. The capture of a Germany defender would certainly have been helpful. Finding a path through the minefield was critical.

The four Rangers had silently worked their way through the pillboxes and were about to retrace their steps to American lines when Sergeant Courtney said, "I see a way through the minefield," and took off at a run. There was no "Sir, I'd like to recommend that we . . ." or "Sir, I have an idea that if we . . ." At that moment, leadership of the patrol passed from Lieutenant Edlin to Sergeant Courtney. His brother Rangers followed. The four burst into a pillbox close to the battery and captured nineteen German paratroopers without firing a shot. Lieutenant Edlin forced a German soldier at gunpoint to take him to the commanding officer. There, again at gunpoint, he demanded the surrender of the battery. When the German commander refused, Edlin pulled the pin of a grenade and held it to the officer's chest. The commander relented and ordered the battery garrison to surrender. The rest of the 2nd Battalion was brought up to secure the battery, along with Lieutenant Colonel Rudder to formally accept the surrender. Thanks to Sergeant William Courtney's bold leadership, a 4-man Ranger patrol captured 850 German prisoners. Courageous? Most certainly—above and beyond. But in my view, it was the culture within the 2nd Battalion that recognized, encouraged, and trusted the leadership of this fine Ranger sergeant. This same culture is found today in the 75th Ranger Regiment; every Ranger is a leader.

The Ranger battalions that so gallantly fought in World War II were either disbanded or absorbed into larger infantry units. The Rangers of the 1st, 3rd, and 4th were so decimated by combat losses that they literally ceased to exist as battalions. Even as these bloodied and surviving Rangers passed into the ranks of line infantry battalions, their contribution as Rangers did not end. As the veteran German army gave ground in the final days of the Third Reich, there was no shortage of dangerous objectives that had to be taken. American commanders now knew of the Rangers, and if they were available to them, their Rangers, the Rangers sprinkled through the ranks of their conventional units, often spearheaded the attack. These Rangers continued to lead the way until the end of the war.

Put into the stark accounting of killed and wounded in action, the World War II Rangers paid a staggering price. Five Ranger battalions saw combat in Europe and the Mediterranean (the 29th Ranger Battalion was activated and trained in England for a short time but never saw active combat), to which some six thousand Rangers were assigned. Accounting for those who became prisoners of war, the Rangers of those five battalions had an attrition rate on the order of 70 percent. The 6th Battalion in the Pacific fared much better, but it had joined the war late. Following the war, the Ranger battalions, like many others that were activated for the war, simply disappeared. Given today's standing all-volunteer force, the continuous engagement in Iraq and Afghanistan, and the emergence of SOF as a part of our standing military force, it is hard to imagine the scale of demobilization that took place following World War II. Unlike today, when our economy and much of our contemporary culture evolves independently from our national wartime commitments, our nation wanted the boys home—all the boys.

In late June 1950, the North Korean army swarmed across the 38th Parallel, which divided North and South Korea. The North Koreans pushed the reeling South Koreans and their American advisers south, ultimately to a defensive position around the city of Pusan. There, the hard-pressed South Koreans and their United Nations allies were able to stabilize their position while planning a counterattack strategy. General Douglas MacArthur, Supreme Allied Commander and Commander, Far East Command, cast about for some offensive weapon in this defensive struggle. There was none, so he ordered the organization of unconventional units for behind-the-lines operations to disrupt enemy supply routes, to conduct diversion operations, and to combat escalating North Korean guerrilla activity. To serve in those roles, MacArthur turned to a battalion of Army Raiders, the Navy's Underwater Demolition Teams, British commandos, and a single company of Army Rangers.

The Ranger story in Korea can be told in the brief and violent history of the Eighth Army Rangers and a gallant young second lieutenant named Ralph Puckett. Given the arduous training of Darby's and Rudder's Rangers, and the detailed preparation of those Rangers headed for battle, it was incredible what Puckett and his men were able to accomplish in such a short time. Ralph Puckett grew up in Tifton, Georgia, and graduated from West Point in 1949. At the outbreak of the Korean War, he was assigned to the 24th Infantry Division, awaiting transport from Japan to the division then fighting in Korea. Puckett volunteered for Ranger duty and was selected, along with two of his U.S. Military Academy classmates, Barnard Cummings and Charles Bunn, as the officer corps for the Eighth Army Ranger Company. Puckett was further selected as the first among equals as the company commander, with Cummings and Bunn as his platoon commanders. Together, the three young officers recruited the balance of their seventy-four enlisted volunteers in Japan. Few of these volunteers had seen combat.

The Eighth Army Ranger Company was activated on August 29, 1950, and shipped to Korea in early September. One can imagine what was going through Lieutenant Puckett's mind while crossing the Sea of Japan to Korea. He and his classmates entered West Point just as World War II ended; they were in high school while their fathers, uncles, and older brothers went to war. Now they were headed into battle in a two-month-old war with green troops and the prospect of immediate combat. Once in Korea, Puckett trained his new Rangers relentlessly in fundamental infantry tactics. In his words, "The officers set the example and either taught the class or participated as a trainee. We shared the same hardships and became hot, cold, wet, dusty, tired, and dirty along with our men." On October 8, not six weeks after the unit's formation, the Eighth Army Rangers were pronounced ready for combat and joined the 24th Infantry Division.

If Ralph Puckett epitomized the Eighth Army Rangers, then the battle for Hill 205 firmly entrenched the Korean War Rangers in Ranger lore. On the night of November 26, 1950, Puckett and fifty-one of his Rangers dug in to hold the hill in subzero temperatures. That night, they withstood five Chinese attacks, fighting with grenades and bayonets when their ammunition ran low. On the sixth attack, the Rangers were overwhelmed and driven from Hill 205. Puckett, himself badly wounded, told his Rangers to leave him and seek safety, but they dragged him bleeding from the hill. Ten Rangers died fighting while thirty-one others were wounded. Ralph Puckett, wounded multiple times, was evacuated to the United States for extended recovery. Like their brothers from the 1st, 3rd, and 4th Ranger battalions of World War II, the Eighth Army Ranger Company ceased to be and was disbanded soon after the battle. Lieutenant Cummings died on Hill 205 and Lieutenant Bunn was assigned to the new Ranger Training Center at Fort Benning. Ralph Puckett, following a lengthy recovery from his battle wounds, went on to serve in Vietnam, and after retirement, to serve as the honorary colonel of the 75th Ranger Regiment. He now takes a well-deserved place with William Darby, Earl Rudder, and Robert Prince on the honor role of Ranger leaders. Today Colonel Puckett lives in Columbus, Georgia, and is a distinguished guest at all Ranger functions.

A total of fourteen Ranger companies were trained and activated at Fort Benning for the Korean War. They existed for just fourteen months or a part thereof, and only six saw combat. Most of those were used in the role of light infantry in support of divisional objectives. Two historical notes will complete this short overview of the Korean War Rangers. Shortly before their deactivation, First Lieutenant Ralph Puckett was succeeded in command of the Eighth Army Rangers by Captain John Paul Vann. Vann's controversial and iconic career in Vietnam was the subject of Neil Sheehan's Pulitzer Prize–winning history of Vietnam, *A Bright Shining Lie* (1988). Second, one of the companies that saw combat was the 2nd Ranger Company, which was made up of black volunteers from the 101st Airborne Division and the 505th Airborne Regiment. It was the only all-black Ranger unit in history, and their exploits on the battlefield are a proud segment of Korean War Ranger history.

The training of Rangers and Ranger companies led to the establishment in 1950 of what is now the U.S. Army Ranger School, an Army leadership school that trains individual soldiers in combat leadership and awards the coveted Ranger Tab. During the time of the Vietnam War, fifteen Ranger companies were organized under the 75th Infantry Regiment, and all but two served in Vietnam. These Vietnam-era Ranger companies were formed with veterans from the Army's Long Range Patrol Scouts (LRPS), and served as the eyes and ears of main-force elements both in Vietnam and Laos. Beyond their reconnaissance role, these Rangers also went behind enemy lines to disrupt North Vietnamese supply and communications lines and to perform selective hunter-killer operations. Individually Tabbed Rangers served in nearly every ground-combat unit in Vietnam, and it was these soldiers who carried the Tab on their shoulder that kept the Ranger legacy alive following Vietnam.

On October 1, 1974, General Creighton Abrams, the Army's chief of staff, revived the Rangers as a combat unit with the activation of the 1st Ranger Battalion at Fort Benning and the 2nd Ranger Battalion at Fort Lewis, Washington. Elements of the 1st Battalion participated in Operation Eagle Claw, the failed rescue of our diplomatic corps taken hostage in Iran in 1980. The two Ranger battalions led the invasion of Grenada in 1983. In 1984, the 3rd Ranger Battalion was activated. Later that year, the three battalions came under the command of the 75th Ranger Regiment at Fort Benning. In 1989, the entire Regiment parachuted into Panama during Operation Just Cause, spearheading the seizure of that country and the removal of strongman Manuel Noriega. From this first action of the newly formed 75th Ranger Regiment, our Rangers have been in virtually every American engagement since: Operation Desert Storm in Saudi Arabia and Kuwait (1991); Operation Restore Hope in Somalia (1993), where six Rangers from the Regiment were killed in action; Operation Uphold Democracy in Haiti (1994); and Operation Joint Guardian in Kosovo (2000–2001). Since 9/11, they have been continuously deployed in various operations in the now decade-long Global War on Terrorism.

General Abrams's concept of the Rangers was that it was to be the premier light-infantry unit in the U.S. Army. In what is known as the Abrams Charter, the general stated his vision for the Rangers in plain soldier's language: "The Ranger battalion is to be an elite, light, and most proficient infantry battalion in the world; A battalion that can do things with its hands and weapons better than any-one. The battalion will not contain any 'Hoodlums' or 'Brigands' and if the battalion is formed of such persons, it will be disbanded. Wherever the battalion goes, it will be apparent that it is the best."

Before we move onto the recruiting and training of Army Rang-ers, let us talk briefly about the current organization of the 75th Ranger Regiment. Today, the regiment looks not unlike it did in 1984, with three line rifle battalions: the 1st Battalion, located at Hunter Army Airfield in Savannah, Georgia; the 2nd, at Fort Lewis, near Tacoma, Washington; and the 3rd, colocated with the regimen-tal headquarters at Fort Benning, Georgia. In the Regiment and in this book, these battalions will often be referred to in military short-hand as one, seven, five (pronounced one-seven-five) for the 1st Bat-talion, 2/75 for the 2nd, and 3/75 for the 3rd. Each rifle battalion has four rifle companies, a support company, and a headquarters company. Only a few years ago, there were but three rifle companies per battalion with the supporting elements integral to each com-pany. The need for Rangers in the current battlespace has led to the recent plus-up of the additional rifle company and a stand-alone support company. In 2006, the Regimental Special Troops Battalion was added to the regiment to support the line rifle battalions in their deployment rotations. The RSTB, located at Fort Benning, has indi-vidual companies that specialize in communications, intelligence, special weapons, and other Ranger-centric skills. The Regimental Special Troops Battalion is the only battalion that does not deploy as a battalion. Nonetheless, the specially skilled Rangers from the RSTB spend a great deal of time overseas. Special teams and ele-ments from this battalion rotate independently and with the rifle battalions. This keeps one-third of these talented Regimental Spe-cial Troops Battalion Rangers overseas at any given time. We will get to the combat training and integration of the RSTB Rangers with the rifle-battalion Rangers later in this work. More immediately, there is a single company in the Regimental Special Troops Battalion that has an exclusively stateside mission. It is the RSTB's Ranger Selection and Training Company, or, simply, the S&T Company. The S&T Company is tasked with the assessment and selection of all new Rangers entering the regiment. (During the time I was at Fort Benning, this training company was designated as the Ranger Operations Company.)

All Rangers who soldier with the 75th Ranger Regiment receive their qualification at Fort Benning, Georgia. Fort Benning itself is a huge military base near Columbus in southwestern Georgia and the site of the Army's Maneuver Center of Excellence. The National Infantry Museum, located just off post, is one of the finest military museums in the nation. Fort Benning also is home to the 3rd Heavy Brigade Combat Team of the 3rd Infantry Division, the parent base for U.S. Army Maneuver Center for Excellence, and the location of numerous infantry-related support commands. Close to 150,000 military personnel and their families call Fort Benning home, which is about half the civilian population of the nearby greater-Columbus metropolitan area. In addition to the training and qualification Rangers for the 75th Regiment, Fort Benning hosts a number of Army training venues, including the Army's Officer Candidate School, a Noncommissioned Officer Academy, the Basic Airborne School, and the U.S. Army Ranger School. The 75th Ranger Regimental Headquarters, the Regimental Commanding Officer (RCO), and the headquarters staff are colocated with the 3rd Ranger Battalion and the Regimental Special Troops Battalion at Fort Benning. The headquarters and the two battalions occupy the same compound. Also in this compound is the Ranger Selection and Training Company.

The Regiment awards the Tan Beret and Scroll to new Rangers on the recommendation of the S&T Company. Within the S&T Company, a cadre of veteran Ranger sergeants determine who will and who will not soldier with the 75th Ranger Regiment. While writing *Sua Sponte*, I was assigned to the Ranger Selection and Training Company and was detailed out to the company's various training venues.

In the fall of 2010, the company's cadre sergeants went about the business of assessing and selecting new Rangers for the Regiment while instructing one aging Navy SEAL in the process.

As previously mentioned, the process by which enlisted soldiers and officers enter the Regiment is through the Ranger Assessment and Selection Program, or RASP. For the enlisted soldiers, it is by way of RASP Level One; for officers and senior NCOs, it's RASP Level Two. Both of these venues serve as reentry programs for soldiers returning to the regiment. In *Sua Sponte*, we will explore both in some detail. I need to point out that my RASP, and even the term *RASP*, is but a point in time. Ranger assessment and selection, and the associated skill-based training, are evolving, dynamic programs. Only a few years ago, it was different than during my time with the Regiment. In speaking with the Regimental Commanding Officer and his subordinate leaders tasked with the training of new rangers, it may well be different in the years ahead. Lessons learned on the battlefield and future operational requirements will drive the Ranger assessment and training pipelines. In this work, I will sometimes refer to the way it was, and even to anticipated changes for future Ranger selection classes. However, this is the way it was in the fall of 2010. I am confident that goals of the process have not changed and will never change. That goal is the assessment, selection, and training of Regimental Rangers for the business of light airborne infantry and light-infantry assault. They will be expected, often on short notice, to go anywhere in the world and to win that fight.

Before we join the Selection and Training Company and business of Ranger selection, we will explore just where we find the men who qualify to be Ranger candidates, and what must take place during RASP in order for them to serve with the 75th Rangers.

CHAPTER TWO

RECRUITING FOR
THE REGIMENT

An Army recruiter once told me that we do not, in fact, have an all-volunteer force; he said we have an all-recruited force. The 75th Ranger Regiment, like the Army-at-large and the other services, are looking for quality individuals to fill its ranks. Indeed, all the services compete with corporate America for available talent. Many of the same attributes that make for a good hire at Starbucks, FedEx, or the local fire department also make for a good Ranger. The Rangers are looking for their share of these good people—good young men, to be specific, because ground combat in the Army and Marine Corps, by congressional dictate, is an all-male enterprise. So while the Rangers are looking for good men, "good" is just a starting point. They must also have some distinct traits and special aptitudes.

Perhaps a reasonable place to begin the recruiting process is to cast a wide net: the universe of available young men of military service age. In my work *A Tactical Ethic: Moral Conduct in the Insurgent Battlespace* (Naval Institute Press, 2010), I focused on this group with respect to the talents as well as the shortcomings this generation brings to military service. From that work:

> *As a general grouping, the young men who are candidates for our ground-force components are the Millennials—those born between roughly 1980 and 2000. They've also been labeled as Generation Y or the Echo Boomers. There are plenty of them in uniform, and more are coming. As with all generational classes, they are special and distinctive, with their own positive and negative characteristics as those relate to military service. Applying generalizations to individual conduct is always a dangerous business, but Millennials seem, when compared to other generations, to be more ambitious, more brand conscious, more mobile in that they move more often, and have more experience with family breakdown and divorce. They seem to be more highly influenced by their peers and their workplace culture. This generation is more open-minded about sexual and romantic encounters and personal attachments, and they are more tolerant of alternative lifestyles. They are exponentially more tech savvy than any previous generation. Their loyalties can be fierce and shifting. A great deal has been written about the Millennials— by employers, journalists, sociologists, and philosophers. They've been variously described as hardworking, impatient, clever, resourceful, lazy, team-orientated, and incorrigible. They are said to be self-centered and narcissist—the "me" generation. So it's the military's task, as with any employer, to find a way to harness the Millennials' potential as well as to effectively deal with any baggage that may accompany them into the workplace. Demanding that they be different or insisting that they summarily disregard the factors that shaped them is simply not an option. The extent to which the military can deal with the Millennials' array of characteristics and potentially conflicting values will have a great bearing in the success of that generation's soldiers, sailors, airmen, and marines, and how they function in our ground-combat units.*

So this is the group from which the 75th Rangers must plumb and extract their successful Ranger candidates. As a universe, it includes some 20 million American males. Yet again, as a premier SOF combat force, the Rangers have a set of elevated requirements and expectations—qualities that dramatically cut into that seemingly large pool. In my close association with SOF training venues over the past two decades, I have identified six areas of aptitude or excellence that apply variously to all SOF ground-combat components and most certainly to the recruiting and training of a modern American Ranger.

1. *Physical fitness.* While it is highly intuitive that a Ranger has to be fit, that requirement is not so easily met as one might think. Young Americans now grow up neither eating as well nor exercising as much as previous generations. Fast food and sedentary lifestyles (TVs and computers) have rendered many young males unfit for the physical demands of military service. It's been my observation that aside from all-around fitness, "durability" is the key component in the physical makeup of a SOF warrior. Durability in military-speak is hard to define, but carrying sixty pounds on an all-night forced march and being able to fight throughout the following day is a good start. Being a star high school athlete does not always make a young man durable. A great deal of Army basic training, which we will briefly address later, is designed around promoting durability and teaching good eating habits. Many of today's high school graduates are simply physically unsuited to basic entry-level military training, let alone the elevated standards of a serving special operator.

Perhaps more than any other SOF unit, physical fitness is a way of life in the 75th Ranger Regiment. Many senior Ranger leaders believe it is the most important of the Big Five. As you will see during RASP, physical fitness and durability are the first qualities assessed in the selection of a young Ranger.

2. *Intelligence*. Soldiering is not brain surgery, but I contend that intelligence is a key factor in nearly every endeavor, whether you're a counter jockey at Burger King or a paralegal in a law office or a special operator. The single most competitive commodity for those looking for new hires is smarts. A large body of evidence suggests that the best barbers, waiters, police officers, health-care workers, computer programmers, and soldiers are the smart ones—those who learn quickly and are able to apply that learning to operational tasks. The armed forces are prohibited from giving IQ tests, but they do use the Armed Services Vocational Aptitude Battery (ASVAB). This test identifies certain suitability factors for service-related specialties, but it's basically an IQ test. Along with intelligence it identifies related mental abilities like judgment, problem solving, and decision making. A great many attributes that make for a good soldier can be taught through drill and conditioning. Unfortunately, intelligence is not one of them. The Rangers, like SEALs, Special Forces, and the Marine Corps, are looking for candidates who are smart. Those charged with the assessment and training of Rangers look closely at ASVAB scores as well as other personality and psychological testing instruments.

God-given intelligence aside, a great many Americans have been pushed through a primary and secondary educational system that has left them intellectually unsuited for even basic military training. Many high school graduates simply don't have the education to get into the Army, let alone shoulder the intellectual requirements of a special operations unit.

3. *Mental toughness*. This is a difficult attribute to measure, and it's different from intelligence, but drill sergeants and military trainers the world over recognize it when they see it in a young recruit. Perhaps it is a blend of confidence and determination. I believe it comes from a young person's parenting. Parents who have raised their children with high expectations and discipline have predisposed

them to mental toughness. Mental toughness can be demonstrated by something as simple as having a pattern of finishing what one starts. It conditions a young person to expect success and not to be a quitter. This can be a powerful force for success in basic military and special operations training. I've been to more than a few SOF-component graduations and have made it a point to meet the parents of those young men I considered mentally tough. These were proud parents, but, without exception, none were surprised that their son had completed a difficult and highly selective training regime. It's how they raised their children.

Mental toughness and intelligence seem to be qualities found in those who set goals and accomplish them. There's a very high degree of success in those young men who are smart enough to clearly see their goal and have the mental toughness to persevere in achieving that goal.

4. *Ethical maturity.* On today's insurgent battlefield, right conduct and strict adherence to specific rules of engagement are becoming increasingly important. The Millennials are a video- and online-centric generation. While that may predispose them to being good with computers, it also exposes them to a great deal of video violence, often gratuitous violence. The business of Rangering deals in real violence, not video violence—a big difference. Sometimes, the decade or so of video games, reality TV shows, and the farce-fighting of professional wrestling in the life of an eighteen-year-old leaves an imprinting that's at odds with reality. To the extent that it exists, this imprinting has to be overcome before a Ranger candidate can become a Ranger warrior. Rangers are in the business of both taking life and exercising the moral restraint to not take life—often on the same operation and perhaps in a single engagement. Ethical grounding is as important as professional combat-arms skills. Young men who want to become Rangers have to come to terms with issues of proportionality and restraint, along with the courage and professionalism to handle mortal combat. Fortunately, there are young

men who can do this—who understand right and wrong in the real world. Many others have simply spent too much time in front of the TV and cannot.

Coincident with ethical maturity is adherence to standards. Service in the 75th Ranger Regiment is all about maintaining high standards of conduct, both in garrison and on the battlefield.

5. *Patriotism.* We don't often think of this as a requisite warrior skill, or one that is necessarily reserved for warriors, but for those serving in ground-combat roles, it is most important. It's not an attribute conferred by waving the flag or a conservative political persuasion. And it's not just a willingness to serve one's country, although that's important. This kind of patriotism is a deep-seated belief that a warrior, in uniform in the service of his nation, has the moral authority to take human life. The military in general and Rangers in particular are in the business of killing people. For those who fly drones or employ standoff weapons, killing is almost an abstraction, because they are physically far removed from the battlefield. This is not so for a Ranger; for him, it's up close and personal. A dead insurgent fighter is part of the job; so is the unintended and unfortunate death of a noncombatant. In casual soldier's banter, killing can be trivialized or the enemy can be so demeaned as to appear less than human. If this casual banter leads to motive, then the warrior is potentially on a slippery ethical slope. Patriotism is the primary moral armor of our ground combatants. Their professional skill gets the job done and gets them home physically intact. Patriotism—the belief in a righteous fight—is what returns them home mentally and morally intact.

It's been my experience that those seeking to serve in SOF-related units with no patriotic grounding usually do so for some misplaced, macho reason or to prove something to themselves. These men are usually incomplete and ineffective warriors. Patriotism leads to self-sacrifice and team orientation—both solid Ranger attributes.

6. *Culture suitability.* This is an awkward term and perhaps an imprecise one, but one that applies to SOF ground combatants— Special Forces, Marine special operators, SEALs, and certainly to Rangers. It's the bonding of warriors. SOF units are part fraternity, part brotherhood, and part family. It also has something of the pack or gang mentality—a comfort that comes from being among one's own. It's something shared by Rangers, SEALs, and street gangs. You belong; this is your tribe. Culture suitability is not restricted to SOF units; it can be found in a conventional military platoon or even with extended family or lifelong friends. All that's required is a common goal, a challenging rite of passage, and a need to belong. In the context of military training, such rites of passage can be transformational for a young soldier. Add to this mix the prospect of mortal combat and there exists the fertile ground for a male warrior bonding that is unique and quite powerful.

While this culture suitability leads to bonding that makes for brothers-in-arms, it can come at a cost. In the case of a young Ranger, his spouse, girlfriend, and/or family sometimes get less from their soldier and feel slighted. They have to share their Ranger with his Ranger brothers. A Ranger (or any SOF operator) needs both his family and his brother Rangers to become a fully formed warrior. To become that fully formed warrior, he must carefully manage these two important and vital influences in his life.

This issue of culture suitability, or the reasons for the lack of it, is a compelling theme. The regimental psychologist said it this way: "I think one of the challenges for Ranger candidates and their inability to mesh into the Ranger culture is that they never played pickup games as kids. They've been supervised in play and organized sports all their life. Personal issues that arise between players and opponents in sports were settled by adults or adult authority figures. In pickup games, jerklike behavior on the part of one kid is settled by the other kids. They deal with it. We see it in the peer review process in RASP. Some soldiers just don't know how to deal with a problem that develops between them and another soldier. They've never had to.

"Another issue is the self-esteem thing. A lot of these kids have either been the best athlete in school or in many cases have been led to believe they were the best. They've played on soccer teams where everyone gets a trophy. In the Ranger assessment and selection process, we're not overly complimentary for success and can get downright hostile with the underperformers and underachievers. Some of these soldiers have never had someone tell them they are weak or that their performance was unsatisfactory. We do that a lot here. We do it a lot in the battalions; it's called maintaining a standard. If you're not living up to or performing up to a standard, someone is going to call it to your attention."

The source of Ranger candidates, enlisted soldiers and officers, is the United States Army. The process by which a young soldier or officer becomes a Ranger is the very well formatted Ranger Assessment and Selection Program—RASP Level One for junior enlisted men and RASP Level Two for officers and senior noncommissioned officers. The RASP programs recently took the place of the Ranger Indoctrination Program for enlisted soldiers and the Ranger Orientation Program for officers and NCOs. Currently, the gateway to the Regiment is RASP. Before a young enlisted volunteer can become a Ranger, he must first become a soldier. Before a young officer can serve in the 75th Ranger Regiment, he must first become branch (infantry, armor, signal corps) qualified and then prove himself as a leader or specialist in a conventional Army unit. Let's look at the process that gets a young man or young enlisted soldier to the Ranger Assessment and Selection Program.

The majority of young men who volunteer for the 75th Rangers must first graduate from one of the Army's entry-level training venues. Army entry-level training is a two-step process. The first step is the nine-week Basic Combat Training (BCT) course that makes a soldier out of a civilian. Following Basic Combat Training, our new soldier will receive Advanced Individual Training (AIT). AIT trains the soldier in one of the Army's many needed skills, called a military occupational specialty (MOS). These specialties include supply (Quartermaster Corps), ordnance, engineering, intelligence, combat medic, and infantry, to name a few. Since the Rangers serve in a self-contained regiment, they have a need for a variety of specialties. The Regiment recruits for these specialties while soldiers complete their Basic Combat Training at facilities located across the country at various Army bases. The key MOS in the 75th Ranger Regiment is the infantry MOS. Infantrymen are created at Fort Benning, Georgia, in a process called One Station Unit Training (OSUT). OSUT is a rather strange acronym for Army entry-level training; it comes from the merging of the two core training programs for new infantrymen. The first portion of OSUT is Basic Combat Training. Following BCT, the infantry-soldier trainees go immediately into Advanced Individual Training to become an infantryman. BCT and infantry AIT are conducted at the same facility, or "one station," which is Fort Benning.

Infantry is a branch of the Army, and there are those in uniform who would claim that it is *the* branch of the Army. But then those in the armor, artillery, and aviation branches would make that same claim. The Fort Benning One Station Unit Training creates infantrymen and confers the 11B Infantry MOS. These 11B-trained Infantry Branch soldiers are simply called "Eleven Bravos." These are infantry*men*, as there are no female Eleven Bravos in the Army. Because infantry skills are basic to the tasking of the 75th Ranger Regiment, a great many Rangers carry the 11B MOS. The Eleven Bravo RASP candidates, along with soldiers with other MOS designations, will go through the Ranger assessment and selection process together. No distinction is made between infantrymen and noninfantrymen in RASP. All must qualify as Rangers.

The first nine weeks of Basic Combat Training for all new soldiers

in the Army is essentially the same. This includes basic soldieriza-
tion skills and orientation to service life, such as learning to wear
the uniform, drill and ceremony, and classes on Army heritage and
Army Core Values. There is training in combat-related skills such
as first aid, map reading, land navigation, and communications, and
the traditional battlefield skills of marksmanship and hand-to-hand
combat—now known as combatives. Some 124 hours are devoted
to individual rifle and weapons training. And, of course, there's a
generous dose of physical conditioning, including calisthenics, road
marches, and the obstacle course. For many new enlistees, the Army
chow halls provide the first nutritionally balanced diet they've ever
known.

The Fort Benning graduates of the BCT who are in OSUT will
seamlessly continue on with an additional five weeks of infantry-
centric AIT. Building on the BCT skill set, the new soldiers train in
infantry-squad tactics, urban combat, and fire-and-maneuver drills,
and participate in a seven-day field-training exercise. Fourteen weeks
ago, these young men were civilians; now they are both soldiers and
infantrymen. Soldiers who graduate from other Basic Combat Training courses will go on to receive training in such disciplines as medicine, communications, artillery, chemical warfare, or other military
occupational specialties.

About 75 percent of all enlisted Rangers are infantrymen and
carry the 11B MOS. Many of those attending OSUT and who are
heading for RASP are on what is known as a Ranger contract. This
provides a young man enlisting in the Army a guaranteed place in
a RASP class, subject to his successful completion of BCT, infantry
AIT, and Airborne School, and his passing the testing and security
requirements for service in the Regiment. There are Ranger contracts
available to new enlistees seeking training in other selected MOSs
as well. Until the beginning of 2010, those entering the Army on
Ranger contracts constituted a significant number of each RASP
class. Since then, the number of these contracts offered new recruits

has been drastically reduced. In a review of its recruiting and training methodology, the Regiment decided that it would reduce those
guarantees of Ranger training for new enlistees and focus on looking
for promising candidates in OSUT and other BCT/AIT venues. This
places the responsibility and burden of finding good men for the
Regiment on Ranger recruiters, rather than leaving it to the Army
recruiting stations across the country.

"This is a new process for us," says Sergeant First Class Don Vandenbark, the lead Ranger recruiter at Fort Benning, "but it gives us
a chance to select from a population of soldiers rather than have that
first cut made by some recruiter out in Chicago who is signing up
civilians for the Regiment. It shifts our recruiting effort to looking
for a few good soldiers rather than a few good high school graduates.
It's like this," Vandenbark continues. "The Army wants the top one
percent of America and we want the top one percent from the Army.
That's our goal. That goal is driven by the numbers needed, but it's
also driven by quality. So far, this new program seems to be working for us."

Recruits attending OSUT will learn about the 75th Ranger Regiment twice during their basic combat and infantry training—once
during their first week of OSUT and again during week eight. These
recruiting pitches are conducted by one of the three 75th Ranger
Regiment staff recruiters. A second source of input to the RASP
process is the specialty or non-11B MOS soldiers needed by the Regiment. These include the cooks, intelligence specialists, supply personnel, combat medics, truck drivers, and the like that help to make
the Regiment function. The Regiment keeps a staff Ranger recruiter
on the road visiting other BCT and AIT venues around the nation
to find these specialists for RASP and duty in the Regiment.

Not all soldiers who want to serve in the Regiment are new soldiers. Approximately 5 percent of those junior candidates coming
to the Regiment for assessment and selection are from the regular
Army. Most of those are Eleven Bravos from other infantry units,

like the 3rd Infantry or 82nd Airborne divisions. After a decade of war, nearly all these men are combat veterans who have decided that they want to return to the fight as Rangers. Others are soldiers with MOS skills and experience needed by the regiment. And a few of these soldiers are junior noncommissioned officers, young NCO sergeants. These veteran candidates are welcome additions to each RASP class and often form the core class leadership of a RASP class.

Regarding the BCT/AIT process, it is well known that this entry-level training can be a difficult adjustment for a young man. Even for those who are physically prepared for the demands of military service, the loss of freedoms, regimentation, and confined living can be new and difficult. Yet for those headed for Ranger assessment and selection, it is but a preparation for the ordeal of RASP. While this may be the case, entry-level Army training does a remarkable job of training competent and capable soldiers. And it's not easy training. A young Ranger-bound soldier would make a mistake not to take his time in OSUT (or BCT/AIT) seriously. It's a progression—soldier, infantryman (or other specialty), airborne soldier, then Ranger candidate. Beyond providing trained infantrymen for the Army's line combat divisions and those relatively few who volunteer for Ranger selection, the Fort Benning OSUT also trains infantrymen headed for Army Special Forces selection and training. I recall one new infantryman I met at Fort Bragg while he was in Special Forces selection. His name was Tim Kennedy, and before and after his active Army service, which included Ranger School, he was a ranked professional martial artist. Tim is still in the Army Reserve and is now an infantry officer.

"OSUT was hard," he told me. "I'm used to a demanding training regime, but all the running in boots was difficult for me. And there's a lot to learn—taking care of your feet, taking care of your buddy, taking care of your equipment, how to pack a rucksack, and how to carry a heavy rucksack. The list goes on. I'd advise anyone headed for Special Forces or Rangers not to overlook their time in BCT or

AIT. It's the foundation of everything you will need to be successful as a Ranger or a Green Beret."

I was able to spend a few days at OSUT while I was at Fort Benning, and I met a number of recruit-company first sergeants. They're among America's finest soldiers and role models. All are combat veterans, and all take their difficult job seriously. Their time in the battlespace has made them better soldiers and trainers, but it also has made some much more measured—even melancholy—about just what they have to accomplish in a very short time. One senior cadre sergeant put it best. He was the company first sergeant and had previously served for close to a decade in the Regiment. I've never met a more stressed-out military trainer, and I've known quite a few.

"Sir," he told me candidly, "I don't worry about the young troopers headed for the Rangers or SF [Special Forces]; they'll get more training and they'll soldier with the best. But I do worry about the kids headed for the 4th ID [4th Infantry Division] or the 101st Airborne. As replacement troops, some of them will join their operational units and be in combat within sixty days after they leave here. When one of my new soldiers is killed, and we know about combat deaths immediately, a part of me dies with him. Sir, it's eating me up. My wife wants me to quit pushing recruits and go back to combat rotation. She says this is too stressful; I think she's right. Getting shot at is not half so bad as preparing these young soldiers to get shot at."

All RASP Level One candidates, unless they are airborne qualified, will attend Army Airborne School before "classing up" in a Ranger Assessment and Selection Program class. Airborne School, or "jump school," is conducted at Fort Benning and makes airborne troopers out of earthbound soldiers. It's another one of those rites of passage in the U.S. Army. A young man or woman must volunteer to join the Army and again volunteer to attend Airborne School. Airborne School is yet another Army training course in which the

Ranger recruiters find good candidates for RASP and duty in the Regiment. Jumping out of a perfectly good airplane seems to add a measure of maturity and esprit de corps to a soldier, and the Regiment finds a surprising number of good soldiers in airborne training who volunteer yet a third time—this time for Ranger assessment and selection. Jump school awards the silver Airborne Wings, a badge that is worn on the left side of a soldier's uniform. Airborne training is one of those formatted Army institutions that changes little with time. As I watched this three-week training at Benning, there was little to distinguish it from my Army airborne training more than forty years before. The drop aircraft are newer, as are the parachutes, but the training is the same—complete with lean cadre sergeants in black ball caps barking orders at airborne trainees.

So these are the young, and in some cases not-so-young, enlisted soldiers who will begin Ranger assessment and selection together. The Ranger culturalization process will also begin there—in RASP. If these Ranger hopefuls are successful, they've taken the first step to entering the Ranger brotherhood. It is as much or more a period of testing as it is one of training. Each RASP class has its own character—its own personality. Individually, each candidate must find it within himself to soldier through this trying period. Yet, collectively, these men will endure the trial of Ranger selection together—as a class. The Tan Beret and Ranger Scroll awarded successful Ranger candidates do not distinguish between infantrymen and noninfantrymen or between the veterans and new soldiers. Once the candidates successfully complete RASP—or, in the case of the junior enlisted soldiers, RASP Level One—they are Rangers.

Officer candidates and senior noncommissioned officers headed for the 75th Ranger Regiment have a different path—in part because of their training and in part because of their experience at this point in their Army careers. As with the junior enlisted men, soldiering with the 75th Rangers is an infantry-centric business, and most of the officers are Infantry Branch officers. Those in the noninfantry minority include officers from the Quartermaster Corps and the Corps of Engineers, as well as the Armor and Artillery branches. There is a regimental nutritionist along with the regimental psychologist, who we've already heard from—both Medical Service Corps officers. Like their Infantry Branch brothers, they will be expected to successfully complete RASP Level Two and to later complete Airborne School and Ranger School, if they've not already done so. All of these noninfantry officers are selected for candidacy to the Regiment because of their specialty training, maturity, and experience.

Each infantry officer who finds his way to the Regiment will have followed a different route. Army officers are commissioned as second lieutenants by way of West Point, civilian university ROTC programs, or the twelve-week Officer Candidate School at Fort Benning. Those entering the commissioned ranks from OCS may be warrant officers or soldiers with former enlisted service. Those officer candidates coming out of college with no prior military service must first become soldiers, and that means nine weeks of Basic Combat Training.

New second lieutenants electing the Infantry Branch attend the sixteen-week Infantry Basic Officer Leadership Course. During the IBOLC, the new officers are trained and qualified on infantry weapons, vehicle maintenance, nuclear-chemical-biological defense, land navigation, supporting arms, call-for-fire procedures, tactics, leadership, and physical fitness. Following the IBOLC, each infantry officer is expected to complete Airborne School and Ranger School. Additional courses for new infantry officers may include Jumpmaster, Pathfinder, and Reconnaissance and Surveillance Leaders courses. It is not unusual for a newly minted second lieutenant of infantry to spend up to a year or more in training before seeing operational service.

At this stage of his career, our new Infantry Branch lieutenant is trained and qualified to lead an infantry platoon. Over the course of the past decade, to lead an infantry platoon has come to mean to lead an infantry platoon in combat. It could be with the 1st Infantry

Division, the 10th Mountain Division, or any number of combat-bound units. Most second lieutenants who are looking to serve with the 75th Ranger Regiment will look for a combat/infantry-unit assignment. Their initial tour will usually take them through their infantry platoon's work-up, or predeployment training, and then on deployment rotations to Afghanistan or Iraq. This initial tour of duty may have them in combat for a part of the time. After their first platoon-leader tour, they can then put in for a transfer to the 75th Ranger Regiment. Unlike the enlisted Rangers, officers will rotate between the Regiment and other Army leadership positions outside the Regiment.

The Regiment is currently doubly blessed with its officer-rotation protocol. First, it benefits from a "second-time" policy for most of their rifle-battalion officer billets. Their platoon leaders are seasoned first lieutenants who have had a tour as a rifle-platoon leader in a conventional infantry unit. This conventional-tour-then-Ranger-tour system applies up the line to executive officers, company commanders, and so on through the battalion-commander level. The 75th Ranger Regiment enjoys experienced and proven leaders at all levels. Throughout a career in the Infantry Branch, an officer may leave and return several times—a tour with the Regiment, then a tour or two with a conventional infantry brigade, then back to the Regiment. Most often, the Ranger tour will be his second tour at that same level of command.

The second blessing comes from fighting a long war. Beginning soon after the U.S. invasion of Iraq, conventional infantry divisions began to provide the 75th Ranger Regiment with a steady stream of combat-veteran platoon leaders—first lieutenants and captains who had been to the fight. A few years later, the Regiment began to see majors who had combat experience at the platoon and company level. Now, after close to a decade of war, the Rangers have the benefit of battalion-level leaders who have deployed in harm's way throughout their entire career. Nearly every officer in the regiment now wears a Combat Infantryman Badge, something that was not all that common in the fall of 2001.

This officer-rotation policy has created something of a symbiotic relationship between the conventional Army and the 75th Rangers. When a good first lieutenant puts in for a transfer to the 75th, he is essentially "leaving" the Army for an SOF component. Yet the Army knows it will get him back in a few years, probably as a captain, well-seasoned, and with more combat experience. The conventional Army battalion and brigade commanders know these returning Regimental Rangers are hard-chargers and capable leaders—role models for their other officers. So this rotation policy serves both the 75th Rangers and the Army, working to the advantage of each.

This is not so with the 75th Rangers' brother SOF ground component, Army Special Forces. Special Forces recruit its officers from the ranks of the Army, and these officers are usually captains with four or five year of experience—soldiers and combat leaders with multitour experience. Quite often, they are outstanding officers, and their experience and contribution to "Big Army" is lost. Army Special Forces, while an SOF unit, is also a branch of the Army, just as is the infantry or armor. Typically, a Special Forces officer will never return to duty in a conventional Army unit—he's gone for good. So picture yourself as a battalion commander in the 508th Parachute Infantry Regiment. One of your captains puts in for Special Forces duty; he's one of your best, and you'll never see him again in the 508th or any line Army unit. In the minds of many commanders, this is almost like desertion—going to the dark side. But a captain leaving for the 75th Ranger Regiment is very different. It's a bit political and a bit parochial, but it's a factor in Big Army's affection for the 75th Rangers that does not always extend to Army Special Forces. The 75th is an infantry regiment. The Commander of the 75th Ranger Regiment routinely signs official correspondence over his typed name. Below his name is his professional calling: "Colonel, Infantry."

Officers and senior NCOs participate in a three-week course

called RASP Level Two. Three weeks may seem like a very short time when compared with the eight-week RASP 1 course for the junior enlisted Ranger candidates, but it serves the Regiment well. First, the officers and senior noncoms bring a level of experience well above that of a recent OSUT graduate, or even a junior soldier from an infantry division. And that experience in the case of the infantry officers is by way of multiple infantry combat tours, so these solid leaders are not new to the game. In the words of the current Regimental Commanding Officer, RASP 2 is designed to inventory and assess an officer or NCO's "physical performance, mental clarity, critical thinking, and psychological profile." These candidates will also be introduced to or reacquainted with the updated Ranger organization and current operations, tactics, communications, and procedures. Senior noncommissioned officers will only on occasion leave the Regiment, but they must still reenter duty with the Regiment by way of RASP 2. A new battalion commander may be attending RASP 2, or one of its preceding courses, for the fourth time. Yet this prospective battalion commander, a lieutenant colonel, will be expected to perform physically with the new twenty-four-year-old first lieutenant and the new twenty-eight-year-old Army medical officer—as well as the thirty-eight-year-old prospective command sergeant major returning from a tour with the 82nd Airborne. All are Ranger leaders, and they are expected to lead from the front.

A recent change within the Regiment now requires that all prospective platoon sergeants must attend RASP Level Two. The platoon sergeant is a key player in Ranger deployment preparation and operational taskings, and is in a position of increased responsibility from his previous duties as a Ranger squad leader. So for the new platoon sergeants, RASP 2 is both a validation of their Ranger skill set and a recognition of their promotion to this new and important role. This same "revalidation" applies to company first sergeants and battalion command sergeants major as well.

"At first, this didn't go over very well," a RASP 2 cadre sergeant told me. "For the platoon sergeants, these guys are all E-7s [sergeant first class] and some are E-8 [master sergeant] promotables. Most have ten, or more, combat rotations behind them. Early on, a few came to RASP 2 with an attitude of 'I've been a Ranger for twelve years. What do I have to do to prove myself?' There's only one answer to that: 'You have to earn your Scroll every day.' It's also an initiation of sorts into the senior leadership of the Regiment, and mixes them in with our new and returning officer leadership. The new platoon sergeants we now see come to us with the right attitude—ready to learn and ready to step up to their new responsibilities. It's all good."

This is who they are and where they come from—those new to the Regiment and those who are not so new. In the next chapter, we'll begin with those junior first-timers who want to soldier in the Regiment. We'll explore what has to take place before an airborne-qualified soldier can call himself a Ranger in the 75th Ranger Regiment and what it takes for a young warrior to earn his Tan Beret and Scroll.

Before we begin with the Ranger Assessment and Selection Program, I need to outline my rules of engagement during my time with the Regiment. The Ranger candidates you are going to meet are real, as are the cadre sergeants who conduct RASP. Their challenges, struggles, successes, and failures are presented just as they happened in RASP while I was there. I was granted full access to RASP, and what follows is an accurate portrayal of this difficult and demanding process. But the names in this work are not real. The photos in the work have been chosen to defeat face-recognition software. As a premier special operations force, this regiment is engaged in daily combat in a global war against a very determined enemy. Their individual privacy on deployment and at home is to be respected. This work was carefully reviewed by the 75th Ranger Regiment, but unaltered in any significant way. It is the story of the molding of the modern American Ranger.

CHAPTER THREE

RANGER ASSESSMENT AND SELECTION LEVEL ONE, PHASE ONE

The 75th Ranger Regiment is just one of the tenant units on the sprawling 182,000-acre Fort Benning Army installation. The regimental complex is a scattering of modern two- and three-story buildings on a built-up area called the Main Post. This complex, in soldier-speak, is said to be behind the brown fence. The fence is a high chain-link enclosure with slats snaked diagonally through metal link to afford privacy and exclusion. It is home to the Regimental Headquarters, the 3rd Ranger Battalion, and the Regimental Special Troops Battalion. Next to this Ranger complex, also shrouded in a brown chain-link fence, are two dated, three-story cinder-block buildings. This smaller compound houses the Ranger Assessment and Selection Level One or, simply, RASP 1. One of these buildings is dedicated to the business of the assessment and selection of young enlisted soldiers who want to become Rangers. The other building houses those waiting for their RASP class to begin and those who, having failed in the assessment and selection process, are awaiting assignment to another Army unit. This second building is called the Holdover building.

Holdover is both a place and an entity with cadre offices on the first floor and barracks on the second and third. One of the entities and stations in Holdover is the place where anxious and hopeful soldiers wait and prepare to begin RASP 1; it's called the Pre-RASP section. The other section is for those who have failed selection and are awaiting orders to another unit in the Army—a unit other than the 75th Ranger Regiment. Those in this latter category are in the Worldwide section, or just plain Worldwide, as they can be sent to an Army unit anywhere in the world. The needs of the Army will govern their immediate military future.

Those in Holdover, whether in Pre-RASP or Worldwide, belong to the Selection and Training Company, or S&T Company, which in turn is a part of the Regimental Special Troops Battalion. The S&T Company headquarters is across the street and behind the Ranger main-complex fence. The other Ranger companies assigned to the Special Troops Battalion have a responsibility to provide direct combat support to the three operational rifle battalions of the Regiment. The S&T Company is responsible for, among other programs, the assessment and selection of the soldiers who will become the Regiment's new Rangers. They are the gatekeepers, and nowhere in the S&T Company is that responsibility more keenly felt than by those cadre sergeants assigned to RASP.

"Our job here in Pre-RASP," Staff Sergeant John Martinez told me, "is to receive those soldiers from OSUT, AIT, or wherever, and in the time allowed, get them ready for the RASP 1. Sometimes they're with us for a week, sometimes a month or more. Over at RASP 1, they can handle 160 Ranger candidates per class. Nine times a year, we try to give them 160 motivated soldiers who want to become Rangers. We don't always make that number, but we usually get close. The maxim number is 165, and we occasionally convene classes with less than 100."

Martinez is a prototype of the Ranger assessment and selection cadre: five feet nine, 160 pounds, polite, measured, competent. Like all cadre sergeants, he's wearing the standard Army Combat Uniform, or ACU, with jump wings—master jump wings in his case—his rank, the Ranger Tab, the Combat Infantryman Badge, and the Scrolls of the 75th Ranger Regiment. Martinez exemplifies what those nearly fifteen hundred soldiers who now come through RASP 1 each year want to be: an Army Ranger.

"Our focus here is preparing soldiers for the assessment and selection process," Sergeant Martinez continues, "but we still have a responsibility to the soldiers who, for one reason or another, are unsuccessful in RASP One. They drop from their RASP class and come back Holdover. We then do our best to see that those who can, and are willing, get recycled to a future class. Those who've had enough or know this is not for them go to Worldwide, and we try to get them to their new Army unit as quickly as possible. But while they're here, we try to see that they stay in shape physically and that they continue to focus on Army Core Values and core soldiering skills. We want them to leave here better soldiers than when they arrived."

While in Pre-RASP, Ranger candidates complete course prerequisites that include physical conditioning, body-fat assessment, immunizations, and a security screening. They are also given study materials on common Ranger skills and introduced to good nutrition and hydration habits that will prepare them for the demands of RASP 1. The candidates must meet a minimum score of 60 percent on the Army Physical Fitness Test (APFT) in each of the four tested categories to begin RASP 1. Those scores will have to increase dramatically if they are to meet Ranger Physical Fitness Test (RPFT) standards. These Ranger prospects-in-waiting are also encouraged to attend to any administrative and personal issues that might distract them when RASP begins.

The candidates are also given an exhaustive battery of psychological tests. The first of these is the standard Minnesota Multiphasic Personality Inventory, Second Revision–Restructured format. The MMPI-2 is the most frequently used mental-health testing instrument. It gauges personality structure and looks for pathologies. Another test, the Shipley Institute of Living Scale, is designed to measure intellectual ability. Commonly referred to as the Shipley, it's basically an IQ test. The third test in the psych battery is the Jackson Personality Inventory, which seeks to measure an individual's capacity for leadership, discipline, resolve, and social-value orientation. And, finally, there is a basic pre-lie-detector test, in which the candidate is asked simple background questions and some not-so-simple ones, such as about drug usage prior to entering the Army.

"Our purpose with this lengthy evaluation is twofold," says Captain John Miller, the regimental psychologist. We've spoken often on this fascinating subject of the psychology of Rangers and Ranger candidates. "First of all, we want to weed out any soldiers who really shouldn't be here, and who are unsuited to the regiment and maybe even to the Army. In a standard RASP One class, maybe six or eight will surface as potential problems. We call in those soldiers for an interview and usually the issues raised by the testing can be resolved satisfactorily—that is, there's a good reason or explanation for our concerns. Sometimes there is not, and that soldier is removed from RASP. Currently, we have maybe one or two who are dropped each class due to the psychological screening.

"The other purpose of the testing is to compile a body of knowledge on Ranger candidates. The individual we want to select is different from the man on the street and even from the average Army soldier. We want to identify what traits make for a successful Ranger and what traits may be problematic for service in the Regiment. Right now, we use the psych evaluation process to identify potential problems and to 'select out' those soldiers that are unsuited for Ranger duty. In the future, we hope to use the information in our database to identify the psychological profile of a successful Ranger so we can 'select in' as well as select out our RASP candidates."

"Have you noticed any trend with the extended RASP One process?" I ask, referring to the recently instituted eight-week RASP Level One.

"Actually, we've recently experienced far fewer RASP One candidates being flagged for a psych interview and fewer being released for suitability issues. I don't think either of these has to do with the length of the RASP One program. I think the Army is doing a better job of screening those who come into the Army. It might just be that the civilian economy is giving us more and better recruits, so there are higher-quality individuals entering service. There's also the shift in Ranger recruiting away from the Army recruiting stations and a greater focus on finding good soldiers in the basic training programs and Airborne School. We just seem to be getting better people, or at least more suitable people from a psychological standpoint."

"You seem to like this job?" I venture, knowing the answer.

"Like it? I love it. I like fieldwork more than clinical work, and it's great to be with an organization where soldiers want to get into the outfit and stay in the outfit. A lot of Army psychs like the clinical work, and that often means dealing with soldiers who are looking to get out of the Army. And there are only three Ranger Tabbed psychologists in the Army—the guy I relieved, a former enlisted Ranger who went back to school to become a psychologist, and myself. I have the best job in the Army. It'll be a sad day for me when I have to rotate out."

At 0600 on Thursday morning, September 9, 2010, Staff Sergeant John Martinez musters 143 Holdover soldiers and turns them over to the RASP 1 training cadre. This is RASP 1 Class 09-10—so designated because it's the ninth and final RASP 1 class to convene in fiscal year 2010. The previous Monday, there had been 159 in this group—one shy of the 160-soldier goal for a class. But the rigors of

RASP 1, by rumor if not by experience, have already caused some soldiers to rethink their goal of becoming a Ranger.

"It's an intimidating process," Martinez says of those who drop before the assessment and selection process even begins. "Those in Pre-RASP who are recycles from a previous class probably exaggerate the difficulty. But it is hard, and hard by design. Above all, it requires mental toughness. These kids know something of what's ahead for them. In that regard, it's a self-selecting process. If you're afraid to even try, we don't want you." He turns and walks back into the Holdover building. These soldiers are no longer his.

The 143 soldiers stand loosely in formation awaiting the first of two cadre teams that will put them through RASP 1. The first of these is the Phase One cadre. They will be charged with Class 09-10 during Phase One—the first four weeks of RASP 1. A great deal of what is now Phase One was the entire junior-enlisted Ranger selection process known as the Ranger Indoctrination Program. One of the candidates in formation sees a cadre sergeant step from the RASP building.

"At ease!" he calls out, as is convention when a cadre sergeant approaches, and the entire class snaps to a rigid position of parade rest. A file of cadre sergeants emerge from the building.

A clone of Martinez steps in front of the class. He takes a long moment to measure the candidates before speaking. "Gentlemen, my name is Sergeant First Class Iselin. I'm the noncommissioned officer in charge for RASP One, Phase One. Over the next four weeks, you and I are going to get to know each other very well."

Walt Iselin is a serious, straightforward Army professional from Michigan. He has regular, choirboylike features and an almost kindly manner about him. While in the Army and between his combat rotations, five of them with the 3rd Ranger Battalion, he managed to earn a bachelor's degree in business administration. He's been with RASP for going on two years, and helped with the transition from the Ranger Indoctrination Program to the current RASP 1.

Arranged behind Iselin are the six RASP 1, Phase One cadre sergeants. Two are perhaps six feet, several under five feet nine, but all of them have that same unsmiling and competent look of special operations professionals I've seen at other SOF training and assessment venues.

"Class, ten-hut," barks Iselin.

"RAN-GER!" shouts the class as they come to attention.

"Class leader."

"CLASS LEADER!" repeats the class.

A tall specialist and his Ranger buddy break ranks and sprint up to Sergeant Iselin. "Put the class into a column of sixes and double-time them over to the Peden Field classroom."

"Roger that, Sergeant," replies the class leader.

The RASP 1 classroom is a large temporary modular structure in the middle of the nearby Peden athletic field. Peden Field is but 150 yards from the RASP 1 compound. The classroom itself has a linoleum floor, rows of tables and chairs to accommodate 160 soldiers, and the blessing of an excellent air-conditioning system. Once the men are settled into their seats, Sergeant Iselin assaults them with a series of PowerPoint slides that cover the administrative matters, routines, and cadre expectations for Phase One. Most of these relate to formation protocols, getting to chow, detailing of the barracks, and the standards of conduct and performance. There are a great many "don'ts" and prohibitions, whether inside the RASP compound or on one of the brief periods they are allowed to venture onto the Fort Benning Main Post. No alcohol, no tobacco, no caffeine, no cell phones, no electronic devices, no over-the-counter drugs (prescription only), no food in the barracks, no visitors, no talking in formation, no talking with candidates in Phase Two or with soldiers in Holdover, no talking in the chow hall, no modifications to equipment, uniforms, or standard-issue boots, and so on. The "dos" address issues of personal hygiene, the use of laundry facilities, the wearing of clean and proper uniforms, and observing military courtesies and specific RASP 1 class protocols. Sergeant Iselin clicks off the overhead projector and begins to pace in front of the class.

"These rules will be posted in your barracks. Follow them to the letter or you'll never get to Phase Two, let alone to the Regiment." Iselin pauses before continuing. "Gentlemen, it's like this. Phase One of RASP is a gut check. We are not here to train you; we're here to assess and select you. You are here to show us that you have the heart for this job. You are here to show us that you have within you, as it says in the Ranger Creed, the ability to be mentally alert, physically strong, and morally straight. Nothing less is acceptable. We want you to succeed; we need you in the Ranger Regiment. But no one—*I repeat, no one*—will leave here and go to Phase Two without his showing us that he has the heart of a Ranger. I have no quota or minimum numbers that I have to send forward." Iselin pauses for another long moment before continuing. "The next four weeks are going to be difficult and demanding. You may wonder about some of the things we're going to ask you to do. On the surface, they may seem mindless—nothing more than general harassment or an admission slip to this fraternity or some arcane rite of passage. Not so. There's a reason behind everything we're going to ask of you. Let me give you just one.

"So far this year, fourteen Rangers have been killed in combat. Literally dozens more have been wounded, many of them seriously. We're at war with a deadly and determined enemy, and the Seventy-fifth Ranger Regiment now conducts more direct-action operations than any other unit in the battlespace. A significant amount of this war is being fought by Rangers. We are what Shakespeare had in mind when he wrote about 'We few, we happy few, we band of brothers.' In close combat, we have only our Ranger buddies to rely on.

"So over the next few weeks, when you're tired, beat, you haven't slept, and the suck factor is off the chart, I want you to give a thought to those Rangers deployed in harm's way. While it may hurt, ours is a safe little world here. So never forget that the men you want to call your Ranger brothers are inbound to target, on target, or coming off target. If you want to be one of them, show us you have heart." Another pause. "We clear on this, men?"

"ROGER THAT, SERGEANT!" the class roars.

"Good. Class leader."

"CLASS LEADER!" There is a scraping as two men push back and stand. One is the assigned class leader and the other the class first sergeant. Even in RASP, candidates go everywhere as a class or as a Ranger buddy pair.

"Take charge of the class and get them to chow." Iselin consults his watch. "Have them back in formation on the RASP rocks at zero-nine-thirty, and we'll begin the move from the Pre-RASP building barracks to the RASP building barracks."

"Roger that, Sergeant."

And so it begins for Class 09-10. RASP Level One, Phase One. Phase One of Ranger assessment and selection is a very closed and insulated world. During the next four weeks, with limited exception, the candidates will be confined to the barracks and the training areas, except for a family emergency. Their movements will be proscribed and severely restricted. As a RASP 1, Phase One candidate, they will run at all times and never go anywhere without their Ranger buddy. All uniforms, boots, eyewear, and equipment are proscribed. They are required to wear a watch and be on time, individually and collectively. There is the expectation of honor in this RASP world; if a candidate lies, is untruthful, cheats, steals, or takes unauthorized leave, he will be immediately disenrolled.

There is really no such thing as a "typical Ranger class." All are in their own way unique. A class may have an overage of Eleven Bravos or it may have more new soldiers than usual or there may be fewer soldiers coming from other units on in-service transfers. There may be a half dozen or more E-5 sergeants in a class or only a few, or none. Of the 143 soldiers who left Pre-RASP for Phase One in Class 09-10, 105 are Eleven Bravo infantrymen, and most of them are coming directly from OSUT. The candidates that carry other specialty MOSs break out as follows: Fourteen are combat medics. Following their BCT, these soldiers trained as medics in AIT to earn the Army combat medic MOS. There are six fire-support special-ists, five radio operators, four communications specialists (all with technical subspecialties), three cooks, two intelligence analysts, one truck driver, one human-resources specialist, one chemical-warfare specialist, and one chaplain's assistant. Of those same 143 Phase One entrants, seventeen are back for another try; they are recycles from previous RASP 1 classes. They range in height from five feet one to six feet six and in age from eighteen to forty. The heaviest is 235 pounds; the lightest, 128. Fourteen are married, sixteen have college degrees, and close to three times that many have some college edu-cation. Four were not born in the United States and are naturalized citizens.

One hundred and eight candidates are new soldiers who arrived at RASP on a Ranger contract of some sort. A few obtained their con-tract as a part of their enlistment package, but most earned their contract after they joined the Army for their superior performance in BCT or AIT. Most of the contract holders come from OSUT, and nearly all in the specialty MOSs have Ranger contracts. "I had to walk out of the recruiter's office three times," one of the medics told me. "I wanted to be a Ranger medic, and that meant a guarantee of medical training at AIT, Airborne School, RASP, and the Special Operations Combat Medic Course when I finish RASP. When the recruiter finally agreed to this, I signed up." Thirty soldiers volun-teered for Rangers during Airborne School. Only five soldiers are prior-service/in-service transfers. Two of those have been to Ranger School and are Tabbed Rangers.

It's a busy first two days for Class 09-10, as the pace of their life picks up dramatically from the routine in Pre-RASP. Physically, the first few days are relatively easy. The cadre leads them in physical training, or PT, and conditioning runs each morning. The days are spent in preparation and administration for the formal beginning of Phase One on Monday. They've been thoroughly briefed on what is expected of them if they are to complete RASP 1. The S&T Company commander and company first sergeant take a few minutes with the class. They tell them there is a place in the regiment for each of them if they can find it within themselves to get through the next eight weeks. Yet for some candidates, this busy but gentle beginning has proved to be overwhelming. At their final formation on Friday, there are 139 Ranger candidates. Four soldiers have decided this is not for them. At this final formation, Class 09-10 is addressed by the noncommissioned officer in charge of all of RASP 1.

"My name is Sergeant First Class Collier. I am the RASP One NCOIC. I hope to see all of you in ranks when you finish Phase One of RASP." Tad Collier folds his arms as he surveys the class, then says, "Okay, guys, bring it in close and take a knee." The class breaks ranks and closes in around Collier, each man going to one knee. They're like sheep flocking to the shepherd. Collier is six feet, with a round, congenial face. Like Sergeant Iselin, he's a 3rd Battalion veteran and has *twelve* combat rotations behind him—four as a fire-team leader, four as a squad leader, and four as a platoon sergeant. Prior to this assignment, he had been in continuous combat rotation since 9/11. There's a quiet authority about him, one that is not lost on these Ranger hopefuls.

"Selection and assessment begins for real on Monday," Collier tells them, "so here's a few things to keep in mind over the weekend. First of all, stay motivated! Remember why you came here, and use these next two days to get mentally right for what's ahead. Secondly, don't quit. I know what it takes to be a Ranger; you don't. I cannot assess your qualifications to be a Ranger if you quit, so don't quit. Stay with your class; stay in training. You do your job, and I'll do mine. Sergeant Iselin and his cadre will do theirs. And, finally,

RASP is a hard program. It's hard by design because Rangering is a hard business. If you want to serve in the Regiment, you have to show us that you have the heart to be a Ranger, and Rangers never quit. Do your best, don't quit, and leave the rest up to the cadre."

The class falls back into formation and Sergeant Iselin takes charge. Off to the side, Sergeant Collier says to me in a low voice, "This is the hardest thing most of these guys will ever do on a purely physical level—harder than Ranger School, harder than combat. It's not really training, it's testing, and we have four short weeks here in Phase One to see who can and cannot man up to this demanding physical and emotional ordeal. These next two weeks will be a make or break for most of the candidates in this class. If we can get them through the first two weeks, we have a real shot at getting those who remain all the way through. Sergeant Iselin and his cadre have a tough job. They'll deal with the heaviest volume of withdrawals. As you're going to see, unless a soldier really wants to be a Ranger in his heart, he has no business here and little chance of making it through RASP."

On Monday morning at 0530, Sergeant Walt Iselin musters his cadre and gives them their final briefing before the first formal evolution for Class 09-10. "Stay professional," he tells them. "Keep the pressure on, the profanity down, and keep it impersonal. Do corrective training as needed, but don't 'smoke' these candidates. We're here to assess and select. Respect them as candidates and demand that they respect you. There are some future Rangers out there and some soldiers who need to find another way to serve their country. Our job is to find out who wants to be here and who doesn't, so let's stay focused on the mission."

In addition to Sergeant First Class Iselin, there are currently seven Phase One cadre sergeants, all E-6 staff sergeants and all but one of those an Eleven Bravo. They are assisted by two TAC (training and counseling) sergeants who are on four-week temporary assignment from one of the rifle battalions. Both are E-5 sergeants. The TAC sergeants come to RASP just for a candidate phase cycle and will then rotate back to their battalion. They're here to help manage the class and to take back to their battalions something of what they learn of the current assessment and selection process.

Class 09-10 is standing tall at 0600 for physical training. Overnight, the temperature fell into the high seventies, but by 1000, it will have climbed back up into the nineties. That's southwestern Georgia in early September—hot and humid. The class forms up on a patch of gravel simply known as the rocks. The rocks are between the RASP 1 building and the Holdover building, but on the RASP side of a broad sidewalk that separates the two. The Phase One cadre has its offices on the first floor of the RASP building; the Ranger candidates' barracks occupy the top two floors.

Off to one side of the formation on the rocks are nine men who, over the weekend, decided that this was not for them and have quit; they are voluntary withdrawals, or VWs. Perhaps they took Sergeant Collier's words to heart and withdrew before the pain begins. These nine, and four others who dropped between the initial class formation on Thursday and final formation on Friday, have cut the class to 130. Those in formation are in shorts, T-shirts, and commercial running shoes of their own choosing—the only nonreg attire I was to see on any RASP candidate. All have shaved heads. All have two-quart canteens slung over one shoulder and across their backs.

"At ease!" a candidate yells as the cadre pours from the building. The class snaps to as Sergeant Iselin steps before the class.

"Good morning gentlemen. Today we begin. You've heard this before, but I'll say it again. While you're here, you will be assessed on your ability to follow directions and exhibit Ranger attributes. Your job is to show us that you're mentally alert, physically strong, and morally straight. Physical ability alone will not get you successfully through this program. You will have to show us that you have the heart of a Ranger."

After Sergeant Iselin introduces me to the class, one of the cadre sergeants leads the class at an easy double-time to the nearby Peden Field. There the class is made to do several rounds of push-ups and a great deal of stretching. The stretching is methodical and comprehensive, working each muscle group. Then 09-10 sets out on a two-mile run that is brisk—close to a seven-minute-mile pace. At the two-mile mark, the line of candidates snakes through a wooded area and down to a level grassy field surrounded by pre–Civil War stonework. Both cadre and students refer to it as the snake pit. It's said to be an area where at one time slaves were auctioned. There the PT gets aggressive—even punishing. Along with the jumping jacks, close to two hundred of them, there is the standard fare of calisthenics, and lots and lots of push-ups and flutter kicks. All these exercises come in twenty-five-count waves. Those candidates who can't do the exercises properly or can't stay with the count are made to bear-crawl around the formation on their hands and feet. Cadre sergeants roam the ranks of sweating candidates, sometimes encouraging them, always challenging them.

"Do it right, soldier. Don't cheat yourself."

"Don't you quit on me. Quit now and you'll quit on your Ranger buddy in combat."

"If you want this, show us. Suck it up, get your back straight, and do it right."

"Are you a little girl? Oh, you're not? Then knock off with the little-girl noises."

"The guy next to you is doing it right, why can't you!"

Along with the physical and verbal harassment dished out by the cadre, they also see that the candidates continue to drink from their canteens to stay hydrated. They also watch the candidates closely for any sign of heat exhaustion. Yet this was a kick-ass PT session—as tough as any I've witnessed. Was it up to a SEAL Phase One first-day PT or Special Forces Assessment and Selection (SFAS) day one PT? Absolutely, and then some. Physical conditioning is one of the Big Five. Rangers pride themselves on their physical conditioning and endurance, and that came through in spades during this physical training session. Class 09-10 retraces its route back to the training area, this time at a slower pace. On the final stretch of road, a slight grade, the candidates are made to pair up and carry one another for the last several hundred yards. After a brief cooldown, 09-10 is sent to shower off and grab morning chow.

"We demand that they shower twice a day and keep the barracks spotless," a cadre sergeant tells me. "This program is hard enough on them without health and hygiene issues. We inspect the barracks daily and a cadre medic is on every physical-training evolution. And most Phase One evolutions are physical."

At 0930 the class forms up for gear issue, interspersed with nearly continuous rounds of push-ups and flutter kicks. They are in the standard ACU training uniforms with only their rank and name on their caps and blouses, a U.S. Army Tab over their left breast pocket, and an American flag on their right shoulder. Many have no rank insignia, as they are still E-1 privates. The class is also down a man since the PT formation because one candidate damaged a shoulder muscle during exercise and is medically dropped from the class. But the class gained some new bodies with the late arrival of three in-service transfers. They are inserted without ceremony into a session of push-ups and flutter kicks. Class 09-10 is now 132 strong.

The afternoon's evolution is the Ranger Swim Ability Evaluation. It's done at the installation training pool and is a relatively easy evolution for most candidates. The RSAE requires that each Ranger candidate enter the pool in full uniform with light-armor, flack-type vest, a ceramic-armor plate bib over the vest, and a weapon—in this case, a Bakelite M16 rifle, referred to as a rubber duck. The soldier then must discard his weapon, remove the plate bib and flak vest, and swim the length of the pool. All but six soldiers pass the RSAE. Those that don't are all African and Asian Americans. This is all too familiar. As in other SOF assessment programs, a great many otherwise promising candidates are lost because of their inability to swim. "This is where," a SEAL instructor once told me at poolside during a swim test, "we find out which kids played in the swimming pool and which kids played in the fire hydrant." Many African Americans simply never had the opportunity to learn how to swim or to even be comfortable in the water. Many others are blessed, or in this case cursed, with dense muscle mass, which makes them negatively buoyant.

One candidate, when fitted out for his RSAE, simply said, "Sergeant, I can't swim." And he couldn't. He toppled into the pool and managed to shed his bib and flak vest, but could go no further. He had to be pulled out. It was like jumping out of an airplane without a parachute. This brave soldier will get some training and a retesting, but he will still have to meet standard and pass the RSAE, or the Regiment will lose another otherwise promising Ranger candidate.

The swim test was the last evolution for day one of Class 09-10. While the RSAE itself was easy for some, the additional attentions of the cadre made it somewhat more difficult. Before and after the graded evolution, there was a liberal amount of push-ups and flutter kicks along the edge of the pool—faces in the water for push-ups, boots dipping in the water on flutter kicks. After a while I lost count, but in the course of the first ten hours of training, Class 09-10 did more than a thousand push-ups and more than five hundred four-count flutter kicks. I wonder just how many will be in the voluntary-withdrawal queue tomorrow morning.

"It's a rough PT this first day," Sergeant Iselin tells me, "and we keep at it all day with push-ups and flutter kicks. But it doesn't get any easier on day two—maybe even harder. We try to alternate morning PT with the runs and with the foot marches. Tomorrow we have a six-mile ruck march. A lot of them will be hurting after today, but tomorrow will be a real wake-up call for some of these candidates. Some of these soldiers have prepared themselves and can carry a rucksack—others can't. Day two is something of a gut check. Those who quit tomorrow will be the ones who mentally throw in the towel. It's not that they can't get through these first two days; it's the thought of having to do this for the next three and a half weeks that will make them quit."

At 0600 on day two of Class 09-10's RASP training, there are 129 candidates formed up on the rocks with three off to one side. They've decided to voluntarily withdraw—to VW. As on Monday morning, the class forms up in PT shorts and T-shirts, but they are now wearing boots. In front of each soldier are a rucksack and a rifle. Each ruck must weigh at least thirty-five pounds. In addition to the rucksack, each candidate wears a combat vest, or rack, and will carry six quarts of water along with a rubber-duck M16 rifle. All total, it makes for a fifty-five-pound minimum load. The class seems poorly sorted out this morning, and several candidates are sent back to the barracks for additional training items, something not lost on the watchful Phase One cadre sergeants.

"This is a conditioning march," the lead cadre sergeant for this evolution tells the class. "Stay up with the group or you will be back out here on Saturday, and we'll do this all again. Clear?"

"ROGER THAT, SERGEANT!"

The class breaks into two groups, each group beginning at a fast walk. They move in files on either side of the road—two files of lights, as each soldier carries a red-lensed gooseneck flashlight on his vest. The pace alternates between a fast walk and a jog-trot for most of the six miles. Soon the two groups begin to define themselves— those who can keep pace with the cadre sergeant leading their group and those who cannot. Only about half can keep up. A third group emerges—those who cannot or will not continue with the march.

They are loaded onto a pickup truck that follows each group. All of the Phase One cadre sergeants on this ruck march, with the exception of the pickup drivers, are under rucksacks. They move in and around the files of candidates, sometimes encouraging candidates while berating others to keep pace. I'm also moving along with the group, but under a light hiking pack with only two quarts of water and a camera.

In sizing up the Phase One cadre as a group, two things strike me. One is that they seem to be of a uniform composition; none of them are big men. They are solid, but none appear to have weight-room-generated physiques. The second is that all of them do the evolutions with the candidates. They can run, they can do the PT, and now they easily move up and down the files of candidates under their rucks. I ask one of them about this.

"It's a Ranger thing," he tells me with a grin. "We all do a lot of PT, running, and rucking, so there's a lot of muscle memory. We've been doing this for years, and because it's all we do here in Phase One, we naturally get good at it. In the Regiment, it's not a lot different. It's just the way of life for a Ranger."

Following the six miles under their rucks, Class 09-10 is back on the rocks but in two separate groups. Steam rises in the early morning light from each group. The first group, close to half the class, is made up of those who were able to keep pace with their group cadre sergeant. They are the winners. For this victory, they are made to do calisthenics with their rucks, push-ups under their rucks, and flutter kicks. The second group consists of those who could not keep pace with their group or who completed the evolution in one of the pickups. As a group, they look defeated, and many of them indeed are. Their penalty is the derision of the cadre sergeants who roam the ranks of this group.

"You failed this evolution—what are you going to do on the twelve-mile timed march?"

"How will you get through this training if you can't carry a light ruck for six miles—on paved roads? In Afghanistan, Rangers carry twice your load, twice as far, over rough terrain."

"Your combat kit and ammo will weigh a lot more than that ruck. And, you'll be sprinting, not walking, to get on target."

"Today is just a sample of what's ahead."

"Quit feeling sorry for yourself. Decide to suck it up or find another Army unit."

After getting a good head count, Sergeant Iselin addresses both groups. "Some of you did well this morning, and many of you did not. Some of you might want to reconsider if this kind of soldiering is for you. Some of you may have already done that. If you've made that decision and would like to withdraw, do it now. You can fall out of formation and fall in here to my left." Eleven men from Class 09-10 take him up on this, including one of those from the group of winners. Iselin dismisses the winners and turns to the group who failed to keep pace but did not quit.

"Okay, bring it in and take a knee." When the fiftysome candidates are in close, he continues in a firm, measured tone. "You men are not doing well, and you're not performing up to standard. I want you to think about this tonight and think about it hard. You need to decide on whether this program is really for you. Right now, you're not cutting it. Many of you had trouble with PT yesterday. You're going to have to dig deep and try to find something more inside yourself and become better motivated. If you can do that, fine. If not, then you might want to join those men over there who've already decided this is not for them. We clear on that, men?"

"ROGER THAT, SERGEANT!"

"Any questions?" There are none. "Okay, get a shower and get ready for the next evolution."

With the eleven voluntary withdrawals, he's almost kind. "Are you men sure this is what you want?" They all nod. "All right, then. Leave your gear here and form up outside my office. We'll get you started on your out-processing paperwork and your VW statement.

Just make sure this is what you really want to do. It's your choice. You can still make chow and be back with the class if you want to continue." All eleven file into the building to start their paperwork.

After the morning foot march, the day is spent in the classroom—Ranger history, Ranger standards, Ranger nutrition, and the Ranger Athlete Warrior (RAW) program. The demeanor of the class members, from the precise way they filed on the double into the classroom, to their rigid and focused attention, was as impressive as the lecture material. The Ranger history was a review of chapter 1 of this book and was well presented by Staff Sergeant Bill Bateman. Sergeant Bateman, who led my section of the foot march, is two college semesters away from his degree in history and hopes to teach in high school when he completes his military service. The Ranger standards lecture begins with the Ranger charter as articulated by General Creighton Abrams and moves on to the Regiment's doctrine and directives. Individual Ranger standards, from grooming to standards of conduct, are basically no different from that of the Army. However, the attention that Rangers give to those standards is. The nutrition lecture was a rundown of what to eat and not to eat, as well as the mechanics of proper hydration. Perhaps more than any other combat unit, the Ranger regiment has made a commitment to good eating habits and the maintenance of sustained physical activity. Hydration receives religious attention, including a daily intake of a hydration-salts supplement. Candidates carry two-quart canteens everywhere and at every formation. The cadre sergeants continuously check canteen contents and make candidates drink.

The afternoon classroom instruction concludes with an overview of the Ranger Athlete Warrior program. After civilian studies and pilot programs, the program was introduced to the Ranger battalions in early 2007 and became a part of Ranger selection and assessment soon after that. The RAW program was designed to support the Core Ranger Skills of marksmanship, physical training, medical training, small-unit tactics (or as it is often expressed, battle drills), and mobility. Ranger and light-infantry doctrine hold that the Regiment's most lethal weapon is the individual Ranger. Mission success depends on his performance on the battlefield. In keeping with this, RAW is all about promoting the fitness and the individual performance of each Ranger. It's a program that continues to be refined and to evolve.

There are four basic components of the program. The first is functional fitness, which incorporates strength, endurance, and movement techniques. Next is performance nutrition, which addresses/promotes good nutrition and nutritional supplements that target individual body composition. The third is sports medicine, which deals with injury prevention, early intervention, and rehabilitation. Finally, mental toughness covers mental preparation, mental endurance, and fatigue countermeasures. All of these components are focused on and support the Ranger combat mission and getting Rangers to the fight in optimal physical and mental condition. A RAW assessment of each candidate will be done later this week and again at the end of Phase Two of RASP.

Two more evolutions were to take place on Class 09-10's day two—one for those who have decided to leave RASP and another for those who were hoping to continue. This second day of Phase One generated a total of twenty-two withdrawals, including the eleven who VWed after the ruck march. Four of them were medical drops and eighteen were voluntary. This group is no longer a part of Class 09-10, but what is ahead for them has yet to be decided. On a historical basis, day two produces the largest single-day attrition for a RASP class, so I took the opportunity to follow these soldiers through their withdrawal process. The twenty-two form up in the hallway outside Sergeant Iselin's office. They move to parade rest as he steps from the office to address them, but they are a dejected-looking group of soldiers.

"Okay, men, I want you to stand tall and hold yourself straight—get those heads up and your chests out. This program has simply proved a little tougher and a little more intense than you might have expected. So be it. This is not a training course, so there was no course for you to fail. Phase One at RASP One is the selection process for Phase Two of RASP One. By dropping out of Phase One, you have deselected yourself from Phase Two—no more, no less. Now we have to decide, or you have to decide, what's next. Those of you on a medical drop, I want you to stay here. We'll get to your disposition once the medics have made their final recommendations. The rest of you come with me. The first sergeant wants a word with you."

I follow Iselin and his eighteen VWs on the short walk over to the Ranger Selection and Training Company headquarters. The former candidates are ushered into a conference room and asked to have a seat around a long table. Most of the chairs are cushy, padded swivels and very comfortable. After a few moments, the S&T Company first sergeant enters. He's a sixteen-year veteran of the regiment and the 1st Ranger Battalion with eleven combat tours behind him. He's not a big man, but he's lean and hard with just a trace of a Tennessee accent. I was expecting some strong or even harsh words from the S&T first sergeant, but this was not the case. He looks slowly around the room before beginning in a soft voice.

"Fellows, my name is First Sergeant Jason Walker. Thanks for coming so I can have a word with you. I know it's been a long day. A few of you I've met during your time in Pre-RASP, and for some of you, this is our first meeting. I want to accomplish three things today. First of all, I want to understand why each one of you has decided to leave Ranger assessment and selection. Our objective is to make the program better and not lose some of you good men in future classes. Next, I also want to make sure that you understand just what you're giving up by forfeiting a chance to be in the Regiment. We offer the best soldiering in this or any other army. It's good duty. We kick ass in the battlespace, and we look after each other when here at home. Since each of you are all going to be in the Army for a while, you might want to think again about what kind of outfit you want to serve in and who you want to soldier with. And, finally, I am going to ask you if you want to leave us for good, or if you'll accept an administrative rollback to the next class. Some of you, I'm told, have personal issues that have kept you from focusing on selection. I want to learn more about your specific concerns. If you have a personal problem but still want to be a Ranger, we have ways to help with that. Rangers take care of each other, right men?"

"ROGER THAT, FIRST SERGEANT!"

Walker then asks each man where he's from, what he was doing before he joined the Army, and chats with him for a few minutes before asking the soldier why he withdrew from the class. First Sergeant Walker listens attentively to the soldier's explanation. Usually the reason is the punishment of the morning's ruck march. There's a scattering of "I lost my focus" and "I need to get stronger." Walker then quietly deflects or diffuses each issue.

"I know it was a tough morning," he tells them, "and I don't expect you to be able to ruck with my cadre. But tell me this. How many in the class were dropped for not keeping up on the ruck march? Zero, am I right?"

"ROGER, FIRST SERGEANT!"

"So what's the problem? This was just a warm-up evolution to get you ready for the graded twelve-mile timed ruck march. We have very few candidates fail the twelve-miler. Did you know that? Nearly everyone makes the twelve-miler."

All the while he's *reselling* the Regiment—presenting them with a second chance to succeed where they have just failed. And he's very persuasive. If *I'd* just VWed, *I'd* have wanted to come back and try again. In the final tally, six elected to roll back to the next class for another try. Eight said they did not want to come back, and four said they had to resolve some personal issues before they could make a decision.

"Okay, gentlemen," the first sergeant says in conclusion. "That's it. But before you leave, I what to thank you for volunteering—

volunteering three times. Once to join the Army, then again for Airborne School, and yet again for Rangers. You volunteered to serve your country in time of war. That takes a lot of courage. I joined in '95 and we were not at war; you joined after the fighting started with every expectation of going into combat. As a Ranger, you're guaranteed combat. I'm proud to wear the same uniform that you do. Good luck to each one of you."

From the moment each of these soldiers withdrew from RASP 1, I was both impressed and surprised at how they were handled. They were treated with respect, courtesy, and compassion. Once they said *no mas*, and the assessment/selection switch was turned off, their world changed. When the time comes for First Sergeant Jason Walker to retire from military service, the company that is fortunate enough to recruit him to their marketing team will be getting one hell of a salesman. They must teach persuasive technique in first sergeant's school, because it's not an uncommon talent in Army first sergeants. But in deference to the spell cast over those who said they would accept a recycle to the next class, several, after more careful reflection, decided to leave RASP.

Those who did not withdraw from Class 09-10 will have a difficult conclusion to their second day in Phase One. At the formation for the ruck march that morning, the class was not well organized and several soldiers had to be sent back to their barracks for missing gear. When individuals in a RASP class perform poorly in areas of organization and evolution preparation, the whole class is made to pay. That evening after chow, the class forms on the rocks for some extra instruction. This instruction is administered by Staff Sergeant Brandon Wilson.

"What we have here is a failure to communicate," says Sergeant Wilson, mimicking the famous line in the movie *Cool Hand Luke*. Wilson is a pacer, and he roams up and down the ranks. "This morning, you were hosed up—big time. We posted a packing list for the six-mile ruck march and apparently most of you failed to read it. Or maybe you just don't care. Maybe you just want to eat dinner chow and take it easy. Maybe you just want to go back to the barracks for some light reading. How about you, Garcia, are you here just to take it easy?"

"Negative, Sergeant!"

Wilson prowls the ranks of trainees, working himself into an indignant rage. "How about you, O'Connor, you want to take it easy?"

"Negative, Sergeant."

"As a class, you guys suck. Class leader?"

"CLASS LEADER!" the class echoes.

"Right here, Sergeant."

"You're fired; get back in ranks. You—" He points to a specialist in the front rank. "You think you can lead this class?"

"I'll try, Sergeant."

"You'll try? You'll try!" Sergeant Wilson is really working himself up. "The hell you will. You will or you won't! When your squad leader goes down from enemy fire, are you going to try to take charge of your fire team, or will you take charge and keep your team in the fight!"

"I'll take charge, Sergeant. I'll lead the class."

"Okay, you're hired. Here's what I want you to do." Wilson huddles for a moment with the new class leader.

Commands are then given to the class through the class leadership. The class leadership continues to change often, including the three platoon leaders. Specialist Dan Allen now leads 09-10—the fourth to take charge of the class.

"Listen up," barks Allen, looking at his watch. It's 0815. "You have twenty-five minutes to be back here in formation with everything you own except your mattress. Bag it up, get it down here, and be standing by your gear no later than eighteen-forty. Okay, let's move!"

I watch with Sergeant Wilson as the class races from the rocks, around the building, and up to the barracks. Wilson is a smiling,

easygoing young Ranger from 1st Battalion. He grew up in northern
Georgia and joined the Army right out of high school, coming straight
to the battalion as an Eleven Bravo. He's had five rotations and has
seen Ranger combat as a fire-team leader and a squad leader. Wilson
has been a cadre sergeant with S&T for close to a year. He's married
and has a two-year-old son. When he finishes his tour here, he's considering taking a specialty in Army intelligence to improve his promotion chances. Brandon Wilson is twenty-six years old.

Staff Sergeant Wilson is a hater. This is my personal term for
cadre who can come across as demanding and mean-spirited. In the
case of Sergeant Wilson, it's exact opposite of his actual temperament. I've seen instructors like him in SEAL and Special Forces
cadres, and they are among the most talented and effective special
operations trainers. Basically, they're actors. It's a real knack—almost
a calling—and few SOF instructors do it well. It is not easy to do
rage, and do it convincingly. Oddly enough, SOF trainees seem to
like these passionate and vocal instructors, and will do their best to
meet the instructor's expectations. In ranks, they may whisper, "Oh
no, here comes Sergeant Wilson," but amid the reprimands and mock
tantrums, the students or candidates know that these cadre sergeants
really care, and want only the best effort from them.

"He's one of my best cadre sergeants," Sergeant Walt Iselin says
of Wilson. "And his talent goes well beyond his work here. He graduates at the top of every Army school he attends and his reputation
in First Battalion is solid. A lot of these kids who graduate will tell
stories about Sergeant Wilson. They'll remember that he may have
made life miserable for them, but they'll also remember that he
made them better Rangers."

"Are there ever any lingering hard feelings on the part of these
candidates for people like Wilson or the rest of the cadre?" I ask.

"Not really," Iselin replies. "Those who succeed and graduate will
know that he made them a stronger class and a stronger individual
soldier. They'll more than likely thank him."

Class 09-10 staggers down to the rocks carrying an amazing amount of gear and clothing. Rows of soldiers and mounds of gear begin to appear. "Stop moving," barks Wilson, and the candidates freeze. Some soldiers are standing behind their gear, which is laid out in good order; others are thrashing about in a littering of linens and uniforms. It's a yard sale.

"No, no, no! This is awful—disgraceful! If some of you can do it right, why not all of you?" Again he's on the prowl in a full rant about their failure to move quickly and to work as a team. "Gentlemen, you will, before you leave here, learn to move with a sense of urgency. You—" He points to a man whose gear is in good order. "Good job there."

"Roger that, Sergeant."

"Now put your boots on that nice, neat pile of gear and start to give me some push-ups. You had your gear ready, but why didn't you help your buddy with his gear? And where's your Ranger buddy?"

The soldier looks around wildly from his extended-arm, push-up position. "Ah, he's . . . ah . . ."

"You don't know where your Ranger buddy is? You don't know where . . . where . . ." Wilson is now beside himself with rage. He can barely speak. "Everybody drop!" While they do push-ups, he continues to prowl, lecturing 09-10 on its lack of teamwork and its shortcomings. "One way or another, before you leave here, you will learn that you never leave or abandon your Ranger buddy. And you'll always know where he is. Clear?"

"ROGER THAT, SERGEANT!"

"Class leader!"

"CLASS LEADER!"

"Right here, Sergeant."

Wilson squats next to Allen while he continues to do push-ups. "I want each of you to dig out your PT gear from the rest of your stuff. Then I want you to return to your billets with your PT gear, change out of your ACUs, and put on your PT gear. Next, get back down here carrying your uniforms, stow your uniforms with the rest of your gear, and stand by your gear. You have six minutes to do this. Clear?"

"Roger that, Sergeant."

"Okay, make it happen."

Allen gives the orders, and the candidates extricate themselves and their PT gear from the mounds of equipment and race off. Wilson looks on dispassionately. Then he turns to me with a grin. "They'll make the effort, but six minutes is an impossible time hack."

The class straggles back to the rocks in PT gear and thrashes about stowing uniforms. "Stop moving," Wilson orders. Then he lectures some more on teamwork and the class does more push-ups. He next sends them back to their billets with all their gear to prepare for a formal barracks inspection. He gives them less than the needed time to prepare for a formal inspection. Class 09-10 is finally secured at 2100, but with casualties. In the wake of this after-dinner activity, four more candidates have voluntarily withdrawn. The four of them form up in the hallway outside of Sergeant Iselin's office while waiting for Sergeant Wilson to finish his inspection of the barracks. One of these men I take special note of.

Private Bill Mann grew up in Pittsburgh and was living in Clearwater, Florida, six months earlier when he paid a visit to a nearby Army recruiting office. At the time, he was a busy senior manager working for a restaurant chain, but he was restless in the corporate world and wanted to serve. Much earlier, he had attended college for two years, where he played football and was a track star, running the four hundred meter in under forty-seven seconds. So at one time he had been both strong and fast. Private Mann is a big man at six feet two and 205 pounds, but Bill Mann is now forty years old. Despite his age, he *looks* like a Ranger.

Normally, I don't speak immediately with soldiers who VW, so it wasn't until the following day that I caught up with Private Mann.

"How did you get here?" I begin. We're in the Holdover barracks, off to one side and out of earshot of the other former candidates.

"I told the Army how old I was and that I wanted to serve my country. I've been given a lot, and I wanted to give something back, even at this late stage of the game. I told them that I'd not enlist unless I could be guaranteed Rangers. The recruiters tried to get me to enlist just for infantry training, but I told them it was the Rangers or nothing. Finally, they offered me an enlistment contract with the Ranger option. They had no Eleven Bravo contracts, so I came in as a radio operator. I went through BCT, AIT, and Airborne, and then came here."

"So what happened?"

"Mister Couch," he began earnestly, "I know my body pretty well, and after that bag drag down from the barracks last night, and while I was digging my PT gear from the bottom of my duffel, I felt some new and different pains. I was hurting, but that's no good excuse; we're all hurting. Candidly, I think I just allowed the pain to break my spirit. I gave up mentally. I started to feel sorry for myself, and I quit. I'm not happy about it, but there it is."

"What's next? Admin recycle?" I ask hopefully.

"Last night I did a lot of thinking. I will be returning with the next class," he says with a determined expression. "They've given me some leave to attend to some personal issues at home, but I'll be back, and I'll be ready. I won't quit again. I might not make it through, but I certainly won't quit."

"That's good to hear," I reply. "Class One-Eleven, if I recall the scheduling, forms up on Thursday, October 7."

"That's right," Bill Mann replies. "I know the date well. On 7 October, I turn forty-one."

At the Wednesday morning 0600 formation, Class 09-10 is standing tall and in good order. It's still dark, but they look better formed than they did the previous morning, the one that had earned them such a miserable evening with Sergeant Wilson. They are in PT gear in anticipation of the morning's first evolution—team PT. Each man has his two-quart slung over his right shoulder and resting on his back. The four men who VWed last night are queued up by the cadre door in ACUs. While the class awaits the Phase One cadre, three candidates in PT gear join the four in uniform. They simply drift from the formation to the VW line. I can only assume that they had intended to do PT with the class, but at the last minute had a change of heart. Then a fourth man also leaves formation and joins the VW line. Two Ranger candidates immediately follow him, but he willingly allows them to escort him right back to the PT formation. When the cadre breaks from the building, there's an even hundred Ranger hopefuls standing with Class 09-10.

Wednesday PT begins with a double time to Peden Field and a good twenty minutes of stretching. The cadre then breaks them into eight groups of twelve to thirteen candidates. A cadre sergeant leads each group for a solid hour of physical training—hard PT of the individual cadre's choosing. Some form a circle and do exercises. In some circles, the cadre sergeants lead; in others, candidates take turns leading. Exercises consist of generous repetitions of push-ups, pull-ups, and flutter kicks. There is hand walking on monkey bars, a series of six-foot walls to scale and run between, and thirty-foot climbing ropes. There are sections of telephone poles used for log PT. Bordering the field is a track where some groups run between exercises. Other groups do shuttle runs with push-ups and flutter kicks between sprints. Then more pull-ups and rope climbing. It's a circus, and a punishing one. Yet the cadre is right there leading the exercises and/or doing them with the students. There is little or no shouting or harassment, just one exercise after another. During the course of the evolution, two more candidates fall out—both with injuries from yesterday's ruck march that have only gotten worse with the PT session. By 0900, the class is showered and formed up for the next evolution—morning chow. They're starting to look smart in formation. I notice for the first time, from the names on the backs of their ACU caps, that they form up in alphabetical order.

Before they leave the RASP compound for breakfast each day, the class recites the Ranger Creed. Six candidates are chosen at random, and each is made to lead one stanza of the recitation. In turn, the six leaders shout, "The first [or second or third] stanza of the Ranger Creed; repeat after me!" and deliver verbatim their assigned stanza. If there is any faltering or miscue, the whole class drops for push-ups. This is not a trivial ritual or a RASP-only event. I have been to solemn Ranger ceremonies where the Creed is recited in exactly the same manner as these candidates must do before they eat breakfast.

As with other formation-centric evolutions in RASP, the feeding of Ranger candidates is very formatted. Freshly showered but still breaking a sweat, the class double-times from the rocks formation area some three hundred yards to the Ranger DFAC, which is short for dining facilities administration center. DFAC is a modern military term for a modern military chow hall. By eating breakfast late, after most of the regimental personnel have finished, the RASP candidates get through the service lines with very little waiting. They file in, eat, and file out very quickly. They sit in their own section and are not allowed to talk. The good news is they get to control what they eat and how much. The Ranger DFACs are among the only chow halls in the Army that are serve-yourself facilities—take all you want, eat all you take. I've had some experience with both military and SOF dining facilities, and have found that none exceed the standards of the Fort Benning Ranger Regiment's DFAC—good chow, and plenty of it. The return trip from chow to the RASP area is the only time a candidate formation is allowed *not* to double-time. After they return to the RASP training area, each candidate must do ten pull-ups.

The balance of day three, with a break for noon chow, is devoted to radio familiarization and call-for-fire training. The cadre sergeants

segue from their assessment-selection role to that of military instructors. There is the occasion for push-ups or flutter kicks, but this is
military training. The radio is the all-important MBITR (pronounced
"Em-bitter"). Technically, it's the AN/PRC-148 Multiband Inter/
Intra Team Radio. Developed in the early 1990s to meet the requirement for a secure SOF handheld radio, it's now the most widely used
team radio in the U.S. military. In addition to MBITR mechanics,
programming, and procedures, the candidates are drilled in radio
call-for-fire procedures. Call-for-fire, for this stage of RASP, focuses
on calling for and adjusting artillery fire, and calling in fire support
from a helicopter—both simulated drills. Rangers on deployment
may have occasion to do the former, but they will frequently call for
helicopter gunship support. Artillery support is a luxury, but few
Rangers will get through an operational deployment without having
called in an Apache gunship to make his life easier, or even to save
his life. It's a skill that all Rangers must master. Those younger soldiers in Class 09-10 who are having trouble are helped by their
classmates who carry the MOS for radio operators or fire-support
specialists. They've done this before.

Day four begins again at 0600. The class, now ninety-eight strong,
is in boots, T-shirts, and ACU pants and caps, and wearing
CamelBaks—canvas-covered water bladders carried backpack style
with drinking tubes that snake over one shoulder strap so the wearer
can drink while on the move. Each man carries a lime-green Chem-
lite; they are a formation of Christmas lights. Today is their first
terrain run.

"This will be a tough evolution for them," a cadre sergeant tells
me. "By now, all but a few of them are hurting—some more than
others. Very few have injuries that should keep them from remaining in selection, but they're getting weary and they hurt. Some can
play with pain and others can't or won't. We're looking for the guys
who can manage their pain—those who can soldier on when they're
tired and when they've got an ache or two."

After the ritual pre-PT stretching, the class moves out at a brisk pace for the snake pit—the scene of the brutal day-one PT. There the class is broken into groups, and a cadre sergeant leads them on a series of trails that circle through a wooded area cut by several ravines. One particularly hilly trail is called the Downing Mile, named for the late General Wayne Downing, a former Regimental Commander and Commander of the U.S. Special Operations Command. The final mile of this terrain run is on paved roads, but the candidates run while carrying a Ranger buddy. Periodically, the formation halts and goes into a notional security perimeter to collect stragglers. They swap carrier and carryee, and drive on. After a plunge through a neck-deep stream crossing, the soaked candidates make their way back to the rocks, where they are dismissed to shower and to get into a dry uniform before morning chow formation.

Most of day four is not unlike day three, only each candidate and his Ranger buddy will be tested as a team on their use of the MBITR radio and graded on their ability to call and adjust artillery fire and to call for helicopter fire support.

The final day-four evolution is the initial portion of the Ranger Athlete Warrior assessment. It's an assessment, not a test, and those in 09-10 will be assessed again at the completion of RASP. The first portion is this assessment involves lifting weights—a bench press of 185 pounds and a dead lift of 225 pounds. Capabilities vary widely. Some of the bigger men familiar with weight work knock out multiple repetitions; some of the smaller candidates cannot manage a single rep on either. With the RAW weight assessment behind them, the class is finished for the day.

By 0600 on day five, the class formation has changed. Instead of three platoons, there are now only two. Ninety-seven candidates muster in the two platoons with a single soldier now standing by the cadre door who has decided to VW. The class leadership has also changed. Both platoon leaders, the class first sergeant, and the class leader are new. This is 09-10's sixth class leader. As the new platoon leaders make their muster reports to the class leader, they also report that ten candidates have put in for sick call. With the muster taken, the class shifts uneasily in ranks and await the cadre.

"At ease!" someone calls and the class comes to parade rest. I can feel the class tense as Sergeant Wilson makes his way to them across the rocks.

"What are we doing today?" he asks a candidate.

"I'm not sure, Sergeant."

"You, what are we doing today?" he asks another candidate.

"Continuing with the RAW assessment, Sergeant."

"Was the word put out about the schedule for today?" he asks the class.

"ROGER THAT, SERGEANT!"

"Then why don't some of you know that?" Silence. "Men, every-one should know the schedule for the day. So now everyone drop." After several rounds of push-ups, Sergeant Wilson calls them to their feet. "Men, I am very unhappy today. You are making me more unhappy. You do not want to make me more unhappy. Do you know what will make me more unhappy?"

"NEGATIVE, SERGEANT!"

"You will make me more unhappy by not knowing what your next evolution is, by not keeping your head in the game, and above all by not putting max effort into the RAW assessment we'll do today. Do you understand me?"

"ROGER THAT, SERGEANT!"

"It will behoove you *not* to make me more unhappy. Are we clear on that?"

"ROGER THAT, SERGEANT!"

After more push-ups, the class runs over to Peden Field. Follow-ing stretching and warm-up, they continue with the RAW assess-ment, which includes pull-ups, timed push-ups, timed shuttle runs, a timed agility course, and an eight-pound medicine-ball toss. These graded events will form a baseline for Class 09-10—individually and as a class. In the Ranger battalions, the RAW assessment will include shuttle runs and negotiating obstacles while in full battle kit. The idea behind the RAW assessment program is that it forces Rangers to assess themselves against a physical standard that relates to battle-field performance. And if a Ranger slacks off on his personal PT program, it will show up on his periodic RAW assessment.

After finishing the RAW assessment and morning chow, the class moves over to the training mats at the Smith Fitness Center on the Main Post, a huge modern facility with weight rooms, sports courts, and a rock-climbing wall. For many of these candidates, this is their introduction to the Special Operations Combatives Program, or SOCP (pronounced "sock-pee"). The Special Operations Combat-ives Program is an extension of the Army's Combatives Program. SOCP is a cumulative physical combat skill set developed to aug-ment the special operator's behind-the-gun skill set. It was developed from a combination of martial-arts disciplines and lessons learned on the insurgent battlefield to support the needs of modern ground-combat special operators. The program will be introduced today and continue throughout RASP 1. SOCP will provide an operational tool these future Rangers can take with them into combat.

After a long warm-up session, the candidates of Class 09-10 are introduced to the proper stance and the multidirectional movement made while in this stance. The stance is designed to deflect and absorb blows as well as to provide a platform from which to deliver hand strikes, elbow strikes, and kicks. These are unarmed movements and strikes, but they are designed to create no contradiction when used by a Ranger who is fully armed. The initial moves and strikes are elementary and fundamental, and are primarily defensive in nature. The goal of these basic skills is to create space between the Ranger and his attacker so that he or another Ranger can assess the nature of the attack and resolve it with lethal or nonlethal force. Staff Ser-geant Son Chin is the lead cadre sergeant for combatives. He's a small, compact man with excellent martial-arts technique. Chin was born in Cambodia and raised in the Philippines. He's also a very accomplished Thai kickboxer. Sergeant Chin is the only member of the Phase One cadre team who is not an Eleven Bravo; he's a truck driver. More accurately, he's a Ranger with the truck-driver MOS. Sergeant Chin is from the 2nd Battalion and a veteran of five combat rotations.

Combatives is hands-on training that follows an explanation-demonstration-application format. The candidates learn it, see it, and then do it. It's a break from the assessment and selection routine to an evolution of teaching and learning. Both candidates and cadre seem to enjoy it; it's physically challenging, and it's warrior training.

The candidates take a break for chow—MREs (meals ready to eat) behind the gym complex—then they're back inside for more combatives instruction. They're sitting in the bleachers as the cadre file in. The rush of the morning's training has made Class 09-10 a little boisterous as it awaits the afternoon's evolution. This attracts the attention of Sergeant Brandon Wilson.

"Everyone quit moving." The class freezes. "You are here to learn and perform, not to carry on like a bunch of grade-school kids. Class leader."

"CLASS LEADER!"

"You and your first sergeant get out here. The rest of you sit at attention and watch." The class watches while Sergeant Wilson puts the two candidate leaders through multiple sets of push-ups and flutter kicks. "You screwed up, and now they have to pay for your mistakes. How do you feel about that?" The class leader and class first sergeant push and kick and sweat while their classmates are made to watch. "Are you okay with that? You get to screw off and they have to pay for your mistakes. Is that all right with you?"

"NEGATIVE, SERGEANT."

"Then pull your heads out of your butts and get with the program." Wilson paces before the class; they look straight ahead, trying not to make eye contact with him. "Recover," he calls to the two scapegoats, "and fall back in with your class. The rest of you tighten it up. This is serious business, gentlemen. Quit thinking about the weekend and focus on what we're doing here. These are skills you will use in combat—those few of you who will manage to get to Regiment." He moves away, leaving 09-10 to await the afternoon's combatives in silence.

By the end of the day's training, the class is down by six more men. Morning sick call resulted in the medical drop of two candidates. Of the six men who were scheduled for the Ranger Swim Assessment and Evaluation retesting, only two are able to shed their flak vest and body armor and swim the length of the pool. At the end of five days of assessment and selection, Class 09-10 is able to muster ninety-one candidates.

There is no formal training on this Saturday or Sunday. It's a chance for the survivors of Class 09-10 to recover, work on their uniforms and gear, and to attend to assigned barracks maintenance details. Sickness and infection are taken seriously, and much of candidates' weekend time is devoted to keeping the barracks well-scrubbed and reeking of disinfectant. But for some members of the class, there's a makeup evolution. That previous Tuesday morning, fifty-two candidates "failed" the ungraded six-mile ruck march, in that they were unable to keep up with their cadre sergeant. Of those, just over half, twenty-eight soldiers, are still in training. At 0600, they muster to repeat the march. The makeup ruck march is conducted at Stewart-Watson Field, a series of athletic fields near the Smith Sports Complex and bordered by a one-mile running track. It's a wide scenic gravel path with firm, easy footing. Scenic or not, it's one of the few times that a group of Ranger candidates wish they were about the distasteful task of cleaning the barracks. Of the twenty-eight candidates who began the makeup six-miler, all but one finish the evolution. Due to a painful knee, he drops out from the makeup ruck march. As this is not a graded or critical evolution, his failure to complete the makeup ruck march will not get him dropped from the class.

Most of the cadre do not come in on Saturday, but Sergeant Walt Iselin is not one of them. He was there to take the report at the 0600 formation and to monitor the six-mile ruck repeat. Following the evolution, he puts them back in formation and cautions them about making good use of their time off.

"You have the rest of today and tomorrow to get yourselves ready for next week's training," he tells them. "Use your time well. This program will not get any easier, gentlemen. In fact, when we get to Cole Range, it will get a lot harder." After the candidates leave, Iselin turns to me. "I wasn't kidding. Week two is probably our hardest week. This is where we see our next round of attrition. Those still in training will have to step it up a notch at Cole Range to stay in selection."

On Sunday afternoon, I stop by the barracks. The class now occupies only the second floor; it no longer spills over to the third floor. The barracks are separate, closed-off sleeping bays with between four and fourteen racks—all two-tier bunks. The men bunk in alphabetical order, and each week they compress into fewer rooms as the class shrinks. The candidates I meet are generally in good spirits, and I'm surprised to learn just how structured their "off time" is. They muster three times a day and run to the DFAC. There are assigned barracks maintenance duties, and each man has to do laundry and ready his uniforms and gear for the next week's training. And all are required to drink a hydration shake each morning and two quarts of water each evening. During their limited free time, they study their Ranger guides in preparation for the written test they must pass in Phase One of RASP.

Over this course of this first week, I was able to spend a few minutes with many of the soldiers who left RASP. Their stated reasons for quitting are wide-ranging. Many are honest in their formal withdrawal statements, while I suspect others are not. There are legitimate medical reasons why some soldiers cannot continue, but many who leave are hurting no worse than others who have elected to continue. The pattern I see emerging in the Ranger Assessment and Selection Program is little different from what I've observed during Basic Underwater Demolition/SEAL (BUD/S) training in Coronado, California, and at Special Forces Assessment and Selection (SFAS) at Fort Bragg, North Carolina. Approximately 10 to 15 percent of the candidates simply don't have the physical tools to withstand the punishment this kind of program asks of a young man. Another 5 to 10 percent will not quit unless they are seriously injured, and even then they will go to great lengths to hide their injury; no amount of pain or physical harassment can make them quit. These are the few who, if ever captured by the enemy, will die before divulging secrets. The remaining candidates, about 75 to 85 percent of the class, have the physical tools to succeed. They are in play—up for grabs. If they have or can develop the needed amount of determination and desire, or somehow are able to see their goal clearly enough, they will succeed. For this large percentage of candidates, it simply comes down to who really wants it and who doesn't. If there were a written test for heart, then we wouldn't need SOF entry-level programs like RASP, BUD/S, and SFAS. Until such time, the coin of this realm will continue to be sweat, pain, and desire.

That said, my focus is on those who stay in training—those who don't quit. During breaks in training, over a lunch with an MRE, or on a road march, I'm beginning to get to know the soldiers of RASP Class 09-10. Every candidate has a story that deserves to be heard, but there are just too many soldiers and too few pages to be able to tell them all. While *Sua Sponte* is the journey of a RASP class, I'll occasionally make time in this text to share the personal stories of individuals who have volunteered to serve their country as a Ranger.

Private Jeffery Jennings is a twenty-four-year-old who stands out if for no other reason than he's a lean six feet three. Over an MRE on Friday, I ask him how the course is going for him. He smiles from ear to ear. "So far so good," he tells me. "Looking forward to a few days off this weekend, but no problems." I usually begin my questioning of a candidate by asking what he was doing before he joined the Army. "I was a policeman in Moab, Utah," Jennings says. Moab is a small town in the northern part of the state that is both scenic and touristy. "The job was okay, but it was a small-town force with all the small-town politics that go with the territory. There was little chance I could find a job in a larger metropolitan department until I had at least six years on the job. And I had only two years in. But most police departments count service time, so I decided to join the Army."

"Okay," I reply. "But since you were a policeman, why not the military police—the MPs? Why the Rangers?"

"Well, my initial thought was that it might be fun to go to Airborne School, but my recruiter said he had no MP slots with airborne training. He said he didn't even have airborne slots at that time for infantrymen. But he did have a guaranteed airborne training slot for an Eighty-Eight Mike."

"What's an Eighty-Eight Mike?"

"That's me; I'm a truck driver."

"As I understand it, truck drivers don't get airborne training unless . . ."

"That's right, sir," Jennings says, the smile now a sheepish grin. "Unless they're on a Ranger contract. Later on, when I really read the fine print, I found I'd signed on for Ranger training—BCT, AIT as a truck driver, airborne training, and RASP. I probably should have read it closer before I signed up. Honestly, I feel a little stupid about it."

"Any regrets?"

"No, sir. I really lucked out. I knew nothing about Rangers until I got here. Now I really want to serve in the Regiment. And the timing was perfect. I just missed Class 08-10, so I had five weeks in Pre-RASP. That gave me time to get in shape and to move my family out here. I have a wife and two sons." With the mention of his family, the smile gets even bigger.

"Are you Mormon, Jennings?"

"Yes, sir. There are several in the Regiment, and the local Mormon church has been very supportive in helping us get settled. And when I get to Phase Two, I'll get to see them on the weekends."

I'm not sure that even Phase Two candidates get time off on weekends, but I say nothing. The class is beginning to stir; it's time for formation and more combatives.

"Good luck, Private."

"Thanks, sir. Are you going to be with us the whole time?"

"The whole time. See you at graduation, Jennings."

"You bet, sir. And I'll introduce you to my family." He makes his way back into the sports complex, still smiling.

On Monday morning, the second week of RASP 1, Phase One, ninety-one candidates are on the rocks at 0600 to begin further assessment and selection. Specialist James Neuman is now the class leader. Neither he nor I can recall just how many leadership changes there have been. I do know that at least three of his predecessors are no longer with the class. Neuman is a serious soldier from Missouri who has a degree in psychology and was working in an assisted-care facility before he joined the Army. He's quiet, confident, and seems to be something of a loner, but he gets the job done. I've watched as other class leaders have taken to shouting orders, but Neuman is content to work through his class first sergeant and class platoon leaders. When I ask him about being class leader, he's very measured about it. "All Rangers have to be leaders, and now it's my turn to lead. I'll do the best I can and learn as much as I can until the cadre appoints someone else as class leader."

In addition to two platoon leaders and the eight squad leaders, there is the candidate company first sergeant. This conforms to the company officer/NCO team-leadership model in the Army, where the unit leader is an officer and the unit senior sergeant is the first sergeant. For Class 09-10, the current first sergeant is Private First Class Don McFarland. McFarland is a twenty-four-year-old infantryman from Northern Virginia who was a wind-turbine repair technician. Parachuting and Ranger training, according to McFarland, are only slightly less scary than climbing around on three-hundred-foot-tall windmills.

There's another class leader, one who has yet to be assigned a formal leadership position, but leads from within the ranks of Class 09-10. He's Ranger candidate Mark Ikenboch. Ikenboch has seen this training before—all of it. He's a sergeant who previously served in the Ranger Regiment with the 3rd Battalion. He's also a Tabbed Ranger. Any soldier with more than two years broken service may reenter the Regiment, but he must do so by way of RASP.

"I got out and joined the [National] Guard," he told me. "I went to college for a few years, but that just wasn't for me. I missed the life in the Regiment, so here I am."

"Any problems this time around?" I ask.

"Not really. I'm a little older than most of these guys, but I have good pain-management skills. This is the way it has to be, and I accept it."

"I understand where he's coming from," one of the Phase One cadre sergeants confided to me in referring to the 3-75 veteran candidate. "I wanted to earn my college degree, so I left the Regiment and did just that. After trying my hand at a few civilian jobs, I knew I wanted back in the Regiment, so I had to come back through RASP, or RIP as it was called back then. I had RIP cadre sergeants who had been in my platoon when I was in the Regiment the first time. They told me back then what we now tell Ikenboch: You have to earn your Scroll again. Doing it a second time is somewhat easier, because we second-timers know that where we're going is worth the pain to get there. So, in that sense it may be easier, but it's still very hard."

This morning after formation, following the now-ritual stretching and warm-up and a few sets of push-ups, the class jogs over to the Stewart-Watson Field track for their ungraded five-mile run test. All Rangers in RASP must run five miles in PT gear in forty minutes or less. Four men are unable to finish the run, and another six are not under the forty-minute standard. Two run the five miles under thirty-two minutes, and one of those is just over thirty-one minutes. Sergeant Mark Ikenboch registers the fifth-fastest time in the class. Again, this is not a critical event, so those who did not finish or finished over the forty-minute standard are still with the class. If, however, they are unable to meet this standard on a later timed run, they will be dropped.

The morning and the first part of the afternoon are spent in the classroom on map reading and map orientation. This is a review, as all of these soldiers have had some work with map and compass during their basic training, and most have some familiarity with land navigation. These classroom sessions are in preparation for their land-navigation practical work at Cole Range. Sergeant Brandon Wilson teaches map reading, and he attacks this assignment with the same enthusiasm he had with his class corrective measures. He's as good in the classroom as he is in addressing the shortcomings of Class 09-10. Following the map classes, he gives them a warning.

"Okay, listen up, men. You'll have the rest of the day to get your gear squared away for Cole Range. We have an early morning ruck march, and this one's an eight-miler. The good news is that you'll be out there on the land-nav course for four days enjoying the beautiful Georgia woodlands. The bad news is it's going to be very hot. Everybody take a drink." The candidates snatch up their two-quarts and begin to drink. "Remember," Wilson continues, "it's what you drink this afternoon and tonight that gets you ready for the heat tomorrow. Class leader."

"CLASS LEADER!"

"Get the classroom policed up and then get the class back to the RASP area for Cole Range gear prep."

"Roger that, Sergeant."

Back in the cadre offices, Sergeant Walt Iselin and his cadre are going through their checklists for the Cole Range block of training. "This is where we will see our last flood of VWs," Iselin tells me after the cadre briefing. "The days are long, and they don't get nearly as much sleep as here. And as you may have heard, it's going to be plenty hot."

With all this talk of weather, I thought it might be a good idea to get a forecast, so I checked it online. The good news was that the humidity was, for the first time since the class convened, under 50 percent. The bad news was that the high temperature for Tuesday was to be ninety-eight, and it would be in the mid-nineties for the rest of the week.

In deference to the heat and the length of the march, the class musters on Tuesday morning at 0400 on the rocks. Class 09-10 begins the movement to Cole Range with ninety-one souls. Unlike the previous ruck march, the class forms up in ACUs. There is a new class leader and class first sergeant. Specialist James Neuman led only over the weekend and through Monday; apparently, the cadre liked what they saw from him and installed a new class leader. Specialist Larry Silvers is an infantryman from eastern Pennsylvania. Like many of the candidates tapped by the cadre for class leadership, Silvers is a college graduate. College graduates who enlist are advanced to E-4, or specialist, when they graduate from OSUT or AIT. Two years ago, he earned a degree in business from a small college not far from his hometown. After graduation, Silvers traveled for a year before he enlisted in the Army. "I always knew I wanted to be in the Army, I just wanted to take some time off after school before I joined up." He volunteered for Rangers in Airborne School. Silvers has a preppie look to him, and I guessed him to be much younger than his twenty-three years. The new class first sergeant is, at thirty-three, one of the oldest in Class 09-10. Specialist Rick Petrino is a lean, olive-skinned soldier with sharp features and an easy smile. He has a degree from USC. Before he decided to join the Army for Ranger training, he was tending bar at the Palisades Hotel in Los Angeles. "Life was good," he said of his pre-Army days. "I made good money, I was into surfing and cycling, but I was going nowhere. I think that someday I want a family, but that's a difficult thing for a career bartender. I felt a need to do something more worthwhile, and so here I am."

Leadership changes are initiated by the Phase One cadre, usually with some forethought, and other times not. When there is forethought, there seems to be an attempt to select the older and more senior candidates, but Class 09-10 was a junior class to begin with, and they're running out of rank. Nine-ten began with only five E-5 junior sergeants, and now they are down to two. One has had his term as class leader; the other is Sergeant Ikenboch, who has yet to be tasked with leading the class. I ask Specialist Larry Silvers how the leadership choices flow down from the cadre to the class.

"The cadre select the class leader and the class first sergeant," Silvers tells me. "Class leaders choose who they'd like for the class platoon leaders. The platoon leaders choose their four squad leaders, and the squad leaders pick two guys in their squads to serve as fire-team leaders. There are accountability and formation chores for the platoon and squad leaders and for passing down the word, but most of it is on the class leader and class first sergeant."

As with the six-mile ruck march the previous week, the class forms up in two groups. This is made easier as there are now two platoons, and together with their rucks, they board two buses. The buses will take them to a starting point some eight miles from Cole Range. Cole Range is one of the numerous ranges on Fort Benning some twenty-five miles from the built-up Main Post area. It's used by all the units assigned to the 75th Ranger Regiment for land navigation and small-unit-tactics drill. These four days at Cole Range have acquired a reputation as something of a gut check for RASP 1, Phase One classes. It will prove to be that and then some for Class 09-10.

Three men elect to VW before their classmates board the buses, so eighty-eight candidates begin the eight-mile ruck march. The two groups begin well enough, but soon they string out badly, as many have difficulty holding the pace. Again, the Phase One cadre sergeants are under rucks marching with the students, encouraging them to keep pace, harassing those who fall behind. I'm under the weight of a camera and a CamelBak. With this light load, I'm able to keep up and to visit on occasion with the candidates. The road is paved but winds through gently rolling hills. The moon is still up, illuminating the ghostlike forms laboring under their packs. For the smaller candidates, there seems to be more ruck than soldier. I walk for a while with one of these soldiers, Private First Class Salvador Santos. Santos is third-generation Puerto Rican American and was driving a propane gas truck before he joined the Army. He's keeping up with his group behind the cadre-sergeant leader, but he's struggling. Santos joined the Army to be a Ranger, but he did not get a Ranger contract until he was in OSUT. Santos is twenty-five years old.

"How's it going, soldier."

"No worries, sir," he replies. "I just have to hang in there and keep up with the group."

I don't want him to have to expend energy talking to me, but I have to ask. "Private Santos, how tall are you?"

"Five one, sir."

"And you weigh how much?"

"About one hundred twenty-eight—maybe less now. That was before we classed up."

Although Santos is compact and muscular, he's carrying well over one-third his body weight, and the rucksack does indeed look as big as he does. By volume it probably is.

"My guess is that you'd be all for a program that indexes the weight of the ruck for the weight of the man, right?"

He grins. "That would get my vote all right."

"Good luck, Private. Hang in there."

"Roger that, sir."

As Class 09-10 closes in on Cole Range, the class is very strung out, and a few, nursing injuries, are falling so far behind that they have to be collected by the trailing vans. By 0700, the last of the stragglers arrive, and the class forms up in their two platoons. The lead cadre sergeants are not happy with the class's performance on the ruck march. Once the last man is in formation, the cadre begins some serious corrective PT, most of it involving the candidates lifting their rucksacks from the ground to an overhead, extended-arm position and back—again and again. Between the overhead rucksack presses, there are push-ups and flutter kicks. This goes on for close to an hour before the candidates are allowed to put down their rucks.

Following the post-ruck-march PT session, the class is introduced to a new command: "Hit the wood line." The improved part of Cole Range is a ten-acre meadowlike field that is kept mowed. The field is served by a series of support buildings, open-air classroom facilities, storage bins, a mock-up target area, and a small RASP cadre office—all bordering the southern and western edges of the field. From the RASP assembly and road-access area to the far tree line is close to 250 yards of mowed meadow. At the command to hit the wood line, the class is made to sprint from the assembly area to the wood line and back—a quarter-mile round-trip. I watch as the class makes four trips to the wood line. On the fifth and final trip, they conduct buddy carries. Between these long sprints, there are more push-ups. Following the ruck march and during the trips to the wood line, a line of soldiers begins to queue up in front of the Phase One cadre office.

The class is looking ragged and dispirited. This is when the entire Phase One cadre, led by the RASP NCOIC, Sergeant First Class Tad Collier, takes the pressure up a notch. The class is ranged out in a line across the meadow. Collier has one of the Phase One cadre sergeants place two sandbags some seventy yards into the meadow. The class is now lined up on a starting line with the just-placed sandbags marking the finish. The RASP NCOIC then begins to have the class run wind sprints over the seventy yards. After some ten sprints, Collier begins to pace up and down the line of winded candidates.

"Stand tall, men. Dress it up; keep your hands at your sides." Class 09-10 comes to a semblance of attention. The men all know and respect, and probably fear, Sergeant First Class Collier. He carries an air of authority that is not lost on these tired and sweating candidates. "This is not a game, men. This is preparation for life-and-death combat. There are Rangers going out on combat operations every night—every night. Every one of them depends on his Ranger buddy. If you complete this course, you will be one of them. But first you have to show me that you want to be a Ranger, and I mean really want it. I have no requirement to graduate a single one of you from this phase of the program. Unless things change, none of you will graduate. We'll convene the next RASP class and see if there are some men in that class who want to be Rangers. What does it take to be a Ranger? I'll tell you. It takes everything you've got—every time, all the time. And we'll be out here until I get that from you. Or you all quit and go someplace else. Ready . . . go!"

Class 09-10 is made to do wind sprint after wind sprint—up and back. The sun is climbing into a cloudless sky and the temperature seeps into the nineties. They run a total of forty sprints before the cadre starts calling out the winners. After each sprint, the first two—then the first four—are excused from the runners and made to stand at attention, while the others continue to run. The last two sprinters run a total of fifty-eight times. That's well over two miles of wind sprints. Many are limping, some are just going through the motions, and others are sprinting for all their worth, but they don't have much left.

It's late morning on this first day at Cole Range when Class 09-10 forms up on their rucksacks, but there are not as many as there were earlier. Sergeant Walt Iselin and his cadre sergeants now roam the ranks of trainees.

"If you quit now, you'll quit on your Ranger buddy down range."

"You think this is hard? It will only get harder this week, that I promise you."

"What are you going to do when you have to sprint to an objective at ten thousand feet in Afghanistan, and you're carrying fifty pounds of body armor and combat kit? What are you going to do when you come off target on the run, and you have to carry a wounded Ranger brother?"

"Suck it up and show us you have heart, or go get in the VW line."

"Stop with the teen-age girl noises." Again it's Sergeant Wilson. "We are not assessing little girls here. We are trying to assess Rangers. What about it, men? Are you a little girl, or do you want to be a Ranger? It's up to you; it's your decision."

While the cadre keeps the pressure on, they're watching the candidates carefully, checking canteens, making them drink. "Sip it, don't chug it," I hear time and again, "drink often, a little at a time." The candidates are also made to put hydration salts in their canteens—supplements that are heavy in sodium and potassium. Those who drink too much too fast bring it right back up. By noon of this first day at Cole Range, there are sixty-five men in Class 09-10—twenty-three fewer than when they boarded the buses earlier that morning. A few have medical issues that may or may not force them from the class, but most are voluntary withdrawals. It has been a long day, and it will get longer. Following a break for an MRE lunch, the class begins the afternoon with a block of instruction on land navigation, basic patrolling tactics, another session of combatives, and a class on knot tying. That evening, they set up a patrol base, and are kept on the move by the duty cadre. Cole Range, by design, will test each candidate's ability to perform when he's had very little sleep. The class gets into its patrol base at 0300 in the morning, and the men roll up in their sleeping bags. They are up at 0500 for personal hygiene, an MRE, patrol-base duties, and equipment maintenance.

At 0630 on day three of week two, Class 09-10 forms up for the first of its land-navigation practicals. A new class leader and first sergeant head up a formation that now numbers fifty-six. Nine more candidates can't face another day at Cole Range and have voluntarily dropped from selection. The class leader is now Sergeant Mark Ikenboch, and the class first sergeant is Sergeant Joe Whitmore—the two NCOs that still remain in the class. Whitmore had already had a brief stint as class leader. The cadre now want these two candidate sergeants in the leadership positions. In addition to those who have recently VWed, there are a few candidates who will be seen by the medics. They may be able to rejoin the class, but I've yet to see that happen. If they miss an evolution, even for medical reasons, they will be recycled.

Sergeant Walt Iselin explains this policy. "It's not fair to those who are hurting but manage to stay with it. If we can get a man fixed and get him back with the class without missing a key evolution, we make that happen. Otherwise, we encourage them to take a medical rollback to the next class. We decide this on a case-by-case basis, but we're in the business of looking for men who will not quit—men who can and will soldier on even though they're in pain. And again, it's not fair to the guys who hurt but don't quit."

Later that morning, and armed with map and my old Silva Ranger compass, I'm boring holes in the Georgia woodlands with Private First Class Gary Galdorisi and Private Lorenzo Gonzales. They are Ranger buddies on the first land-nav practical because they follow one another in the class alphabet. They also stand next to each other in formation and are roommates. Gonzales is a stocky nineteen-year-old—he's five feet four, 160 pounds—who only a few months ago became a naturalized U.S. citizen. He was born in El Salvador and has spent the last seven years in Virginia. Gonzales is quiet and tough. His run times are good, and he can do more push-ups and pull-ups than anyone in the class. He told me that his lifelong goal was to be an American soldier. Galdorisi is a twenty-six-year-old former District of Columbia cop who joined the Army to become a Ranger. He has an associate's degree in criminal justice. He, too, is at the top of the class in both running and PT. Both were offered Ranger contracts when they excelled at OSUT. Galdorisi is the most illustrated man in Class 09-10 with highly intricate tattoos on his arms from his wrists to his shoulders. Galdorisi and Gonzales navigate; I follow along behind.

Each Ranger candidate pair is given five sets of eight-digit grid coordinates that represent five precise locations on their maps. The candidates plot their points, then set out to find them using map, compass, pace count, and terrain features. They can locate them in any order they choose. At each point, there's an iron post with a listing of numbers that correspond to those on each nav pair's card. When they find a point, the nav pair notes that number on their card, which will validate that they found that point when they report back to the cadre office. The distance between points can be from five hundred to thirteen hundred meters, so a pair of navigators might walk four miles or more to get all five, if they walk as the crow flies. The terrain is gentle with scrub trees and vined undergrowth, but it's dry, and the ravines have little or no water. Still, the Ranger hopefuls don't walk as the crow flies, and sometimes they get lost. The class has four hours to complete the first land-navigation practical. After four hours of hard walking, Gonzales and Galdorisi, with me in tow, get two of the five. Three of five is the minimum standard, so they'll have to do better if they are going to pass this portion of RASP.

Meals at Cole Range are MREs taken in a ring of sandbags in a wooded area behind the cadre office and just off the meadow. This is their patrol base—their home at Cole Range. The candidates are required to eat *everything*, and the cadre inspects the empty MRE packets to ensure that this happens. Each meal has about 1,200 calories when fully consumed. While 3,600 calories a day seem adequate, a Ranger candidate at Cole Range burns far more than that. It's estimated that a soldier in combat burns up to 4,200 calories a day, and these soldiers are operating at a combat-plus pace. So these Ranger candidates are burning far more than they take in.

After the midday MRE following the first land-nav problem, a cadre medic inspects each candidate's feet. This is not sick call that is voluntary for men with injuries; it's a boots-and-socks-off inspection. Collectively, it's not very pretty; there's a good amount of chafing and more than a few blisters that need attention. The medic applies and distributes a liberal amount of salve, BandAids, and moleskin. The candidates are then made to powder their feet and don dry socks. The relatively minor amount of foot damage, given the pounding these feet have taken, is a function of cadre oversight and modern Army combat-boot technology. When these men get to their Ranger battalions, they'll have a range of types and makes of boots to choose from, but for now they all wear the standard-issue Belleville desert-style boots.

Following the evening meal, the candidates form up in front of the cadre office for their next land-navigation assignments. The Ranger-buddy pairs set out on their second land-nav practical at dusk. Each candidate has a new nav partner, and they have until midnight to find at least three of their five points. Then it's back to their patrol base, patrol-base chores, and another two hours of sleep.

Day four of this second week is a repeat of day three—two land-navigation practicals, afternoon classes on patrolling, small-unit tactics, and combatives. The class is down now only one man to fifty-five. Candidates having trouble on the land-nav course are given extra instruction. When the nav practical is a night evolution, the scores go down dramatically.

"This is all very basic instruction—the land nav, the patrolling, the small-unit tactics, the combatives, all of it," one of the cadre sergeants tells me. "We're out here to keep them moving and to see if they have the heart to drive on, to help their buddy, and to perform simple soldiering tasks when they're beat up and haven't slept in a while. By this time, they all have aches and pains, and they're starting to dream about a good night's sleep and not moving under a ruck, not hurting, and not having to face the cadre. We want to see if they can put those dreams aside and press on. If they can do this, then they're the kind of men we want in the Regiment. If not, they need to be someplace else."

A good many of these apprentice Rangers still move about with no apparent injury, but all are tired and most are nursing multiple ailments. Many others are limping noticeably or they run gingerly like they're on gravel in bare feet. During the afternoon combatives session, the lead cadre sergeant drills them on different types of takedowns, then puts the class in a circle in the meadow.

"All right, men, this is when we clear the air and get rid of any class issues or beefs. Some of you have been whining and complaining, and I know more than a few of you think that some of your Ranger buddies aren't pulling their load. I also know that some of you are pissed at them. Well, this is where we get it all out—this is where it gets settled and put to rest."

This, another cadre sergeant tells me, is the beef circle. Since the entire class suffers if just one or two candidates fall short, animosities can build up. Some in the class have tried to cut corners and brought cadre wrath down on them all. And there are still a few in the class who are not team players. They look after only themselves— once they have their gear in place and ready to go, they don't help their buddy with his gear. The beef circle is to address all of this. I watch as the lead cadre sergeant pulls a man from the rim of the circle into the center. He's a candidate who is performing well, but isn't the best Ranger buddy.

"Okay, who has a beef with Private Smith here? Come on—if you have a gripe, let's get after it." Another soldier steps from the rim of the circle.

"I do, Sergeant."

"All right, get over here." The cadre sergeant puts the two candidates on their knees in the middle of the circle, facing each other. "Okay, these are the rules. No punching, no choking, no kicking, and no groin grabbing. If one guy taps the other, the fight stops. Before we begin, we shake hands. When it's done, we shake hands again. Everybody got that?"

"ROGER THAT, SERGEANT!"

"Okay, shake hands." They do. "Now begin." The two candidates lunge at each other. Given how tired and beat up they are, they grapple with surprising ferocity. They fight with a will. The initial surge of energy soon dissolves into groans and grunts with an occasional flurry of activity as each looks for a means to dominate his opponent.

"In your Ranger platoons," the cadre sergeant says to the rest of the class as they watch the two combatants, "you're going to have issues with your fellow Rangers. Now and then a Ranger buddy is going to piss you off. You think a platoon of Rangers can train, live, fight, and bunk with each other without problems coming up? Well, they can't. Issues come up; guys get pissed at each other. This is how we solve them. We take it out on each other, shake hands, and move on. Got it, men?"

"ROGER THAT, SERGEANT!"

I watch as several more trainees, including Sergeant Ikenboch, the new class leader, are pulled to the center of the circle. Soon he and a classmate with a beef are rolling around on the meadow grass. I know these men are very tired, and I'm surprised at how much energy and passion they put into these matches. At one time, there were four pairs of grapplers in the circle. The contests continue under the watchful eyes of the cadre until one of the cadre sergeants calls time and sends the pair back to the rim of the circle. I even see Gonzales and Galdorisi out there having at each other, and I know they're good friends. I find Galdorisi after they've shaken hands and returned to the circle rim.

"You really have a problem with him?" I ask.

"No way, sir," he replies with a grin. "He's my roommate, and he's a great guy—the best. But now and then he does do some things that piss me off."

The beef circle goes on for another half hour. Some have beefs, others don't. Those who do grapple in the circle and shake hands when it's over. I even see an occasional buddy hug.

"All right, men," the lead cadre sergeant says when the final two grapplers return to the circle rim, "anymore beefs? Anybody else have an issue?" No one steps forward. "Fair enough, but that's it. No more whining, no more bitching, no more bellyaching. You drive on and work as a team. Class leader."

"CLASS LEADER!"

Sergeant Ikenboch and his first sergeant Ranger buddy break from the circle.

"Form the class up on their rucks for the next evolution."

"Roger that, Sergeant."

The sun is almost down. The class gets a final review of land navigation before they pair up with yet a different nav partner, and head out on their fourth nav practical. After boring holes in the Georgia woodlands for four hours, followed by some cadre attention, they get to their patrol base at 0230.

Day five of the week is the final day at Cole Range for Class 09-10. Reveille is held at 0530, and the men are out in the woods by 0600 for their fifth and final land-navigation practical. Fifty-three Ranger candidates jog, hobble, and stagger into the woods. Two candidates are medically unable to make the last nav practical and are held out of the final land-nav problem. By 1000, the remaining fifty-three are back at the Cole Range RASP formation area, and all but two pairs have found at least three of five points. Those two nav pairs are given a passing grade because the four soldiers have demonstrated proficiency during previous land-nav practicals. It's the last evolution for Class 09-10—almost. After the cadre medic conducts another boots-off inspection and finds a number of well-blistered feet that need attention, the class gathers on their rucks for a final time. The class leader, still Sergeant Mark Ikenboch, turns to the survivors.

"Okay, guys, listen up. Most of the hard times are behind us. Not all of them, but most of them. From here on out, we have to heal up and keep up with the program. A function of just how hard or how easy that is will be on us. How much slack the cadre cuts us will depend on our performance as a class. We screw up individually or as a class, then we all pay the price. Paying that price, for some of us, will be the difference between making it or not making it. You guys with me on this?"

"ROGER THAT!"

"Good. Because our past performance as a class will not be good enough going forward. What can we do to tighten things up? We got a few minutes here, and it's time for a little self-critique. Let's hear it—from anyone. Where have we been screwing up? What can we do to fix it? C'mon guys—speak up." One of the privates stands up. "Okay, Thompson, let's have it."

"Well, Sergeant, I've been pretty good about having my gear staged, but maybe not so good at helping other guys once I'm good to go. The first guys ready for a formation, me or anyone else, have to dump their gear in place and help the others. Once you're good to go, help a buddy."

He sits as another candidate hand goes up. "I've been late for my share of formations, but the times I'm not it's because I get my ruck and my uniforms laid out before I hit the rack—here or back in the barracks. We can't leave the details to the last minute. It's killing us. We gotta get our gear set up and ready for the next evolution, then eat, sleep, or whatever."

Yet another. "We have to quit cutting corners. When we do, we screw the class—we screw our buddies. I was the guy who tied an extra pad on my ruck trying to make it more comfortable. I cheated. I got caught, and you all had to pay the price in cadre push-ups, so I apologize to all of you. I let you down; I let the team down. But I won't let that happen again."

"Speaking of screwing your buddy," says another, "we have to stop doing that. Like on the runs to the woods on Wednesday. Most of us went all the way to the wood line before turning back. Some of you stopped twenty yards from the tree line to make the turn. The cadre couldn't see that, but the rest of us could. You beat the rest of us back, won the race, and got cut some slack. But you cheated your buddies. That shit's gotta cease; we're in this together. You know who you are; stop it now."

There were other complaints; some of them small, others not so small. Finally, Sergeant Ikenboch raises a hand. "Okay, men. All good comments and all things we have to focus on. Like Sergeant Iselin said, it's not about you and it's not about me; it's about your Ranger buddy. Anyone else?" There is no one else. "So we look out for each other and we tighten it up. I get the word from the cadre, we pass the word down the line quickly, and we hop to it. Fair enough?"

"ROGER THAT!"

The cadre has one more surprise for them—this time a good one. It's a DogEx, or dog exercise. The relief cadre coming out to Cole Range have brought hot dogs, buns, condiments, chips, and several cases of soft drinks from the Ranger DFAC. They fire up the barbecue, and each Ranger candidate gets two hot dogs, some chips, and a Pepsi for having survived Cole Range. Late Friday morning, the fifty-three remaining members of Class 09-10 return to the Main Post and the RASP barracks. The class can now fit onto a single bus.

Following the DogEx on Cole Range, and just before the bus arrived, I had a chance to speak with Private First Class Brendan O'Connor. Like everyone in 09-10, he's tired and it's an effort to speak, but he's not lost his broad, easy smile. He's five feet ten and a very solid 185. Quiet and affable describe O'Connor. Physically, he's one of the strongest in the class, and his PT scores are consistently at the top. The cadre is careful not to play favorites, but if they have one I suspect it might be Brendan O'Connor. But Cole Range has taken its toll even on this strong candidate.

Brendan O'Connor grew up in the Washington, D.C., area and was a standout high school wrestler. He wrestled in college for a year, but then left school. At twenty-seven, he still has the build of a wrestler with broad shoulders and a deep, muscular chest. I ask him what he was doing between college and the Army.

"A little of this and some of that," he says vaguely. "I was in security work for a while. Actually, most of that security work was as a bouncer. I also worked for a while at a camp for kids—kids with psychological problems." When I inquire about this, he says, "I was a swimming instructor. I taught kids how to swim."

"So the Ranger swim test was not a problem for you."

Again the easy smile. "No problem there. I do all right in the water."

O'Connor knows why I ask this. Most of the African Americans in the class left by way of not being able to pass the Ranger Swim Assessment and Evaluation. Brendan O'Connor is the only remaining African American with Class 09-10. He gets kidded about his race and his name on occasion, but O'Connor just smiles, handling it as easily as he seems to be handling Ranger assessment and selection.

"So why the Rangers?"

"In Airborne School, they asked for volunteers for Ranger training. I didn't know much about Rangers then, other than the presentations we had in OSUT. So I stepped up and raised my hand."

"Any regrets about that?" I ask.

"Not really. It's hard—probably the hardest thing I've ever done—but I'll see it through. Right now I'm just looking for a little sleep over the weekend."

"Good luck, Private."

"Thanks, sir. You, too."

The continuous pain of Cole Range is behind Class 09-10, but not the effects of the ordeal. Of the fifty-three survivors, eighteen of them were unable to keep up with their cadre leaders on the eight-mile ruck march to the range. Those eighteen soldiers must complete the eight-mile ruck march makeup on Saturday. At 0600 on Saturday morning, those eighteen weary soldiers form up and march over to the Stewart-Watson one-mile track for eight more miles under their ruck. One of those soldiers is Private First Class Salvador Santos. Given the ordeal at Cole Range, these soldiers, in my opinion, are eighteen very courageous men. Sergeant Iselin is not there this time. He's at the hospital with his wife, who has gone into labor with their fourth child. In his place is Staff Sergeant Bill Bateman. Seventeen of these candidates manage to finish the eight miles under two hours, while a single candidate simply can't hold the pace, and is unable to complete the eight-mile ruck makeup.

The first two weeks of Phase One were hot and humid. Week three begins warm, but wet. It rained all the previous night and at 0600, Sergeant Ikenboch musters the fifty-two members of Class 09-10. The candidate that could not make his time on the eight-mile ruck march makeup is still having trouble and is medically dropped from the class. They are in good formation, in PT gear, and their two-quarts are uniformly slung over their left shoulder. Every Sunday evening, the class barbers break out the clippers. Fifty-two freshly shaved heads glisten in the rain under the single arc light that illuminates the rocks formation area.

The Monday morning PT is civilized. The class runs over to Peden Field and stretches for fifteen minutes. The cadre then takes them through focused repetitions that involve only push-ups, modified sit-ups, and pull-ups. They exercise in the rain, but for Class 09-10, it's a merciful beginning of the week. After an hour of PT, they run back to the barracks for a shower and morning chow formation. One candidate, the same soldier who couldn't complete the eight-mile ruck or the makeup, stands apart from the formation. He's back in Holdover and not allowed to muster with his former classmates.

The morning and afternoon training sessions focus on the basic weapons of the Ranger arsenal. The training is conducted at Honor Field, a Ranger training field behind the brown fence on the compound shared by the Regimental Headquarters, the Ranger 3rd Battalion, and the Regimental Special Troops Battalion. Honor Field is a football-sized area surrounded by tree lines. It has an obstacle course, mock aircraft fuselages for airborne training, a rappelling tower, and stadium lighting. All the candidates have had weapons training, and except for three in Class 09-10, all the weapons training took place during their basic training. For the Eleven Bravo infantrymen, they've trained with the M4 rifle, the M249 squad assault weapon (SAW), the AT-4 rocket launcher, the M240B medium machine gun, the Mk-19 and M203 grenade launchers, and the M2 .50-caliber heavy machine gun. They all qualified on the standard Army M4 rifle with only a familiarization firing of the other weapons. "At most, we only got about two hundred rounds through the M4," one of the class Eleven Bravos tells me. "I know of six guys from my OSUT class who are now in Afghanistan. That's scary—two hundred training rounds in basic, and they're already deployed."

The MOS candidates who came to RASP from BCT/AIT received training on these same weapons, except for the Mk-19 grenade launcher. Most, but not all, fired the .50-caliber heavy machine gun. Many trained and qualified with the now-obsolete M16 rifle. None of these soldiers fired a pistol during their basic training.

The weapons-familiarization training in Phase One is basic and confined to five weapons: the M4 rifle, the Mk46 SAW—a SOF variant of the M249 SAW—the M240B, the AK-47, and the .50-caliber machine gun. After disassembling and reassembling each of the first four, they conduct jamming and malfunction drills with blank ammunition with the M4, the Mk46, and the M204B. They all seem to look comfortable behind the weapons, but, initially, they're somewhat clumsy and hesitant when it comes to clearing jams. Dummy rounds are sprinkled among blank training rounds, forcing the gunner to clear each weapon and get it back into action. Entirely new to them are the standard SOF modifications to the M4 rifle, which include the EOTech holographic sight, the LA-5 target pointer/ illuminator/aiming device, and a high-intensity light. All these appendages are rail mounted on the forestock of the M4. With the .50 cal, they learn how to disassemble, assemble, change barrels, and set the head spacing on the big machine gun. There are timed clearing drills with the blank ammunition on all but the AK-47.

Most of these weapons are relatively modern. The venerable .50-caliber machine gun was around before these soldiers were born; it was around before *I* was born, and is essentially unchanged. "Wow," exclaimed one of the candidates when I share this with him. "I had no idea it was *that* old."

Tuesday PT begins at Peden Field and is again restrained—a brisk three-mile run and cadre-led exercises that focus on Ranger physical fitness regimen of push-ups, pull-ups, and sit-ups. Behind the rain that moved through Fort Benning on Monday is cooler weather. For Tuesday PT, it's in the low fifties.

"We usually keep it a bit light after Cole Range," one of the cadre sergeants tells me. "Give them time to burn off a little lactic acid. It'll pick up later in the week. The cold front that moved through is supposed to persist, so it'll not be so hot this week and that will help."

After PT and morning chow, the class, still numbering fifty-two candidates, is again off to Honor Field for more weapons drills. On Tuesday, the men work primarily with the heavy .50-caliber machine gun—clearing jams with belts of blank ammunition. Even with blanks, the bark of the big gun is ferocious.

Wednesday PT is much like Tuesday's, with the intensity dialed up. There are some general calisthenics, but mostly its abs and arms. For the arms, there's set after set of push-ups. For the abdominals, there's a variety of stomach crunches and multiple sets of flutter kicks. Periodically, the class is sent out on a dash around the quarter-mile running track. For the class in general, there were four of these dashes. For those doing poorly on the exercises, there were many more.

Wednesday's evolutions are devoted to preparing for the two-day FTX, or field-training exercise, to be conducted Thursday and Friday—the only such exercise in RASP 1. This Phase One FTX is conducted with the RASP 2 candidates and is built around a parachute drop. For all but three candidates in Class 09-10, this is their first parachute jump since Airborne School, which makes it the sixth jump of their military career. For these new airborne soldiers, it's fresh in their minds. For the three prior-service candidates in the class, the two sergeants and one specialist, the time since their last military parachute jump varies widely. One has not parachuted in five years, another not in three, while the third made a jump three months ago. During the morning and early afternoon, the class reviews jump commands, jump procedures, parachute malfunction procedures, emergency procedures, and drop-zone procedures. One of the great American organizational enterprises—military or corporate—is Army parachuting. The Army, which develops and oversees all military parachuting, has made a seemingly hazardous undertaking extremely safe and commonplace—day or night, with or without a rucksack, rifle, and combat load. Each year, thousands of soldiers are airborne qualified and tens of thousands make military parachute jumps, seldom with incident.

Following the basic airborne refresher and drill on the aircraft mock-ups at Honor Field, the class makes its way to the 75th Ranger Regiment riggers' shed to get fitted for and briefed on the T-11 parachute. The T-11 is the new standard Army parachute, with improved performance and load-bearing capabilities. The 75th Ranger Regiment was the first Army unit to get the new chutes. Each Ranger battalion has their own parachute riggers. These crews of riggers not only support battalion and regimental airborne training operations, but they keep staged and palletized the equipment that must parachute with a company or battalion of Rangers who may have to jump into harm's way on short notice. The Phase One candidates are given a refresher on how to prepare ruck and rifle for a combat drop, but they will jump without any equipment on this evolution. This is one of the few times in their Ranger careers they will jump Hollywood—that is to say, they will jump without rucksack, rifle, and a combat load. In the Regiment, Rangers will almost always jump with full combat load. On many of these equipment jumps, their gear load will exceed their own weight.

The purpose of the FTX is more for and about the candidates in RASP 2 Class 10-10 than the soldiers in RASP 1, Phase One. The RASP 2 candidates, whose journey will be covered later in this book, will plan, lead, and be graded on the FTX, and it's an important part of the RASP 2 assessment process. For the junior enlisted members of Class 09-10, they are training support for the RASP 2 assessment. It's also a parachute jump and a chance to meet and interact in a training environment with officers and senior NCOs headed for the Regiment.

Thursday morning begins at 0600 with the killer PT of the week led by the RASP 2 candidates. The combined classes are broken down into small fire teams with an officer or senior NCO from RASP 2 and two or three soldiers from RASP 1 per team. They total twenty-two from RASP 2 and now fifty-one from RASP 1—a single candidate has been dropped for medical reasons. The teams break off, get acquainted, and begin to stretch. The young Phase One soldiers respond immediately to the senior candidates. For the first time since they began RASP, the Phase One candidates will be coached and led by someone other than their cadre sergeants. The combined teams begin a route laid out for them by the RASP cadre. Basically, it's a four-mile run over two obstacle courses, and finishing at Honor

Field, with a third obstacle course. The teams have to finish together, so no team is faster than its slowest man. In Ranger-speak, it's a smoker, and as each candidate team comes off the final obstacle, they're steaming in the moist morning chill.

After hot morning chow behind the Selection and Training Company headquarters, the teams return to Honor Field for their final jump briefings. One of the reasons the combined classes jump Hollywood is that a few RASP 2 candidates, along with the two in RASP 1, have not jumped in a year or more. Army regulations state that a familiarization or nonequipment jump must precede any with equipment for these soldiers. The jump from Air Force C-130s is routine. A military parachute jump, with all its formalities and procedures, is a choreographed ritual. It's also a brief moment of bonding between those who have only a few jumps and those who may have hundreds. They may not actually cheat death, but for a few moments, they defy gravity. It's exhilarating. After the final jump, candidates and cadre alike are all smiles as they trek off the drop zone and load their chutes onto a waiting truck. The combined-class teams board buses that will take them to Cole Range for the balance of the FTX. All have their rucks and combat load staged aboard the buses.

Just before dark, the combined teams go into the woods for a series of evolutions that will assess both the leadership and the professional knowledge of the RASP 2 candidates. For the young soldiers of RASP 1, they will act under the direction of the senior candidates and learn from their assessment drills. In some ways, it's just another evolution and a long night's tramp in the woods for the junior candidates. Yet it's more than that. For this short block of time, while they are in their RASP 2–led teams, they work with and train alongside future Ranger leaders. This is far different than being put through their paces by the Phase One cadre. This is their first taste of what it might be like to be a Ranger, and it's intoxicating. It's also a long evolution, with the RASP 1 candidates reaching their barracks just after 0500.

On the final day of week three there is no PT, and the men are allowed to sleep until the indecent hour of 0800. After formation and morning chow, they disassemble, clean, and reassemble all the weapons they fired during the week. Blank ammunition is notoriously dirty, and a very grimy pile of weapons awaits the class. As they scrape, clean, oil, and reassemble, they are becoming more familiar with the tools of their trade. Just before lunch, they all take the Phase One written examination. It's the one-hundred-question RASP 1 General Standards Test, which covers Ranger standards and Ranger history. The last six questions require that the candidates write verbatim the six stanzas of the Ranger Creed. All but eight of the fifty-one candidates pass. The unlucky eight will be retested the following week. This is a critical event; if they are unable to make this standard, they will be dropped from RASP.

Saturday, for this particular class, is the Mogadishu Mile. Each year the Ranger Assistance Foundation and the 3rd Ranger Battalion sponsor a five-kilometer run-walk to commemorate the thirteen Rangers who perished during the Battle of Mogadishu in 1993. The event is called Mogadishu Mile because the Rangers who fought on that terrible day were without transport and had to fight on the run as they made their way from the Somali capital back to their base on the outskirts of the city. Fifty-one Ranger candidates make the commemorative five-kilometer run in formation, all wearing thirty pounds of body armor, to honor those fallen Rangers from 3rd Battalion. Running with them are the Phase One cadre, along with the S&T Company first sergeant—all wearing their body armor.

When Class 09-10 convened, there were close to a dozen eighteen-year-old Ranger candidates. Now there is only one. The last of the youngest men standing is Private First Class Garth Palco. Palco is from just outside Columbia, South Carolina, and he joined the Army a few days after he graduated from high school. He was a good student and completed his high school curricula in three and a half years before taking a semester of Advanced Placement courses his final semester. The AP courses earned Palco some college credits. These credits, and the fact that he participated in high school ROTC, allowed him to enter the Army as a private first class. He is one of triplets, and his twin brother and sister are both in college.

"Your choosing to join the Army must have generated some interesting dinner-table conversation at home," I say to him.

Garth Palco gives me a cautious smile. He's five feet eight, weighs less than 150 pounds, and has striking green eyes—all of which make him look younger than eighteen. "It did come up, and I think my parents would rather that I'd have gone to college. But I knew I wanted to join the Army, and I wasn't all that interested in going to college. My best friend in high school and I went in together. We were in OSUT together, and he's already in Afghanistan."

"How did you decide to come here?"

"The pastor of our church was a Ranger, and I've always admired him. When he learned I was joining the Army, he said I should think about becoming a Ranger. I was able to get a Ranger contract when I enlisted. My high school buddy couldn't get a contract on enlistment or in OSUT, so he's already gone forward."

Private First Class Palco is performing well in RASP and is one of the better runners in the class. I later learn that he was a high school standout in track and cross country, and that he had run eight hundred meters in just over one minute and fifty-six seconds—a very respectable schoolboy half mile.

"You know, Private, with your high school grades and running times, you could have easily gone to college on a track scholarship."

Again, the cautious smile. "Maybe, but I didn't want to wait. I've always wanted to be a soldier, and now I want to be a Ranger."

Week four—the final week of RASP 1, Phase One. The end of this first milestone in becoming a Ranger is in sight. Those in Class 09-10 know that most of the attrition is behind them—that most of them will make it to Phase Two. And most in Phase Two will graduate and earn their Scroll and Tan Beret. But there are critical events in week four that they must still pass. Historically, at least a few candidates who get through week three do not always make it through week four.

The physical events of week four of Phase One, with the exception of the twelve-mile ruck march, focus on building up the candidates individually while keeping a certain amount of pressure and tension on the class as a whole. Before a candidate can move on to Phase Two, he must first score 75 percent on the Ranger Physical Fitness Test. Three candidates have yet to do that. Candidates must have run five miles in less than forty minutes. Two candidates still in training have yet to do that as well. All have to complete the twelve-mile ruck march in under three hours. This is not a cadre-led march, but it is a timed, critical evolution, and the candidates know they will not move on to Phase Two unless they make time. On the written-test side, the eight candidates who failed the General Standards Test will have to pass that exam or they will not move on. Also ahead in week four is the Ranger First Responder training with its written test and practical application. Most in the class are performing to standard, and their prospects for moving on to Phase Two are good. For some, this is not the case. They will have to step it up and perform to standard, or they will not become Rangers—at least not with Class 09-10. Finally, there is the Phase One Review Board. Marginal candidates, even if they manage to achieve the minimums, may be asked to appear before this board and speak to their weak performance.

It's an unusually cold morning on this first Monday in October—in the high thirties. Forty-nine candidates muster with their class on the rocks. They are in PT gear with their two-quarts, and the formation is tightly packed for collective warmth. Two candidates are not in formation but not out of the class. They have blisters that became infected to the extent that they will not be allowed to continue without the approval of the medics. "We have to watch them closely at this stage of the training," a cadre sergeant tells me. "They've come far enough that they're sometimes reluctant to bring up a medical issue that may roll them back to another class."

Medical issues in Ranger assessment and selection can be something of a catch-22. On one hand, the candidates are expected to drive on when they're tired and hurting. Yet they're told to go to sick call and see the medics when they have a problem—to get it fixed and get back in training. Blisters are a chancy business. If they can be treated with moleskin, bandages, dressings, and ointments, a candidate can continue if he can soldier through the pain. If the blisters lead to infection, as in the case of these two, their well-being will take precedence over their desire to stay in selection. Shortly after formation, these two candidates in 09-10 are dropped from RASP; their blisters are judged to be too serious to continue. If they are to become Rangers, it will be with a follow-on class. Both were performing to standard, and it is very difficult for them. It's hard on me as well as I'm getting to know these young men, and I feel their disappointment.

Following the morning PT and breakfast, the class heads for the Peden Field classroom and the medical-training portion of RASP 1 training. In lieu of their morning PT evolution, the three candidates who were deficient on their Ranger Physical Fitness Test are retested. All make the 75 percent cutoff, but one of them just barely passes. He'll have to do better in Phase Two. The men file into the classroom, and while they await the medical cadre who will conduct the training, Staff Sergeant Brandon Wilson makes his way to the front of the room. The class collectively sits a little straighter, and you can sense an elevated level of tension. Attention from Sergeant Wilson is not always a welcome thing.

"Okay, guys, while we wait for the medics, I have a question for you." As is his practice, Sergeant Wilson begins to pace. "How many of you are considering a career in the Army? C'mon, let's see a show of hands." A smattering of hands go up. "And how many of you are in for your initial tour, then out?" There are only one or two hands, probably because most think they smell a trap and wonder where Wilson is going with this. "Okay, hands down. Consider this, men. I'm a staff sergeant, an E-6, and I've been in the Army for seven years. With my base pay, bonuses, housing allowance, and combat pay, I make about sixty-five thousand dollars a year. I own a house, my wife has a wallet full of credit cards, and when we want something, we buy it. We take a vacation once a year, and each payday I'm able to save a little. My family and I have full medical care. When our little boy was born, there were some complications—nothing serious, but the bill came to about ten thousand dollars. You can run up a bill in a hospital very quickly these days. Know what it cost me? Zero, right? No worries; all the bills were paid by the military.

"So," Wilson continues, "you see what I'm getting at? How many of you know someone who is out of work, who lost their job, or who is having trouble finding a job?" All hands go up. "Everyone, right? Now, that sixty-five thousand dollars comes with some strings. I have to leave home and I have to go to war. I love my brother Rangers, yet a lot of the time I'd rather be home with my family. But that's the deal I made. The money is decent and my family is taken care of. So I want you to give this some thought, men. Maybe this is the life for you. Maybe not. But think about it; some of you guys could do a lot worse. Ten-HUT!"

"RAN-GER!" the men yell, amid a scraping of chairs.

"Take your seats and carry on, men. The medical cadre will be along shortly. You *will* stay awake for this training. I catch you sleeping and I will become unhappy, and you don't want me unhappy. This medical training is important. It allows you to save a Ranger buddy's life and for him to save yours. Clear?"

"ROGER THAT, SERGEANT!"

The next two and a half days of Phase One are devoted to the Ranger First Responder course. RFR training, qualification, and periodic requalification is mandatory for all who serve in the Regiment. Again and again, Rangers and Ranger candidates are told that everyone is a medic, and that the man who goes down could well be the platoon's special-operations-trained combat medic. The RFR course lays down the treatment protocol for combat casualty care under fire, which initially calls for getting the wounded man safely out of harm's way before administering medical attention. Win the fight or suppress the fire, then move the downed man to safety and treat him. Rangers are taught how to respond if they are the casualty or they are treating a casualty. Medical training is one of the Ranger Big Five.

The RFR training follows the MARCH-E formatted treatment procedure—massive bleeding, airway, respiratory, circulation, head trauma/hypothermia, and evacuation. Combat care puts a premium on bleeding—keep the blood inside. Great strides were made in controlling bleeding on the battlefield after the Ranger experience in Mogadishu. It's been estimated that if the current state of training in this one area was in place during the Vietnam War, half of the fifty-seven thousand Americans killed in action could have been saved. The main weapon to control massive bleeding is the immediate and skillful use of a tourniquet. Tourniquets are followed by the proper use of pressure bandages and hemostatic (blood-clotting) dressings. Next is the airway—how to open and clear the esophagus, and the use of the nasopharyngeal airway (NPG). This device is a simple rubber hose that is slid into and down one nostril, an unpleasant procedure the candidates perform on each other during the RFR practical drills. Respiratory treatment focuses on life-threatening torso injuries and the use of dressings that provide an air seal, as well as needle decompression. Needle decompression is a lifesaving procedure for a chest-cavity wound. RFR has the candidates practice needle decompression, but on a training mannequin. Circulation treatment involves a constant reassessment for bleeding, and head trauma/hypothermia often involves giving an IV under battlefield conditions. RFR training requires that each candidate give and receive an IV. Evacuation involves the steps taken to get a casualty ready for transport and the procedures for air evacuation.

Initially, the instruction takes place in the Peden classroom with a parade of PowerPoint slides. Many of them are both graphic and grisly, but then so are battlefield wounds. The instruction then moves outdoors, where the candidates treat each other. They practice the techniques for trauma assessment as well as treatment, and how to move casualties and prep them for medevac. First and foremost is the proper use of tourniquets. All Rangers carry tourniquets, and those tourniquets are carried in the same place on every Ranger's combat vest. All Rangers carry medical kits, appropriately called bleed kits, with the same standard bandages, hemostatic dressings, and combat pill packs. Ranger combat medics will carry the larger squad casualty response kits, which are equipped to deal with multiple trauma issues and extended battlefield care.

Following the classroom instruction and the practice drills, the class is given a written test and a practical exam on a trauma lane. By noon on Wednesday, the forty-nine candidates of Class 09-10 are all qualified as Ranger First Responders.

Tuesday PT, like that on Monday, is cadre-led squad PT, and the emphasis is again on abs, arms, and running, although today there is minimal running in anticipation of the twelve-mile ruck march scheduled for Wednesday. Two in the class who were deficient on the five-mile run are able to make the distance in less than forty minutes and remain with the class.

There is no PT on Wednesday. At 0500, the forty-nine members of Class 09-10 are on the rocks in ACUs and a combat rack vest, carrying six quarts of water, a rifle, and a thirty-five-pound rucksack. Each man has the required reflective belt slung around his ruck and a red-lensed flashlight on his rack. For this ruck march, there are no cadre members with them, urging them to pick up the pace or berating them for falling back. It's just six miles out and six back. They must make this round-trip in three hours, or they will not move on to Phase Two. All the candidates make it. The first to return to the starting point does so in two hours and thirteen minutes. The last in makes it in two hours and forty-nine minutes. Later that morning, the eight candidates who were deficient on the General Standards Test are retested and pass. There is but one more hurdle for Class 09–10 in Phase One, one that will affect only the marginal performers in the class: the Phase One Review Board.

After noon formation and chow, the candidates move into the classroom to complete their peer reviews. This is done in different ways and in different formats, but basically the candidates are asked to rate or rank one another. For RASP 1, Phase One, each candidate is asked to name the top two candidates in the class—the two with whom they would most like to serve. They are asked to rate the bottom two as well—the candidates they would least like to serve with. Then they are asked to justify and explain why they ranked these peers as best or worst.

A word about the peer-review process. It's a common practice in Army training venues, including Basic Combat Training and Advanced Individual Training, although the peer-review results are not nearly so influential in the entry-level training as it is in RASP. This practice of asking peers to rank classmates in a training environment and to speak frankly to their shortcomings gets to issues in the barracks and interpersonal issues that might otherwise escape cadre attention.

"We sometimes know who will peer high but not always who will peer low," Sergeant Iselin says of the peering process, "and we get fooled. We don't always know what goes on when we're not around, up in the barracks or out on the land-nav course. We had one candidate who was moving through selection with seemingly no problems. He was strong; to us he looked like a stud. But his class peered him low, saying that he cheated and that he was a terrible Ranger buddy. He wouldn't lift a finger to help anyone. We brought him in and questioned him, and he admitted to cheating. So we rolled him back to day one in the next class, and he smoked it. He never had to cheat, and he became a good Ranger buddy—even got a few top peer ratings.

"And there's the flip side of that," Iselin continues. "Sometimes we're all over a guy who we think is weak and screwed up and not putting out, but he does well when we're not around. He helps with the barracks details and is willing to help others with their gear and to study for the written exams. This happens infrequently, but it does happen."

Eight candidates will appear before the Phase One Review Board, and peer ratings are an important factor in determining who will appear. The Phase One board is chaired by Sergeant First Class Tad Collier. The other members are Sergeant First Class Iselin, Staff Sergeant Bateman, and Staff Sergeant Paul Cook. Cook is the lead weapons instructor at Phase One and a six-combat-tour veteran from 3rd Battalion. The board is held in Sergeant Iselin's office. The setting is informal—four cadre sergeants seated around a sparsely furnished office. But for the candidates who must appear and be questioned about their performance, it's an inquisition.

Of the eight candidates, three must appear for reasons of marginal performance and/or low peer rankings. One is there for low peer rankings and insubordination—talking back to a cadre sergeant. One must answer for an honor offense; when asked a direct question by a cadre sergeant, he lied. And one of the candidate sergeants must come before the board for reasons of performance and leadership. Had he been a specialist or a private, he would not be there, but the RASP cadre in both phases expect a higher standard from sergeants. Two of the candidates are not there for performance reasons. In fact, they are performing well above standard. But the cadre sergeants have cited them for being cocky and arrogant. Their appearance before the board is to bring them down a peg or two, and make them better team players and Ranger buddies.

I'll not take the reader through these individual board appearances, but I will say they were all strained, confrontational, and emotional. That was certainly the case for the candidates, to a lesser degree for me, and to some extent for the four cadre sergeants. These cadre sergeants are, after all, deciding the fate of young soldiers. But I sense that those on the board, who between them have thirty some combat deployments, are more than qualified to decide who should and should not be passed on to Phase Two of RASP 1, and who will and will not be an asset to the Regiment. That said, they are not without compassion, and they know there is sometimes very little daylight between those who they allow to move on and those who they do not.

The board chastises the two strong performers and sends them on to Phase Two. Both know the Phase Two cadre will be forewarned of their arrogant behavior. If it continues, they will appear before the Phase Two Review Board and may not be so lucky. Two in the low peer/marginal performance category are sent forward on a probationary basis. Again, the Phase Two cadre will know of their issues and their weak performance profile. Two are offered and accept a day-one recycle. This means they will begin Phase One anew with Class 01-11, which convenes the next day. The sergeant and the soldier with the honor violation, after much discussion, are both offered a day-one recycle with Class 01-11. Both decline and are gone.

With the conclusion of the board, the books are closed on Phase One for this class. At one time there were 159 soldiers on the roster of Class 09-10—less when their training actually began. Now there are forty-five. On Thursday of week four, Class 09-10 is handed off to the Phase Two cadre.

One of those headed for Phase Two is Private First Class John Zeaman. He is probably having fewer problems than most of his classmates in 09-10. He's measured, focused, and, from what I've seen of him in training, a very serious soldier. He's also a little more mature than the average Army private first class. Zeaman grew up in Savannah, Georgia, and spent five years in college before joining the Army. He's twenty-five. For two of those years, he played line-backer at the NCAA Division I level. At six feet one and 190 pounds, he's one of the bigger men to remain with Class 09-10.

"I was on my third change of major," he told me, "and I still had a semester to go before I could graduate. I guess I just got tired of going to school and was really ready to do something else."

"So why the Army and why Rangers?"

"I got here by a process of elimination. I wanted to be a medic, and I first approached the Air Force. I wanted to volunteer for the PJs [the Air Force pararescue team], but the Air Force recruiter was really unhelpful, and when I did finally pin him down on their programs, he said he didn't have any openings. I went to the Navy, but their medical or corpsman billets were filled up for the next year or more. So I went to the Army, and they said they could guarantee me a place in the sixteen-week Army medic program for AIT. The company first sergeant in my advanced training was the one who told me about Rangers and the Special Operations Combat Medic Course for Rangers, so I volunteered for Rangers in AIT."

"Why did you want to become a medic?"

"One of my majors in college was public health, so I've had some training in a related field. I want to put in for the physician assistant program. Again, my first sergeant in AIT said being trained as a special operations combat medic and serving as a Ranger would go a long way in helping me get selected for the PA program."

"Looking for an assignment with 1/75 [the 1st Battalion of the 75th Rangers is located in Savannah] and getting back home?"

Zeaman gives that some thought. Again, he's a very serious soldier. "I don't know. I'm a little afraid that if I go to First Batt, I might start to hang out with some of my friends and lose my focus. We'll have to see. If I can get through RASP, I'll go wherever they send me."

So Phase One is over. Private First Class John Zeaman, forty-four of his classmates from Class 09-10, and I are headed for Phase Two.

CHAPTER FOUR

RANGER ASSESSMENT AND SELECTION LEVEL ONE, PHASE TWO

Phase Two of RASP 1 begins for Class 09-10 on a Thursday morning at 0700. The Phase One cadre hand them off to the Phase Two cadre and then immediately return to their offices. Phase One will receive RASP 1 Class 01-11 from Pre-RASP at 0900, and the changeover is paperwork intensive. Class 09-10 was up early this morning, one of the few mornings with no PT. Prior to their 0700 formation, they turned in the equipment issued to them from Phase One. Following morning chow formation, they draw a different set of equipment for Phase Two. The class shifts barracks space from one end of the RASP building to the other to make room for the new RASP class. The two RASP classes, 09-10 and 01-11, live together in alphabetical communes on the second and third floors of the RASP building, but they are to have no interaction. At 0930, the members of 09-10 find themselves back in the Peden Field classroom awaiting their in-brief for Phase Two. Not once since the handover have they been made to do a single push-up, nor has any cadre sergeant spoken to them in anything other than a civil tone. For most in 09-10, this is almost a surreal experience—for most, not all.

Four candidates from the Class 08-10's Phase Two have been rolled back to Class 09-10—two sergeants and two privates first class. For one of the sergeants, a computer specialist coming from another Army unit, it was felt that he could use another pass through Phase Two to lock down his Ranger-centric skills. For the second, an Eleven Bravo, the cadre wanted him to better demonstrate his leadership skills. The two privates first class had medical issues and were pulled from the previous class to heal, and are now back to complete Phase Two. With the new additions, the class is back up to forty-nine, with Sergeant Mark Ikenboch still the class leader.

Two cadre Phase Two sergeants enter the classroom. "At ease!" someone calls out, and the class quickly rises to a position of parade rest. The taller of the two cadre sergeants waves them to their seats with a casual "Carry on." He comes to the front of the room and begins to fiddle with the remote control for the overhead projector. A few moments go by before a "Welcome to Phase Two of RASP 1" slide blossoms onto the large flat-screen monitor.

"I'm Staff Sergeant Simmons, and in addition to being your lead cadre instructor for the mobility portion of Phase Two, I'll be giving you your Phase Two in-brief. Sergeant First Class Sedwick would normally be giving this briefing and welcoming you to the phase, but he's recovering from knee surgery." He begins to flick through a series of slides with an itemized listings of dos and don'ts that very closely resemble those from Phase One. Sergeant Joel Simmons moves through them, some more quickly than others, highlighting those rules and restrictions that may have changed or that merit emphasis. He then turns from the flat screen to the class.

"All the rules and prohibitions from Phase One are still in place. Keep it tight, be where you're supposed to be in the right uniform with the right gear, and be ready to conduct training. Keep to yourselves and don't talk to the guys in Phase One. You can't help them, just like no one could help you when you were in Phase One. They have to suck it up and do it themselves, just like you did. We'll give you some time off on the weekends unless you show us that you're not taking this training seriously. Weekends are for rest, study, and conducting PT. As for morning physical training during the week, we're not going to smoke you with killer PTs, nor are we here to break you down. The PT evolutions are designed to make you stronger so you can pass the Army Physical Fitness Test. As you know, you have to score eighty percent or higher on each of the four graded events in the APFT. Here, that eighty percent is just the minimum standard, but PT is a big thing in the Regiment. The physical training we do here will get you ready to do PT with your Ranger squad.

"Phase Two is all about training you in basic Ranger skill sets so when you get to your Ranger fire teams and squads, you're ready to train with them for war. We're here to teach you, and there's a lot of important material that you'll need to lock down before you leave here. This material will demand your focus and attention to detail. Give us that attention and focus. If you don't, we can resort to Phase One correction drills, but you don't want that and neither do we. Put forth your best effort on a consistent basis or you'll find yourself over in Worldwide and looking for another way to serve your country. Never forget that while the focus here is on teaching you, you're still in RASP, and you're still being assessed. We clear on that?"

"ROGER THAT, SERGEANT!"

"It's like this, guys," Simmons continues. "In Phase One, you were too dumb to quit. Here in Phase Two, we're going to see if you're smart enough to stay and learn what we're going to teach, so you can serve in the Regiment. We're going to concentrate on three things—mobility, shooting, and breaching. During week one, you'll get mobility training and a chance to drive Humvees [HMMWVs, or high-mobility multipurpose wheeled vehicles]. This is not a combat driving course, but you'll get your military license and some time behind the wheel. More importantly, you'll get some training in maintenance procedures—the care and feeding of our Humvees. Humvees can do a lot of things, and there are a lot of things they can't do. You'll learn some of this as well.

"During weeks two and three, we'll split you into two sections. Half of you will go to the shooting range and half to the breaching range. On the shooting range, you'll all qualify with the nine-millimeter pistol and the M4 rifle. You'll also get an introduction to combat shooting. We have some of the best marksmen instructors in the Army here in Phase Two. You're not going to believe how well you'll be shooting at the end the week—on the range and on the move. On the breaching range, you're going to learn about explosive entry and some of the entry tools we use to enter and clear buildings. Some of this work involves building charges and some very cool and high-speed stuff—things you're all going to be doing while you're on deployment. But hear me on this, guys; you have to stay in your lane and pay attention. We expect you to stay focused, work hard, and learn. Again, Phase Two is all about preparing yourself to be a productive member of a Ranger fire team. We clear on that?"

"ROGER THAT, SERGEANT!" There's a bit more enthusiasm behind this acknowledgment. The members of 09-10 like what they're hearing.

"Class leader."

"CLASS LEADER!"

Sergeant Simmons hands Ikenboch a small, lumpy mesh laundry bag. It contains the cell phones that the candidates turned in on day one of Phase One. "Get these back to their owners. They're not to be carried at any time during the training day. Understood?"

"Roger that, Sergeant," Ikenboch replies.

"You'll have the rest of the morning to square away your rooms and get to noon chow. We'll be up to inspect the barracks at thirteen hundred."

"Roger that, Sergeant."

Friday is a training holiday, and Monday is Columbus Day. The candidates from Class 09-10 are restricted to Fort Benning, but they have a rare and welcome four-day break from the RASP routine. Phase Two training will begin the following Tuesday. It's a break from the normal training routine, but there are still barracks duties and a new daily weekend requirement—two class-led PT sessions a day. The class runs three miles in the morning with cross-training, upper-body workouts in the late afternoon. The class sergeants lead these sessions. Over the extended weekend, they're also made to write out in longhand the Ranger Creed, the Abrams Charter, and Rogers' Rangers Standing Orders—ten times each. I ask if this measure was some form of punishment or corrective action, given the seemingly more Socratic approach in Phase Two of RASP 1.

"No, it is not a punishment," Sergeant Simmons tells me. "We do this with all the classes. We want them to know their roots and to know their role in the Army as detailed in the charter. As for the Creed, if they say it and write it enough, they'll begin to live it."

Phase Two, week one begins at the leisurely hour of 0630. Class 09-10 musters on "the grass" instead of the rocks—a plot of grass on the opposite side of the RASP 1 building from the rocks where Class 01-11 earlier began their day. The temperature is in the high forties, which has the candidates moving in place to stay warm. They are in two platoons, with Sergeant Ikenboch still the class leader. The two other class sergeants now serve as platoon leaders.

"We up?" Ikenboch asks his platoon leaders.

"We're up," they answer in unison.

"Okay, let's do it. Class, ten-hut!"

"RAN-GER!"

Sergeant Ikenboch puts the class in a single formation and double-times them over to Peden Field. There he puts the class through the familiar Ranger warm-up exercises. For the first time since Class 09-10 began RASP 1, the PT warm-up is left to the class leadership.

I could see no difference in this warm-up from the cadre-led warm-ups of the previous weeks. At 0645, the Phase Two cadre joins the class. The class is cut into seven- to eight-man groups, and they set out on a brisk cadre-led four-mile run.

Physical training throughout Phase Two falls into a distinct rhythm. The class alternates between running workouts and upper-body workouts. The running workouts vary somewhat. Sometimes the candidates run at close to a seven-minute-mile pace for three to five miles, pausing on occasion to collect any stragglers. As often as once a week, they jog over to the Stewart-Watson one-mile track and do interval or fartlek running—alternating a quarter-mile jog with a quarter-mile sprint. On occasion, they muster in boots for a terrain run, usually accompanied by a climb up a hill or two while carrying their Ranger buddy. The upper-body workouts are all about abs, arms, and overall conditioning. A typical upper-body workout is heavy on pull-ups, push-ups, and sit-up conditioning exercises. Sit-ups are a part of the Army and Ranger physical testing requirements, but I seldom see the cadre having the candidates actually do sit-ups unless it's on an incline board with their feet held by a bar restraint and with their legs bent. Otherwise, the abs are attacked with flutter kicks and stomach crunches. Upper-body exercises are often done in breakdowns. At the pull-up bars, for example, a squad will line up with the lead man doing ten pull-ups. He then drops from the bar to be replaced by the next man. When the first man remounts the bar in his turn, he does eight pull-ups, and so on. For conditioning, they may do wind sprints between turns on the bar. This run-exercise rotation works the same for other upper-body exercises.

Most of this physical training is done in cadre-led groups of seven to nine candidates. "This gets them ready for PT with their Ranger squads," a cadre sergeant tells me. "Most of the PT in regiment is done in squads, and we want our RASP graduates to be able to fit right into the running and PT when they get their squad. A lot of them think this daily PT is just for harassment purposes here in RASP. Not so. They'll do daily squad PT, often a lot harder than we do it here." I can believe this. I see Ranger squads from 3rd Battalion running all over Fort Benning. When they circle up on Peden or Honor field for PT, they do some serious and punishing exercise.

Following morning chow, the men are in the classroom for the start of their mobility training. I will handle this particular week differently from the other weeks of training in that this week of Phase Two training is in the midst of change. What took place for Class 09-10 was different from what took place for previous classes, and it will be handled differently for subsequent classes. Normally, the "mobility week" is split between mobility training and combatives training.

Combatives training is relatively new in the Army, and the Special Operations Combatives Program (SOCP) is newer still to the Ranger Regiment. Army-wide, the whole phenomena of the popular mixed-martial-arts industry has had an impact on the young soldiers joining the Army and young soldiers in the Army. This, for want of a better term, is a cultural force that has to be reckoned with. Yet some distinction has to be made between entertainment and utility. From a conditioning perspective, martial-arts training has great value. It's also a form of fighting, and serious fighting is something very few young Americans have experienced before they joined the Army. And combatives training has shown to build confidence and personal courage. So there's good rationale for a venue in which a soldier can fight—really fight—in a nonlethal environment. There's also something to be said for getting your face pushed into the mat, rather than the mud, or the chance to push your opponent's face in the mat. Yet Rangers, like the other ground combatants, do their business behind a gun. More specifically, behind an M4 rifle or a squad assault weapon. Their secondary weapon is a Beretta pistol, not their fists. Yet while a martial skill set may be useful in conditioning or on the battlefield, any proficiency in this area of combatives has to come at the cost of taking time from some other training imperative.

Perhaps the key question that has to be answered is, what is the utility of this skill set in today's battlespace? And if there is some utility, where in priority does it fall among those traditional basic military skills that relate to moving, shooting, and communicating? One of the knocks against combatives-type skill sets is that a military fight is a fight to the death—winners live and losers die. Is there utility in combatives-type training, where there are rules, while in mortal combat there are none? The second issue I've heard raised is that it takes a great deal of time to reach a proficiency that is useful in combat—time that our soldiers simply do not have between deployments. Or that this precious training time is better allotted to more useful training, like training behind the gun. Those who support combatives training say that combatives is also about controlling your opponent through nonlethal means when shooting someone is not authorized within the rules of engagement. Rangers need to be able to deal with a variety of threats that don't require use of their primary or alternate weapons.

This is all to say that there are changes coming to RASP, and the assessment and selection of Rangers regarding combatives. The Special Operations Combatives Program is now in the process of developing curricula and certifying instructors to teach this skill in RASP. I can only assume that like shooting, breaching, and mobility, the skill level taught in RASP 1 will be such that a new Ranger can master the SOCP basics sufficiently to allow him to seamlessly integrate with his squad or fire team for combatives training. Combatives training for RASP 1 Class 09-10 covered only those basics that were taught in Phase One. So the mobility/combatives week for this class focused only on mobility.

Mobility for RASP 1 is all about Humvees—often called GMVs (government military vehicles). "We're not trying to make combat drivers out of these guys," Sergeant Simmons tells me, "but we want them to know how to drive a Humvee and to have their military driver's license. Past that, we want them to know how to do basic preventive maintenance on the vehicles and operate them in a safe and appropriate manner."

Joel Simmons is a solid six-foot staff sergeant from the 2nd Ranger Battalion. He's had ten combat rotations with 2/75. He is also living proof that Ranger First Responder training really works. After a combat wound, a Ranger medic treated him in the field with needle decompression for a tension pneumothorax, a condition that could have been fatal had it not been immediately treated. Simmons now has only one lung, but he has recovered well enough to return to combat rotation when he finishes his tour at RASP. Combat wounds and Purple Hearts are not uncommon among RASP cadre sergeants.

The regimental motor pool is conveniently located across the street from the RASP barracks. Within the motor-pool bays are several Humvees in for maintenance. Under Sergeant Simmons' supervision, the candidates swarm over the vehicles. After allowing them time to explore the burly tan armored trucks on their own, he calls them in for a class on periodic maintenance schedules for these vehicles. They then work through the predriving checklist, which calls for ensuring that fluid levels are within spec and that the vehicle running gear is in good order. Prior to the driving portion of the course, they review safety, emergency, and operating procedures, and go over the function and purpose of the controls, gauges, and warning lights. All Army personnel in any Humvee must wear helmets and gloves.

The Humvee of today is unlike its predecessor, the venerable jeep, and very different from the original unarmored vehicles that first came into service in 1981. They're even different from those that went to war after 9/11. The original basic unarmored vehicle weighed just over fifty-five hundred pounds, only slightly heavier than a full-sized SUV. The current armored version, the M1151A1 expanded-capacity model, is a fully armored twelve-thousand-pound monster powered by a 6.5-liter turbo-diesel engine. The Humvee comes in many versions and configurations, but this armored version carries a driver, three passengers, and a gunner stationed in the ring turret, which mounts a .50-caliber machine gun or an MK-19 grenade launcher.

The students and five of the regimental Humvees set out in a mini convoy and drive the paved and unpaved roads on Fort Benning. The focus is on safety, basic driving instruction, and towing. Students practice hooking up the tow bars and tow straps to simulate the rescue of a wounded Humvee, something most will do as a deployed Ranger. They don't actually change a tire, but they break out the jacks and get a wheel off the ground. Simmons also has each of them lift a Humvee spare wheel to understand that it's a lot heavier than the wheel on their SUV or pickup. Each student gets eight to ten hours in the vehicle and close to two hours behind the wheel.

"This is where I left off in civilian life," Private Jim Parcell says of his introduction to Humvees. Parcell is a twenty-one-year-old infantryman. "I had just finished my associate's degree in automotive mechanics and was all set to go to work on civilian cars and trucks. Now here I am learning about and driving Hummers. These are awesome vehicles."

"So what made you decide on the Army in favor of becoming a mechanic?"

"I always wanted to be in the Army, but I had a thyroid condition that kept me out when I tried to enlist after high school. While I was in college, I was on a strict medication regime that seemed to take care of things. Before I went out to look for a job, I thought I'd try the Army one more time. This time they accepted me. I like cars, but this is what I really want to do."

"In the future, some of them may get special mobility training in Humvees," Sergeant Simmons says, "training that will get into some serious off-road and tactical urban-driving techniques. For now we just want them to have a military driver's license, and to be able to care for the vehicles and operate them safely."

The mobility week unexpectedly claims three more candidates. Two of them, both young infantrymen, were dealing with lingering medical issues from Class 09-10 that carried over from Phase One. They were not improving, and the medics recommended that these two soldiers be pulled from training and allowed to heal. They will become future Phase Two inserts and will, if they can successfully complete Phase Two, graduate with a future class. The third withdrawal was a cadre-mandated drop. It involved a misleading statement that on close review was determined to be an honor violation. At this stage of the RASP process this is rare, but honorable conduct is as much a part of the assessment process as physical and professional competence—perhaps more so. The soldier is dropped from the program and will not serve as a Ranger. Class 09-10 completes mobility week of Phase Two with forty-six Ranger candidates. One of those candidates is Private First Class Eldon Northridge.

Northridge is a twenty-one-year-old Army medic from Texas who wants to be a Ranger medic. Northridge is a wiry, bespectacled, scholarly looking soldier who is deceptively fit. He is the fastest runner in Class 09-10, and he posted the best time on the twelve-mile ruck march. Private First Class Northridge was home-schooled and had completed a year with the Army ROTC program at Texas A&M before he enlisted. I asked him about this decision to leave one military training venue for yet another—specifically, Ranger training.

"I liked the program at A&M, but last year for our summer military training, I served as a role player at Robin Sage." Robin Sage is the huge Army Special Forces unconventional-warfare training exercise out of Fort Bragg that is the final phase of the Special Forces Assessment and Selection process. "I got to know some of the SF medics and was blown away by their skills. Those guys were really impressive. Then, when I was getting ready to head back to school, it just didn't seem worthwhile to go back to classes when I could be in the regular Army doing something interesting and important."

We talked a bit about the Special Forces medical training. It's a twelve-month course, broken into two six-month portions. The first six months is spent in the Special Operations Combat Medic Course, or SOCM (pronounced "sock-em"), which is the same six-month course that qualifies RASP graduates who are Army medics as Ranger medics. "So why didn't you apply for the Special Forces Eighteen X-Ray program. Then you could have gone to Special Forces Assessment and Selection after OSUT and on to the full-year SF medic program?"

"My recruiter said he could get me a contract for the X-Ray program, but that Special Forces choose their medics during SF assessment and selection—no guarantees up front. But he did say he could offer me a contract for basic training and AIT as an Army medic. My contract also guaranteed me RASP after airborne training. The Ranger contract was the only way I could be assured of special operations medical training on completion of assessment and selection. Now that I'm here, I'm glad I took that route."

"You're still pretty young. Maybe Special Forces and the full SF medical program are in the future?"

"Perhaps," he replies. "Whatever God has planned for me."

This reply gives me pause. "I take it from your response that you're a Christian—a practicing Christian?"

"Yes, sir."

"How many others in the class share this with you?"

"There are a few," Northridge replies. "There are about five or six of us who regularly get together for Bible study."

Week six begins with class formation at 0630. The men still form up in two platoons, and Sergeant Ikenboch is still the class leader. This morning he stands in front of one platoon that, for this week, will be the marksmanship platoon. There are forty-six candidates in the class—twenty-three men in each platoon. Another candidate sergeant heads the breaching platoon. For the next two weeks of Phase Two, Class 09-10 will be split in two sections—by alphabet. A through M begin marksmanship week, while N through Z will do breaching. They will split for training but not for the start of morning PT. After taking roll, first one platoon and then the other moves from the grass area to the roadway and over to Peden Field at a run. There, the platoon leaders put their men through the familiar Ranger warm-up exercises.

The M through Z platoon is led in its warm-up by an interesting candidate sergeant, Cory Sadler. Like Sergeant Ikenboch, he has a Ranger Tab and a Combat Infantryman Badge, but unlike Ikenboch, he has not served in the 75th Ranger Regiment. Sadler grew up in northern Georgia and attended a small college there. After college, he was commissioned as an infantry second lieutenant. He saw active service in Iraq as an infantry platoon leader before leaving the regular Army for the National Guard. When it became impossible for him to serve in the Regiment as an officer, Captain Sadler traded his bars for stripes and returned to active service, and to RASP, as a sergeant. Since his stripes and the responsibilities of an Army sergeant are relatively new to him, he was asked to repeat Phase Two of RASP 1.

Following the platoon warm-ups, while the class awaits the Phase Two cadre, I ask one of the candidates about their weekend PT.

"The class NCOs lead the runs and PT," he tells me. "We don't punish each other, as some of us are still hurting from the regular PT during the week and healing up from Phase One. We run in the morning and do upper-body work in the afternoon—mostly push-ups, pull-ups, stomach crunches, and flutter kicks. As a group, I think we're getting stronger. What we do on the weekend would pass for a hard workout before I joined the Army or even in basic training."

Following this morning's regular squad PT and morning chow, I elect to go with Sergeant Sadler and the breachers. The N through

Z platoon begins its Ranger Assault Breacher Course in the Peden classroom. The marksmanship students, the As through Ms, have gone their own way. The twenty-three breaching candidates occupy only a single corner of the big classroom. They talk quietly at their tables as they wait for class to begin. A Phase Two cadre sergeant steps to the podium, and the class immediately falls silent.

"Good morning, men. I'm Staff Sergeant Jack Diesing. Welcome to the assault breaching course. Some call this the demo course, and we will be using explosives, but demo is only a part of what we do here. During this week we're going to cover a number of ways we enter buildings and rooms—external entry and internal entry. You're going to learn about mechanical breaching, ballistic breaching, thermal breaching, and, finally, explosive breaching. We'll be doing all of these things. Each has variations and uses, and each has advantages and disadvantages. In most cases, your assault leader will determine how he wants to conduct the entry. It may be using one of the standard techniques or some variation. Once your assault leader chooses the method of entry, it'll be your job to carry it out. You may have breaching responsibilities in your squad and fire team, and you may be called on to help with the assessment and choosing the type of breach. Today in class, we're going to cover mechanical and ballistic breaching."

The series of PowerPoint slides cover the array of standard breaching tools carried by Rangers, including a Hooligan Tool (a simple pry bar with a leverage pick set at a ninety-degree angle from the bar and tool blade), bolt cutters, a sledgehammer, and a rabbit tool (portable pneumatic jaws for opening doors and lifting gates off their hinges).

"These are refinements of the standard burglar's tool kit," Sergeant Diesing continues. "Many have extendable handles so they carry easier and are made of titanium alloy so they're lighter. They're not as sexy as the other breaching methods, but they have the advantage of being silent, or relatively so. We also on occasion use a var-

iety of battery-powered saws and drills, and there's also our big
gas-powered saw. Which tool you use will depend on the mission,
how long of a walk you may have to get on target, and how much
noise you can safely make. You'll get a chance to use most of these
tools in the Ranger inventory out on the range. Questions on any of
this so far?" There are none, but the class is locked onto this material; no heads nodding off to sleep.

Staff Sergeant Jack Diesing is a handsome, athletic Ranger veteran
from 2nd Battalion who has been with the Phase Two cadre for close
to a year. He was born and raised in Iowa, but still calls Tacoma,
Washington, and 2/75 home. "I had six rotations in five years—three
as a squad leader and two as a fire-team leader," he told me. "My
wife and I waited to start our family as she wanted me at home when
we were to expect our first kid. She's now four months old. We work
long hours here, but I get home every night, and that's been really
great. I'll be here for at least another year before heading back to
battalion and back into deployment rotation."

"Next we have ballistic breaching," Diesing continues, "and we
have a great tool for that." He picks up one of the shotguns that are
scattered around the student tables. "This is the twenty-four-inch
Remington M870 twelve-gauge magnum breaching shotgun. It has
a ten-inch barrel and a four-round capacity—three in the magazine
tube and one in the chamber, but we never carry a live round in the
chamber. There are two types of rounds for this gun. The Hatton
round, which is the one we use nearly all the time, is a frangible
round that breaks up on impact. It's good on locks and hinges, and
it doesn't carry too far past the door you're trying to breach. There's
also a double-aught buckshot round available, but we seldom use
that load."

Sergeant Diesing then goes into how to use the breaching shotgun, which amounts to putting the end of the barrel against the lock
or hinge at the proper angle and pulling the trigger. He then goes
into how to load and safely carry the weapon, and how to assemble and

disassemble it. After a break for chow, the class is back in the class-room, dry firing the shotgun. Unlike other weapons systems in the Ranger inventory, the shotgun is never carried with a round in the chamber and the safety is never used. When needed, a round is loaded with the pump action just prior to use. There are no sights on the gun, as the end of the barrel is placed directly on the door lock or hinge. Simplicity itself.

The balance of the afternoon is taken with a quick overview of the standard Ranger explosive breaching charges and how to make the three essential calculations for any of the charges they will use in an explosive breach. These calculations involve the net explosive weight of the charge; the minimum safe distance, or how close one can safely get to the charge when it's detonated; and the safe frag-mentation distance, or how far the effects of the charge may carry into the room or structure you're explosively entering.

"It's not rocket science," Sergeant Diesing tells them. "It's eighth-grade math. Make your calculations and have your Ranger buddy check them, just like he'll check yours." The breaching students are issued handheld calculators, the same kind as they'll find in their demolition kits in their platoons.

After PT and chow the following day, the twenty-three student breachers are bused to the Ranger breaching range and begin to lay out the various tools that will be available to them when on deploy-ment with their Ranger battalions. The Ranger breaching range is a part of the Booker Range complex on Fort Benning, a fifteen-minute bus ride from the RASP barracks. The range itself has two open areas, each half the size of a football field and protected on three sides by fifteen-foot revetments. The training areas are served by several concrete hard-stands and open-sided training sheds. Each area has a line of metal frames with specially designed wood and steel training doors, and multiple lines of standard-construction, prehung doors. Immediately on their arrival on the range, the stu-dent breachers begin to lay out the Ranger breaching tools. In addition to the tools covered in class, there is a full array of DeWalt battery-operated power tools, including drills, circular cutters, skill saws, and saws-alls. The cadre spends a minute with each tool, and the student gets to handle each one. The largest saw is the gasoline-powered Husqvarna cutting, or quickie, saw. It's a tool they will use on the range, so they go over its use and the saw's basic maintenance requirements.

"This saw will usually be carried on the outside of a combat vehicle, and it'll get dirty whether you use it or not," Staff Sergeant Garret Fowler tells them as he breaks down the saw, "so you'll want to give the filters some attention on a regular basis." Sergeant Fowler is the old man of the Phase Two cadre sergeants. He joined the Army when he was thirty-two. He's a veteran of six combat rotations with 1/75. He just turned forty. Fowler grew up on a ranch in northern Texas and, before joining the Army, was a custom-home builder. Prior to that he was a professional bronco rider and a ferrier. Along with a broad working knowledge of tools, engines, construction mechanics, and explosives, he's a fount of knowledge on practical improvisation technique and Ranger lore. The student breachers take to him instantly.

In addition to the tools covered in class, the candidates are briefed by Sergeant Fowler on the use of the Broco torch, the only thermal breaching tool. The Broco is a portable oxygen-magnesium rig used to burn through or melt metal plating, casements, and rebar. It's of limited use in a tactical situation, but very handy for cutting through heavy metal. When a heavy-metal cut is needed, as with a vault or a steel cage, it's indispensable.

One portion of the range is set up for drills on the basic Ranger mechanical breaching tools: the Hooligan Tool, or hoolitool; a one-man battering ram, also called a donker; the sledgehammer; the crowbar; and the jackrabbit breaching tool. A series of metal and wooden doors are hung in metal frames with one-inch by one-inch wooden strips set in as blocking bars to offer resistance. These training doors are set up to take blows and pry bars, and to simulate the failure of a real door. Yet they can quickly be reset for the next student breacher and/or the next tool. The candidates practice forcing doors with the donker and a combination of the hoolitool, the crowbar, and sledge, but the breaching tool of choice is the jackrabbit tool. The jackrabbit is a portable pneumatic device that very forcefully and quietly separates a door from its jamb or defeats a locked gate. In all practical work, the candidates simulate the use of these tools in combat, building muscle memory and developing technique.

"You'll use these mechanical breaching tools and techniques time and time again," Sergeant Fowler tells them. "Practice, practice, practice. Most of the time you'll be doing this at night with gloves and using your NODs [night-observation devices]. Most of it will be by feel. When you're the breacher, you and your Ranger buddy will most likely work as a team. That's why we practice with these tools and techniques in pairs. The quicker you make the breach and get your team through the door, the better chance you have of gaining the element of surprise. So after you make the breach, step aside quickly so your teammates can get through the door and clear the room. Then toss aside your breaching tools, get back on your primary weapon, and get in there. The purpose of the breach is so we can get to the fight. As a new man on the fire team, you'll often handle the breaching duties, so you'll not be first in the door and the first to the fight. But your time will come. Everyone wants to be the first to the fight.

"Furthermore, you talk to any Ranger and the rabbit tool, more than any other, has led to more bad guys waking up in bed surrounded by a Ranger fire team." Fowler gives them a grin. "It's nice to mix it up, but you really like those times when you can cuff them in their rack before they're even awake. Y'see, whenever we can, and that's about half the time, we're able to get the guy we want without firing a shot or blowing anything up. And that's sweet."

Another portion of the range is designed for drill with the breaching shotgun. The door locks and hinges are simulated by flat plastic slugs, so that they can be shot away with the .12-gauge Hatton rounds. Again, the doors are of a special construction so that they can be easily rehabilitated and rehung. For most of the afternoon, the candidates make dry-fire runs on the door. "Remember," Sergeant Diesing cautions them, "the weapon is always on fire—safety off. You chamber a round as you step up to make the breach. Then and only then do you put your finger in the trigger well. If the breach calls for a double-tap to the door lock, don't cycle the third round into the chamber. The weapon is considered safe with an empty round in the chamber. Real world, after a two-round breach, you would feed two more rounds into the feed tube as soon as possible, and you're good to go on to the next door."

"You wait until tomorrow when we do this live," he tells me. "Amid the noise and the kick of the weapon, some may forget themselves and chamber that third round. That's why we do this by the numbers and drill on the safe handling of this weapon."

Wednesday begins with a light rain shower that makes for a wet PT but clears by the time the platoon gets to the breaching range. The breaching section is cut into two groups. One will cut and burn while the other shoots. Sergeant Fowler handles the burning and cutting. The Broco torches, three of them, are hooked up to large commercial oxygen cylinders for this block of training. There are several of the man-portable cylinders the size of small scuba bottles, the ones they will carry on operations, laid out for the candidate breachers to see and try on. But the commercial cylinders are more economical for this training. Sergeant Fowler gives his eleven Ranger candidates a quick refresher, and they're soon burning cuts in quarter-inch steel plating and cutting into sections of railroad track. The torch spits a two-inch blue flame that is ten thousand degrees at the tip. Managing that much heat is all about technique. It takes the candidates a few tries, but soon most are cutting metal to a standard acceptable to the ever-watchful Sergeant Fowler.

The sawing is done with the big gasoline-powered quickie saw. Again, Sergeant Fowler shows them how. "You've got to manhandle the rotary saw, men. You handle it; don't let it handle you. Get into a good stance, then bear down with steady pressure—lean into it. The men cut concrete blocks, expanded metal barricade sheets, half-inch rebar, and steel I-beams. Lots of sparks and dust. As with the torch, they work in pairs with one candidate coaching the other. A third of the students in the class section have experience in welding and two have run a quickie saw, so the cutting and burning are new for most of them.

After an hour and a half of burning and sawing, Sergeant Fowler brings them in. "Okay, men, good job. You were all paying attention out there, and you're all learning. Today, we only covered the basics with these tools. When you get to your battalions, they may do it a little differently. If you get assigned to breaching duties, get this equipment out and practice with it, even if it's just assembly and disassembly. A lot of marksmanship is dry firing. Dry fire this breaching equipment. Get familiar with it and how to best carry it with a combat load. It all builds mental muscle memory. We good on that?"

"ROGER THAT, SERGEANT!"

"Again, good job. Stay motivated, move quickly, and work to improve yourself and your Ranger buddy. You do that and guys like me will have to dream up some new ways to make you do push-ups. Now let's get this area cleaned up and get ready for some shooting."

My section transitions over to the shotgun breaching range, where Sergeant Diesing is waiting for us. Before taking up the breaching shotguns, the men don helmets and body armor. They already have eye and hearing protection in place from the cutting and burning. Here again, the doors and doorframes are a marvel of ingenuity for breaching-shotgun training in that they can be quickly reconfigured between shooters. In addition to the simulated hinges and door locks, the heavy doors are hinged at the bottom so that once the lock or jamb hinges are ballistically defeated, the door can be kicked open, or, in this case, a good kick simply pushes it over. The bottom hinges allow it to be quickly erected and reseated, and the plastic hinges and door locks easily replaced.

"Today will be no different from the dry-fire practice in the class-room on Monday and out here yesterday," Sergeant Diesing tells the section. "It's the same drill, only today we'll do it with live rounds. Remember to move deliberately. Smooth is fast. The key thing is to have the barrel of that weapon tight against the hinge or lock. You can even push on the hinge or lock to take any slack out of the door. Once you've made the breach, roll out of the way so your teammates can move through the door. Make sure you have an empty chamber and you inspect and clear your weapon before you come back off line. Now the weapon will kick, but not as much as you might think. These Hatton rounds have a magnum charge, but the ceramic load is not as heavy as a load of buckshot so the recoil is not bad. You'll soon get the feel for it."

The candidate breachers shoot three breaching cycles, two times. The first is a two-round breach to defeat the lock. The shots are placed close to each other, one over the other in a figure-8 pattern. Diesing demonstrates, then each candidate does it twice. Next they shoot a three-hinged door, one round for each hinge. After each breach, the candidate kicks down the door and rolls to one side, weapon pointed at the ground. The final drill is another double-tap to the lock followed by a kick that does not bring down the door. Each student breacher then feeds two more rounds into his gun to make a total of three. He then shoots the hinges and kicks down the door. Each candidate shooter gets twenty breaching rounds. The time spent during the previous two days of drill and dry firing pays off. There are no live rounds inadvertently chambered, nor are there any major safety violations. The few weapon jams are managed prop-erly by candidates and cadre alike. For me it was a pleasure to see the section handle the evolution so professionally, given that half of the candidates had never before fired a shotgun.

When the student breachers arrive at the Booker Range on Thursday there's a small moving-van-type truck awaiting them. The range has no demolitions-storage capability, so explosives are delivered daily, and if need be, collected daily. After unloading the demolition materials, the candidates gather around a series of large work tables under one of the range sheds. Each table has a demo kit with the standard tools needed to build and prime explosive charges. This is the same kit that will be awaiting them when they get to their squads and platoons. After a quick inventory and explanation of each tool, Sergeant Diesing begins with the explosives.

"This morning we will show you how to build charges. This afternoon each of you will be assigned to build a charge, and we'll blow them all before the end of the day. We okay with that?"

"ROGER THAT, SERGEANT!" Lots of enthusiasm.

"This morning we'll be working with detonating cord and other explosive materials. Some of the explosives come factory ready and others you will have to build. You'll use these basic explosive materials to build various types of charges. These charges will be used in breaching situations to either cut or push, and sized to get the job done with minimum damage to the structure and anyone who may be behind the door you're trying to breach. With just these explosive materials you can build a whole range of charges to defeat any number of doors and entryways. But remember, just because you have all these high-speed explosives doesn't mean you'll use them when a quieter or safer mechanical breach might be a better option." Sergeant Diesing takes each explosive, talks about it for a few moments, then passes it around so each student breacher can feel and examine it. "Now pay attention while we build a simple push charge with explosive materials."

The candidates are locked on, watching Sergeant Diesing attentively while he sets about building the charge. He cuts the sheet explosive to proper size with a pizza cutter, a one-by-eighteen inch strip from a sheet of explosives that is about an eighth of an inch thick. Then he preps it with a hard rubber strip of equal thickness that will rest between the datasheet and the door to achieve the "push" from the explosive. He also attaches a strip of cyropack material (over-the-counter compartmented saline packets used for medical applications as cold packs) to the back of the charge to achieve a tamping effect. By tamping, it concentrates and focuses the charge in the desired direction. These materials are positioned and held in place with liberal amounts of hundred-mile-per-hour tape—a type of military-issue, olive-drab duct tape. Sergeant Diesing then primes his datasheet charge with a booster and short length of detonation cord. The final step is the installation of the hydrogel strip—a double-sided adhesive strip to attach the charge to the door. It is carefully affixed to the charge so the sticky-side protective strip can be easily peeled and attached to the door with gloved hands in a tactical situation.

"This small eighteen-inch charge with just a thin strip of explosive material is about as small a charge as you can build," Sergeant Diesing tells them, "but wait until you see what it can do. And we can go up from there. You can double the amount of explosive by using C-2 datasheet or layer the explosives for more power. It's up to your imagination and the requirements of the breach."

Diesing then builds a charge, explaining about the cutting effect of the V-shaped design of the explosives material. "You also have different sizes of material to choose from, depending on how deep a cut you need to make," he tells them as he works. When he finishes the cutting charge, he sets it to one side. Then he begins to cut six-foot strands of detonation cord. "Det cord is a fast explosive with high relative effectiveness. A charge with just three strands of det cord will shatter most wooden doors, and you can build a long charge that's easy to handle." The det cord is sandwiched between strips of carpet tape and hundred-mile-per-hour tape, then primed. The hydrogel adhesive is put in place just as with the push and cutting charges. Sergeant Diesing holds up his work. "Remember, men, a pretty charge is a happy charge. Keep them neat, and that means a lot of attention to detail with each stage of building your charge. Now what do we do next?"

"Mark the charge?" offers one of the candidates.

"Right, and what are we going to put on the charge?" Diesing says, handing the det-cord charge to one of the candidates.

Another candidate quickly consults his notes and recites: "Name, date, NEW, MSD, and SFD."

"Okay, good," Sergeant Diesing replies. "But on your written exam, you won't have your notes to refer to, so you'd better know it. Your name, date, net explosive weight, minimum safe distance, and safe fragmentation distance. What else might we want to put on our charge?"

"The kind of charge, Sergeant?"

"That's right. Everyone in the squad or the fire team will be carrying two or three of these charges. The breachers will have more than that. Since you make them up in advance, you might want to note the kind of charge it is. Sometimes with all that tape, and a few weeks between the build and the breach, it's hard to tell. We good with this?"

"ROGER THAT, SERGEANT!"

After a quick break for an MRE, the student breachers are back building the charges assigned to them. After completing each one, they bring them to Sergeant Fowler or Sergeant Diesing for inspection. They look for construction technique and the proper placement of the booster charge and det-cord pigtail. They question each candidate about the construction and design of their charge. Usually, they offer a few suggestions on how to improve on it or to do it differently. Occasionally, they tear apart the charge and expose the flaw in the construction. Then the student returns to his table to rebuild his charge. After the charges are built, Sergeant Fowler brings them in for a quick review of the firing systems covered in class.

"Out here and pretty much overseas, you'll be using two types of nonelectric firing systems—both of them dual primed systems with two blasting caps. One of these is the command detonated system." He demonstrates how to marry the blasting caps to the detcord pigtail of the charge, and to set up the hand initiator. "These nonelectric systems feature charge initiation by twelve-gauge shotgun primers and an instantaneous, fast-burning explosive train. It allows you to control when the charge goes off," he continues, "so you're in full control of when to initiate the breach.

"We will also be using this type of nonelectric system with a set time delay. What are the two delays we will use? Private Jones?" Jones rattles off the correct time delays. "Very good. There are longer delays available," Diesing continues, "but those are the two we'll use. Know what they are and which one you're using. When you use these initiators, you will have just that much time to get back away from the blast. And once you initiate the system, it *will* go off, and if someone inside hears those primers go pop, they may have time to dive out the back door, or maybe even come to the front door to see what's up—either way, this may or may not be what you want, understand?"

"ROGER THAT, SERGEANT!"

"Command detonation or timed delay—each of them has its place. It'll depend on the mission. The team leader and the breacher will make that call, along with the kind of charge for taking the door." Sergeant Fowler then goes into the use of the initiators—how to tie in, when to pull the safeties, and how to actuate each initiator. "Okay, men. Let's go and blow down some doors."

Sergeants Diesing and Fowler are good team teachers. One talks while the other demonstrates or moves about the class to give assistance. They're also both quietly observing who is paying close attention and which of them helps their Ranger buddy after they've completed their own charge. They also take special note of who may be borderline in the safe handling of the explosives. While this is an outdoor classroom setting and a learning environment, the assessment continues. This is the first time these RASP candidates have been in a situation where inattention to detail and safety can get someone hurt or killed. On both the breaching and shooting ranges, the cadre sergeants watch their students closely. Who pays close attention to detail and who does not. Who listens carefully and follow directions precisely and who does not.

Both cadre and candidates kit up in body armor, helmets, gloves, ear protection, and safety glasses. They take their charges and move the short distance to the target portion of the demo range. Staff Sergeant Jack Diesing runs the range, and all eyes are on him. Amid the rows of prehung doors that have been wedged in steel frames, he quickly briefs the student breachers on range safety. Then he holds a quick session on charge placement.

"On approaching the door, what's the first thing we do?"

"Recognize and analyze, Sergeant."

"Right. You may or may not know anything about the door you're going to breach. In any case you'll do a quick assessment of the door—does it open outward or inward, what's it made of, where are the hinges, and, depending on the target, what might be the collateral effects to property or people behind the door? You'll then determine what kind of charge you're going to use, how big it needs to be, and where to place it. Are you going to attack the lock or the hinges, or even the center of the door? You've had the basics in this course; the rest will come with time and experience. Now, let's see if one of these works."

Diesing takes the first charge he built for the class as a demonstration, pulls the strip of guard tape from the hydrogel adhesive, and attaches it to the door between the lock and the jamb. He then ties in the initiator—in this case, a command detonation device. A student is by his side, assisting with the placement.

"What is the minimum safe distance for this charge?" he asks his assistant. After the correct student response, he says, "All right, then, that's how far we have to move back. Let's get into place."

With the charge on the door, the class moves back. This, too, is part of the training. They crouch in close to the line of doors, much as they would along the front of a target house in a tactical situation, IED emplacement zone from the breach. As a safety measure, they have riot-type ballistic shields between the student stack and the target door. This is a very new experience for these Ranger candidates. They may have thrown hand grenades from well-bunkered positions in basic training, but none of them have been this close to an explosion. The charge detonates and the shock wave washes over them. They then gather around Sergeant Diesing and the breached door, which is standing neatly open.

"Okay, men," Sergeant Diesing begins. "This was one of the smaller charges you will work with—an eighteen-inch push charge with a single strip of explosive. But we had it tamped with the cyrogel, so we got the most out of this small amount of explosive. It literally shoved the door out of the jamb and even blew the doorknob out of the door. But there was very little damage to the surrounding area, so it was a good breach. Questions? Now's the time, men; we're here to learn."

After a short time of Q&A, Diesing sets in and detonates another charge, and then another. Each time he talks about the door, the charge, the placement, and the type of initiator. At each step, he pauses to ask for questions. After the blast, they talk about the effects of the charge, which in some cases has blown the door completely off, hurling it some distance. Occasionally, the blast sets the insulation in the hollow-core door on fire. For the rest of the afternoon, the student breachers build charges and bring them to Diesing and Fowler for inspection and comment. They are questioned on the charge and what might be the expected result of the breach. Most of the charges are cleared for breaching, while a few are torn apart and sent back to the prep tables to be redone. Before they leave the range that afternoon, they take the written breaching examination. Everyone passes the exam.

Friday is a full day of building and detonating charges on the range. This breaching range is new. Sergeant First Class Tad Collier had much to do with the construction of the range and the contractor-supported, cadre-taught demolition training that takes place here. This Friday, he takes a break from his duties as the NCOIC of RASP 1 and comes to the range to teach explosive breaching for the day. Sergeant Collier has a big job; he's in charge of all of RASP 1. I sense that when he needs a break from his administrative duties, he comes out to his breaching range for a relaxing day of showing RASP 1 students how to properly blow open doors.

"You're building a charge to do a certain job with an expected result," Sergeant Collier tells his student section between rounds of explosive breach. "Sure, it's fun, but it's not just a big bang for the fun of it. A little too much cut or push is better than a charge that is not quite enough. These charges are tools—a means to an end. Know what each of these types of explosives can do and build your charges with the expectation of a given result. This is where we learn. After each explosive breach, we can examine the result. We can see if what happened was what you expected to happen."

On Friday after the range is policed, there are some seventy doors hanging by hinges or blown across the rows of supporting metal jamb casings. After the final breach and breaching critique, Sergeant Diesing calls them in close.

"Okay, men, take a knee." The front ranks drop down. "It's been a good week, and you did well. Remember, we just covered the basics out here. The art of breaching comes with time and experience. Each battalion and each company may do this a little differently, but, fundamentally, it will be the same. Above all, remember the safety precautions of handling and carrying explosives. You will all be involved with building breaching charges and using them in combat. Some of you will become the primary breachers for your squad or fire team, and you'll build a lot of these charges. And keep in mind that most of your breaches will be mechanical, not explosive. With an explosive breach, people can get hurt, and there's always the chance that the wrong people get hurt. We're in the business of getting through the door, not destroying someone's home." He points to a student. "What's the mission of the breacher?"

"A rapid, positive, dynamic breach, Sergeant."

"And what do you do first when coming up to the door?" he asked, pointing to another.

"Recognize, analyze, and then make the breach, Sergeant."

"Fair enough. Again, good job and good luck with the rest of your training. Section leader?"

"SECTION LEADER!" Sergeant Sadler steps forward.

"Let's get a good cleanup on the ranges and load up the bus."

"Roger that, Sergeant."

"As a group, they did well." Sergeant Diesing tells me as the class polices the ranges. It will take a while, as there are mangled doors and debris scattered across a wide area. "But that doesn't mean that we didn't see some things from certain candidates that didn't give us pause—minor safety issues for some and a few failing to follow directions. That's a big thing, following directions. There's a lot of information these guys have to lock down, here and in battalion, and they've got to do it quickly. Within six months, all of them will have been in combat, most of them in a gunfight. Learning quickly and following directions is critical. We've made notes on those we feel may be questionable in this area. If it shows up during marksmanship training or is a pattern for this individual during RASP, then he may not be good Ranger material."

During the range cleanup, I notice one student breacher who has a lingering smile on his face. I also noted that he seemed to pay particular attention during the breaching classes.

"You seem to be having a good time there, Specialist." Typically, a soldier in Ranger training who is a specialist, or E-4, is someone who joined the Army with a college education.

He gives me a comfortable smile. "Mister Couch, this was great. I think I've been wanting to do this ever since I was a little kid."

His name is Jon Edson. He's five feet ten with handsome, regular features and has a knowing way about him. He's youthful, but I sense he is not young—not like the others. "What were you doing before you joined the Army?"

"Actually," he replies with that same easy smile, "I was looking for a job. And to be honest about it, I was running out of options."

"A college graduate?" I ask.

"I grew up in the Seattle area, and I have a degree in business from Washington State. I was married for eight years, but that didn't work out. I was in the real estate business and the bottom fell out of that as well. I lost just about everything. Candidly, I was struggling, and I needed more than a job. I was looking for a change, and, I guess, a way out. So I joined the Army."

"And the Rangers?"

"I did well in OSUT so I was able to go to Airborne School. They asked for volunteers while I was in Airborne, and I said why not. It looked interesting."

He seems comfortable talking about this, so I take it a step further. "So I guess that if you were a Frenchman, you'd be in the Foreign Legion right now."

This brings an immediate smile. "You have that right as well. I just needed to be someplace different from where I was. The French Foreign Legion." He ponders this a moment. "I didn't even think about that. Maybe that was an option I overlooked."

"How old are you, Specialist?"

"I'm thirty-four, sir. I'm the old man in the class."

"You know," I tell him, "there are a lot worse places to be than where you are right now."

"Oh, that's for sure, and I've been to some of those places. I'm very happy to be right where I am; I have no complaints at all. I took this challenge on, and I'm going to see it through."

"Good luck."

"Thank you, sir."

If there's a favorite week at RASP, it's the marksmanship week. A few of the candidates favor breaching, but most like the shooting. After the class NCO-led stretching and a cadre led four-mile run, the class section that finished breaching now draws weapons. The class section that finished their marksmanship training heads off to the Peden Field classroom for their initial breaching class. The new shooters assemble in one of the Ranger Selection and Training Company classrooms with their pistols, rifles, and magazines—all but one. One soldier is not present. I had noticed him hobbling through PT and on runs the previous week, and so did one of the cadre sergeants.

"He didn't want to drop out from the class," the sergeant told me, "but we could see he was hurting. He has some issues with his hips, and rather than break him or have him fail the final PT test, we had him step back. He'll be rolled into the next Phase Two or the one after that after he heals up. He's a good soldier, and we want him in good form when he gets to the Regiment."

Class 09-10 now stands with forty-five candidates—forty-one of them originals who began Phase One together only a few weeks ago. To these candidates, it seems like an eternity.

The recycle of this candidate seems to be in keeping with the attitude of the Phase Two cadre—get them through and teach them as much as possible. Unless it's an issue of honor, attitude, or safety, Phase Two is a teaching environment. The reader may have noted that I now refer to them as students rather than candidates, as it now just seems more appropriate. With two weeks until graduation, there are only two critical events left for them—the final PT test and any issues that may have surfaced in Phase One or Two that could result in an appearance before the board. In addition to a few written exams or proficiency qualifications, the candidate-students are still being assessed. As on the breaching range, there are safety considerations and conventions on the shooting ranges, perhaps more so. With explosives, each individual charge was relatively safe until it was tied in with an initiator. This was always done under the eye of a cadre instructor. On the shooting range, each student has a gun, sometimes two, and with that, each has an individual opportunity to commit an unsafe or dangerous act.

The marksmanship training will focus on two weapons or weapons systems, as they are called: the M9 Beretta 9-millimeter pistol and the M4 rifle. Phase Two is blessed with two superb lead shooting instructors, Staff Sergeant Ed David and Staff Sergeant Dennis Allen. Sergeant David starts them off.

"You've just had a week of breaching, right, men?"

"ROGER THAT, SERGEANT!"

"Breaching is cool—and important. Some of you may even be primary breachers in your squad, but you'll not always be making a breach on a combat operation. You will shoot. Every day on almost every operation, you will be putting rounds on target. That's what Rangers do—we're gunfighters. That's why we go on target. More than any other piece of gear, that rifle is the tool of your trade. If that rifle goes down, then it's you and your pistol." He takes a Beretta from his holster and holds it up. "We're going to start with our secondary weapons system, the nine-millimeter Beretta pistol. It's a good gun. Some will say a Glock or a Sig is better—maybe so. Others will swear by a forty-caliber or a forty-five; they'll say a nine-millimeter doesn't have enough stopping power. But the caliber doesn't matter if you're accurate. If you shoot the guy in the head or center-punch him, he'll go down. And with the Beretta, you'll have fifteen rounds in your magazine to keep on shooting him until he does go down. Right?"

"ROGER THAT, SERGEANT!"

Sergeant Ed David is a competition shooter and known throughout the Regiment as both a superb marksman and marksmanship teacher. He has blond hair and boyish features, but there's a passion about him when he talks about shooting. David began in 1st Battalion, where he had two tours before being assigned to the Regimental Reconnaissance Company at the Ranger Special Troops Battalion. There he had what amounted to four combat rotations doing things that he's not allowed to talk about. But he is one of the best shooters in the Regiment, and it seems reasonable that those skills were put to good use. Sergeant David is a pacer and he roams the front of the classroom. The student shooters follow him with great interest. There are also a few off-duty Phase One and Phase Two cadre sergeants sitting in on the class. It's a chance to get some good instruction from one of the best.

"Men, you will go to your secondary weapons system because your primary is down, or you're jammed up in a tight space and can't get your primary into action. When you draw that pistol, it's to kill somebody. We're not cops, and we don't draw a gun and say, 'Hands up,' or 'Get down on the ground.' When you draw that Beretta, it's to shoot and kill someone—no other reason. So it's important that you listen carefully to what we have to say here this morning. If and when that time does come, and you draw that pistol, it's because you're in deep trouble. And it will be very important that you get your rounds on target, before that target gets his rounds on you. We'll begin with the basics—the fundamentals. Trust me on this, now and for the rest of your Ranger careers, it will always be about the fundamentals—always. Refinements, yes, but always the fundamentals. I'm a good shooter, but when I shoot poorly, I go back to the basics. You master what we teach you here in the next few hours and you will shoot well, I promise you. And when you have to draw that pistol in combat, you'll kill that bad guy before he kills you."

Two and a half days are spent with the Beretta. Instruction begins with the students strapping on their holsters properly so they ride on the upper thigh—high enough for the pistol to be near at hand but under the body armor. Then the class spends nearly an hour on safely handling the weapon and achieving the proper grip. From there they move on to a proper shooting stance. Each move with the pistol, from the holstered carry position to pressing the trigger, is carefully choreographed and rehearsed.

"We begin with the pistol as pistol shooting is new or relatively new to these candidates," says Sergeant Allen. "Handguns are no longer a part of basic training, and less than half of these guys have ever fired a pistol, period. This is actually good as we can start fresh—no bad habits to break. You'll be amazed at their accuracy after only a few days' instruction."

Like Diesing and Fowler over on the breaching range, David and Allen team teach. One demonstrates while the other talks. They do it by the numbers, getting the pistol from the holster to the point of pressing the trigger to fire the round—or, in their words, break the round. Allen, now the demonstrator, faces the class with his Beretta strapped to his right thigh. Sergeant Dennis Allen is close to six feet and weighs a solid two hundred pounds. He's a veteran of eight combat rotations with 1st Battalion and is almost finished with his two-year tour at the Ranger Selection and Training Company. Class 09-10 will be his last. He's from Idaho and will soon be headed back west to join 2/75 in Washington State. Like many Ranger cadre sergeants at RASP, he's anxious to get back to battalion and back into deployment rotation.

"Okay, men, this is what it looks like by the numbers," Sergeant David says. "Watch closely. First, sweep and draw." Allen runs the thumb of his shooting hand along his belt line and drops his hand to the butt of his pistol. "Notice he grips the weapon high on the back-strap with a firm 'C' grip. Next, draw and rotate." Allen releases the holster catch and draws the pistol from the holster, rotates the weapon, and brings it level just above his holster. His left hand comes to the center of his chest. "Okay," David continues, "the gun is out, and as he clears the holster, he releases the decocking lever so the weapon is off safe and in a double-action firing mode. Now, we meet and greet." Allen brings the pistol to the center of his chest and clenches it in a two-handed grip with the pistol still level. "Look closely, men. He's now at the high ready position. Notice that to get there he brought the pistol to his off hand in the center of his chest— not his off hand to the pistol. Here's where he establishes his grip. It's the same every time. He builds a wall around the pistol with both hands, holding it firmly but not with a death grip. Note that since he began the draw, his eyes have never left the target. Now he's ready for the final step to engage the target—extend, prep, and press." Allen moves slowly as David talks. "As he extends the weapon, he preps his trigger, pressing it slowly to bring the hammer back in preparation for the shot. When he gets to the extended firing position, his trigger is fully prepped, and he needs only a few more pounds of pressure to break the shot. All the while, he's been looking only at the target. Now his eyes go to the front sight of his pistol as he aligns his sights to aim in. The target goes out of focus and the sights—primarily the front sight—come into focus. Now he breaks the shot." *Click.* "Also notice that when he aims in, both eyes are open. It's hard at first, but even as your strong eye acquires the sight picture, you keep both eyes open. Why both eyes open, men? Someone? Anyone?" Sergeant David asks a lot of questions.

"Situational awareness, Sergeant?" someone ventures.

"Right. We're in a gunfight. You have to be aware of what's going on to your left and right. You can't afford to lose half your peripheral. Both eyes open."

The two shooting coaches repeat the drill with Allen turning ninety degrees to his left so the class can observe from the side. "Okay," Allen says, holstering his pistol, "On your feet and get into a shooting stance." There's a scraping of chairs as the student shooters comply, crouching like a convention of gunfighters at high noon. "What do we do first? Okay, make it happen." Each student draws his weapon, checks that the chamber is empty, releases the slide, drops the hammer with the decoking lever, and reholsters his pistol. "Now, slowly and by the numbers: sweep and grip . . . draw and rotate . . . meet and greet . . . extend, prep, and press."

While the students practice, the shooting coaches roam the room, helping here, making an adjustment there. "Keep it slow and deliberate," David tells them. "The speed will come. We're not about speed right now; it's all about the mechanics and building muscle memory—the right muscle memory."

The student shooters work in pairs—one going through the drill while the other coaches. Then they switch. The key to good shooting, they are told, is dry firing. For several hours that afternoon and several more that evening after chow, they work in pairs and dry fire their pistols.

The next day on the range begins like the day ended in the classroom—with dry-fire drills. They again work through the draw by the numbers and dry fire the Beretta pistols in both single- and double-action configuration. When they step to the range and begin to fire live rounds, it's once again a by-the-numbers draw of the holstered weapon while observing all the conventions of loading and making the weapon safe between draws and drills. There is no draw-and-shoot; they holster and unholster the weapon for slow fire. For now, it's all about getting the feel for the Beretta, observing weapons safety, and putting shooting groups on target—tight groups. The class shoots for target groups at three, five, seven, and ten meters before stepping back to the twenty-five-meter line, a long shot for the 9-millimeter Beretta. Even at this range, the student shooters are getting groups on target. David and Allen, along with other Phase Two cadre and TAC (training and counseling) sergeants, roam along the line helping those who are having difficulty.

"Take your time men," Allen tells them. "Move slowly and be

aware of your mechanics. Extend and press. If your grip's not right, come back to the high ready and get it right. Get the feeling of that trigger prep so you know what it feels like when you press fully and break the round."

David reminds them, "Both eyes open, but get that front sight in sharp focus. Some of you are digging or fishing. If you anticipate the round, you'll push forward and dig. If your grip is too tight, you'll tend to pull back and fish. The grip is a firm handshake—prep the trigger, then press to break the shot." I never heard these shooting coaches say "squeeze"—always "press."

The morning is magazine after magazine of slow, deliberate familiarization fire. In the afternoon, they pick up the pace. "We're going to speed things up now," David tells them, "but the objective is to show you that just because you're moving faster, the basics still apply. As you build up the speed, here and later in your battalions, you never abandon fundamental shooting mechanics. In practice, in competition, and in combat, it's all about the fundamentals." David shows his not inconsiderable skill; he draws his Beretta very quickly and very smoothly without taking his eyes from the target, and dumps fifteen rounds in a tight group in less than two seconds. It sounds like he's on full automatic fire. "If I'm shooting well, it's because I can maintain my fundamentals at speed. If I'm shooting poorly, it's because I'm not doing the basics. To get back on track, I slow it and get back to doing it right—first with dry firing, then with live rounds. For now, I want all of you to be deliberate; smooth is fast. This is serious business, men. The day may come that your or your Ranger buddy's life will depend you your putting rounds on target with your secondary weapon. If your shooting mechanics are bad, you'll lose the fight."

The first speed drill has them firing five rounds on the stopwatch with the amount of time dependent on distance. At fifteen meters, they have fifteen seconds to fire the five rounds; at ten meters, eleven seconds; at seven meters, eight seconds; at five meters, six seconds;

and at three meters, four seconds. They're now shooting at silhouette targets. "As you can see," David says to them, "at three meters, it's a matter of getting the weapon level and steady after each round, and it's easy to get a center-of-mass hit. Back at fifteen meters, you have to get a sight picture with the front sight in focus to make your rounds count."

On the next drill, they shoot at two silhouettes at seven meters beginning from the holstered position with a magazine of eight rounds. The student shooter draws and engages the silhouettes in a proscribed manner—two rounds to the center or mass of the first target, then two rounds to the head of target two, two to the head of target one, and the final two rounds to the torso of target two. Then they reload with a second magazine of eight and reshoot the targets.

"These drills are designed to challenge their mechanics with movement," Allen tells me. "We want them to move while they readdress their shooting mechanics, but we don't necessarily want them to move fast. But this is a taste of what's to come. In combat, things happen fast. Most of these guys will never have to go for their secondary weapon, but if they do, it'll be life and death. And there's carryover. The basics of target acquisition and engagement with their M4s will be similar to that with a pistol. I sound like a broken record, but it's all about mechanics. When the bad guys shoot back, we still win. Our mechanics are better than theirs. Every one of these cadre sergeants has been there. We win gunfights because we're trained to shoot better. With this movement, we're testing their mechanics while demanding they move through these drills observing safety and situational awareness. In the classroom, we crawled. Now we're walking. Hopefully, by the end of the week, we'll be moving at a fast walk with both the M9 and the M4."

The final fire-and-movement drill of the day with the Beretta is the "El Presidente." I never got a good answer as to why it was called that, but the drill goes like this. The student begins with his back to two silhouette targets at seven meters. His hands are raised in an "I surrender" posture. At the cadre signal, the shooter turns and draws on his targets. It's all center-of-mass shooting with a double-tap to each silhouette. The shooter then reloads with another magazine. This is called a hot reload because the shooter drops the magazine to the ground and replaces it with a fresh one with a round still in the chamber. He then reengages the targets, again double-tapping each one—two targets, eight rounds. It's a timed event with no time being kept. The cadre score the targets. Three of the four rounds have to be clustered in the killing zone of each silhouette for a passing score. Those who pass are excused from the live range, while those who do not must shoot again. Soon David, Allen, and the other cadre sergeants are working with the less-proficient shooters, coaching them and correcting flaws in their shooting mechanics. After the last of the class clear the El Presidente drill, Sergeant David calls them in.

"Okay, men, that's about it for the basics of the pistol. Now you know what to do, and it's now a matter of taking the time to practice. Never underestimate the value of dry firing. Sergeant Allen and I have been shooting competitively for a long time, and we still dry fire. And forget about speed. The speed will come as you build muscle memory into the fundamentals you've learned here. We good with that?"

"ROGER THAT, SERGEANT!"

"And remember, when you're on target and you take that pistol out, it's to kill someone who needs killing—someone who's trying to kill you or kill your Ranger buddy. Okay, let's get this range policed up. Tomorrow we'll be out here for more of this same drill with the nine-mil Beretta. We'll begin in the afternoon with our primary weapons system."

Weapons accountability during marksmanship week is maintained by the class. There is no armory or secure facility available throughout the week. A room in the barracks is designated as the weapons room, and two student shooters are always there guarding the weapons whenever the class is not on the range. Their classmates bring back food for them from the Ranger chow hall; on the range, they eat MREs. Two students will stand duty in two-hour shifts throughout the night and are expected to conduct dry firing during their watch.

Wednesday morning on the range begins with another round of dry-fire and shooting drills with the Beretta. Safety and mechanics; mechanics and safety. There is no scored qualification shoot, but the students are continually assessed on their ability to respond to correction. More emphasis is put on the ability to take instruction than on speed or even accuracy. After the noon MRE, the twenty-two shooters begin work with the standard SOF assault rifle, the M4A1.

Instruction begins on the range. All the candidates in RASP 1 Class 09-10 have fired the M4 or an earlier variant of the M4. The Phase Two issue weapons are equipped with a forestock-mounted LA-5 advanced laser device and a high-intensity light. The high-intensity light is a hands-free flashlight that allows a soldier to keep his weapon pointed in the direction where he is searching in a dark room. The LA-5 is a sighting device that allows the shooter an optical pointer to aim his weapon, day or night. Also mounted to these training weapons is the SU231 EOTech holographic sight—one of the primary Ranger gun sights.

Sergeant David gives the class a quick safety refamiliarization with the weapon and a review of the mechanics for zeroing a rifle. These soldiers know the weapon, but not the EOTech sight. The EOTech is a battery-powered day/night sighting device that features a starburst reticle pattern with a single dot in the center. There are multiple illumination settings for various lighting conditions. The EOTech is an intuitive sight that is typically set or "zeroed" for a given distance and has the advantage of allowing the shooter to quickly acquire his target, establish a sight picture, and get rounds out. As with the M9, the student shooters are taught to shoot with both eyes open.

"Keeping both eyes open is a little more challenging with the rifle as the EOTech sight is close to your eye," Sergeant Allen says, "but in a combat environment, you have to be aware of what's going on around you. This means precision shooting with both eyes open. It's a knack, and once you get used to it, it becomes natural."

After a range safety brief, shooters gather at the twenty-five-meter range to zero in their weapons. There are special zeroing-in targets with grid squares to help the shooters "walk" their rounds to the proper place on the target. Shooting in five-round increments, the students first try to get their rounds in a tight group somewhere on the target. They shoot from a prone position with their weapons resting on sandbags. It's as stable a platform as they will ever shoot from. Then they make adjustments to the EOTech sight to move the rounds up or down, left or right, as needed. For this, their initial shooting course, the shooters zero their M4s for two hundred meters. To do this, they move their shot groupings to a spot on the twenty-five-meter target that is four inches below their target-center aiming point. Given the high-velocity and flat trajectory of the 5.56-millimeter M4 rounds, this impacting of rounds below the target-center aim point will put them on target at two hundred meters. Some in 09-10 are better than others, but eventually all have their weapon zeroed in. It takes time. After each five rounds, the weapons have to be made safe with empty chambers locked to the rear before the class can go forward to inspect their targets and note their sight corrections for the next five rounds. The balance of the afternoon is taken with the zeroing process. It's also about the mechanics of shooting the same way every time.

"The key to shooting tight groups, men," Sergeant David tells them, "is to maintain the same relationship to the gun each time you shoot. That means your cheek is on the same place on the stock with your nose touching the charging handle. This is where we start building the muscle memory for combat. You'll never have the luxury of being in a prone position and propped up like you are now.

You'll seldom have the luxury of shooting without body armor and full combat kit. You'll be shooting on the run, behind a corner, or from under a vehicle, and you'll have sixty pounds of gear strapped on you. But if you can always find that sweet spot behind your gun with your cheek, then those rounds will always follow your sight picture. This same muscle memory applies to the safety on your gun. That safety comes off when you acquire your target and goes back on when you break your last round. We do it religiously here in training so in combat, when the targets are shooting back and you're running and gunning in the fight, it's something you'll do automatically."

As with the M9, shooting with the M4 is driven by shooting commands, range-safety rules, and weapons-safety protocols. All movements between the shooting stations and targets is strictly monitored and orchestrated. There have been no major safety violations to this point on the range with Class 09-10—a violation that calls for a candidate to be immediately dropped from RASP. There have been such violations in the past with other classes. Today on the range, one student shooter touches his M4 when he should have been standing behind it—a minor violation, but a minor *safety* violation nonetheless. Sergeant Allen sees it and is on him immediately.

"You—what's your name!" The unfortunate candidate comes to a rigid parade rest and answers up. Allen chews on him for several minutes, while all in the class stand at parade rest and listen.

"All of you, pull your heads out of your butts," he tells them. "We have a job to do, but range safety is paramount. It keeps us safe while we train and safe on the battlefield. Imagine how you would feel if an unsafe act caused the death of a brother Ranger? How could you live with yourself? I sure as hell couldn't live with myself. You," he says, pointing to the violator. "That's your one alibi. One more safety violation and you are history, understood?"

"Roger that, Sergeant."

"All of you," says Sergeant David, "go touch my gate." The class runs en masse to the range gate that's two hundred meters away and back. When they return, they fall in behind their shooting stations. "Safety is a collective responsibility, men. Smith there may have committed the violation, but where was his Ranger buddy that should have stopped him? Rangers look out for one another—here on the range, in the barracks, out in town, on deployment, wherever. If one guy messes up, we all mess up. Understood?"

"ROGER THAT, SERGEANT!"

Thursday is all about shooting drills with the M4. It's about getting rounds on target from every possible position and angle—on the move and under difficult conditions, day and night. Rangers are raiders, and the shooting drills, beginning here in RASP and continuing into the battalions, are designed to train Rangers to shoot accurately while on the move in the conduct of a raid. Since they move and shoot as a team, safety is paramount to avoid fratricide. Thursday begins with a rezeroing of their M4s with kit—helmets and full body armor. Then they move on to simple battle drills.

"We take a lot of time with this," Sergeant David tells me, "because in their Ranger squads, each combat work-up begins on the range like this. Everyone has to get reacquainted with his combat load and get his work gun zeroed in. Doesn't matter if it's your first rotation or your tenth rotation. If these guys can jump right in and do this with their squads and fire teams, they'll be stepping off on the right foot to integrate with their Ranger brothers. The shooting drills step up from there. The mechanics of combat assault can be complex, but it's not magic or rocket science. To do it well, and as safely as we do it, simply takes practice and attention to detail—and lots of both. The key to being a good combat shooter is to have your shooting mechanics so locked down that you can focus totally on what's going on around you—where the danger is, where the enemy is likely to be, and where your Ranger buddies are at any given time. Then, when a target presents itself, the mechanics take over and we engage effectively—as individuals and as an assault team."

Combat shooting is all about getting rounds on target in a tactical situation, which is sometimes a chaotic and confusing situation. Battle drills and marksmanship, two of the Ranger Big Five, amount to training scenarios like this that get those rounds on target in difficult and increasingly challenging tactical situations. And it starts here. The student shooters begin with barricade shooting—shooting from behind or around the cover of a building corner or over a car hood, all simulated with training barricades. They shoot left-handed and right-handed as to make full use of cover. This is called shooting strong hand and shooting offhand, and the drills have them changing these shooting configurations often. Through each change of position and magazine change, they observe the strict protocols regarding where their barrel is pointed and when the weapon is on and off safe. Much of the drill and procedure these almost-Rangers follow is the same weapons protocol they will follow in Afghanistan in the not-too-distant future.

Movement drills are procedure-driven as well. These drills have them running in a line abreast, then stopping to engage their silhouette targets. Then they begin shooting on the move, engaging targets while they advance on line at a fast walk. They move in a file, stopping and turning to engage targets to their left and right, while taking care not to sweep the man to their front with their barrel. And, finally, moving away from the target, they execute a full half-turn to shoot a target behind them. Shooters then move parallel to a line of targets, engaging them on the command of a cadre sergeant, first pivoting to shoot right, then left—over and over, drill after drill.

"Smooth is fast, guys," Sergeant David reminds them, "and be aware of your Ranger buddy to your left and right at all times. Keep a good interval and stay on line. If you get out front or lag behind, you cut your field of fire or your buddy's field of fire. If you stay on line, everybody's gun is in the fight—everybody brings the pain."

The student shooters are taught to take a knee and bring their weapon barrel-vertical when they execute a magazine change. "Smith is cold!" a shooter in the line or file calls as he takes a knee to reload. Then he says, "Smith, coming up!" when he's back on line with a fresh magazine.

"Don't just crank off rounds while you move," Sergeant Allen says. "You should have a sight picture each time you break a shot. Every shot is a kill shot."

The final shooting drill of the day is an individually scored event with the shooter moving through a formatted drill with a single twenty-round magazine. At the direction of a cadre sergeant calling out each position, he advances and retreats on his target, turning and shooting quickly between five and twenty-five meters. The objective is to have every round a center-of-mass kill shot. Some are able to at least get every round somewhere on the black of the silhouette; others have one or more rounds that stray into the white area around the silhouette torso.

While the shooting exercises put each student through an identical drill, they don't all perform the same. Some get it quickly, others not so quickly. Combat shooting is all about procedure and awareness. To engage a target on the shooter's left, a right-handed shooter turns left and steps toward his target with his left foot as his rifle comes from the high ready position to a shooting position—off safe, sight picture, trigger press, *bang-bang*, safety on, and back to high ready. For a left-handed shooter, this same shot requires a swinging pivot on the left foot and a step toward the target with the right foot, then the same shooting sequence. Each, when done properly, is a balletlike move with smoothness and grace. There are multiple moves to this combat dance, and these new performers are learning the basic steps. Some are just better dancers than others.

Following a long afternoon of drill, the student shooters get ready for nighttime shooting. A great deal of Ranger assault work in the current battlespace is done at night. The saying "We own the night" is more than just a catchy phrase; 88 percent of all Ranger missions are conducted at night. Night shooting is infrared (IR) shooting. This is done with the LA-5 pointer/laser device. The LA-5 mounted on the barrel of the M4 rifles has two lasers. One is a visible laser that puts a red dot on the target. The second is an IR laser that puts a dot on the target that is not visible unless you're looking through an optical device that sees in the infrared spectrum of light—a device such as a night-observation device (NOD). To shoot at night, the shooter first zeros his M4 to his LA-5. This is done by adjusting the visible, red-dot laser to the center of his EOTech sight. Now the visible laser is aligned with the gun; the rounds will go where the red dot goes.

The visible red-dot laser and the IR laser are optically aligned. With the visible laser off and the IR laser on, the shooter now puts the IR laser on the target. At night, while looking through his NOD, the shooter sees the world in varying shades of green with a bright green dot as his aiming point. IR shooting with NODs becomes something of a video game in which the player/shooter finds his target in the green-shaded landscape, puts the green dot on his target's center-of-mass, and presses the trigger. The shooting mechanics and safety protocols are the same. The ballet steps and dance routines are just done in the dark.

"We operate mostly at night, men," Sergeant David tells them, "running and gunning in a green-shaded world, and bringing the pain to the bad guys. Your shooting mechanics are the same. Don't turn your laser on until you have a target. After you take your shot, turn the laser off. The bad guys have their Radio Shack, Sony-made NODs, and that laser is a beacon to locate and shoot at you. The laser comes on as your safety comes off. Break the shot, then turn your laser off as your safety comes back on."

Class 09-10 goes through a series of night-shooting drills that are not unlike the daylight drills of that afternoon. They move slower, as this is their first dance after dark—the first of many for these future Rangers. It's an interesting contrast for this observer. Without a NOD, there's nothing but the crack of gunfire and an occasional muzzle flash. With NODs, there is the monochromatic green world with fireflylike winking dots on the silhouette targets. And the shooters look different. Their heads are up, looking over their rifles with their NODs instead of the cheek-to-stock conformation of a daytime shooter.

"Here again, this is just an introduction to the kind of shooting they'll be doing when they get to their battalions," explains Sergeant Allen. "That's why it's so important that they pay attention to detail. If they understand the basics and do the drills right a few times here, then they'll be able to step into the flow of battle drills with the veteran Rangers in their squads. It's more important that they move well and move safely than it is that they hit the target every time. Accuracy will come as they work up for their first deployment."

Friday is the stress shoot. As the class was on the shooting ranges late the night before, there is no morning PT. There will, however, be a small amount of PT that takes place as a part of the stress-shoot evolution. The stress shoot is designed to pull together the shooting mechanics and range drills that went on during the entire marksmanship week. It's a validation of their marksmanship with the M9 and the M4 as well as their handling of the weapons, weapons safety, and their primary-to-secondary weapons-system transition. The evolution will also expose any glaring errors with their shooting fundamentals.

The course is a shooting gauntlet of sorts that must be negotiated by the student shooters one at a time. In addition to David and Allen, four other cadre sergeants are there to serve as scorers and safety observers.

The action begins with the shooter doing as many push-ups as he can manage in two minutes, followed by a maximum effort in sit-ups in two minutes. He then stands while two of his classmates help him to quickly kit up—helmet, combat vest or rack, and body armor with full plates. In his kit are two Beretta 9-millimeter magazines with two rounds in each mag and two M4 (5.56) magazines—

one with ten rounds and the other with the full thirty rounds. The shooter loads one of the two-round mags in the M9 and holsters the weapon. He then loads the ten-round magazine into his M4, and puts the rifle on "aircraft safe"—magazine in place, weapon on safe, and the bolt home with no round in the chamber. At the starting signal, the stress-shoot contender is on the clock. He must first sprint two hundred meters before coming to the first shooting station.

At station one, he goes to a prone firing position, chambers a round in his M4, and engages a metal head-and-shoulders silhouette at two hundred meters. He must "ping" the silhouette with one of his magazine's ten rounds. A few hit it on their first round. For most, it requires multiple rounds to get a hit. And for yet a few others, there is no hit and a time penalty is added to their running total. Next, the competitor must change mags, make his weapon safe, and run to the next shooting station or stations. With his new thirty-round magazine, he engages three successive stations, each with two targets. At each station, he shoots while walking and double-taps the two targets before sprinting to the next target station. After engaging each of the three twin silhouettes, the shooter must put his weapon on safe and cannot have a finger in its trigger well. A cadre sergeant follows each shooter to score the targets and look for any deviation from safety protocol. Target misses and any safety violations result in time added.

The next station has the shooter atop a berm. There he transitions from his M4 to his M9 Beretta and engages a metal head-and-shoulders silhouette at twenty-five meters. He has to hit it once with one of his two rounds, change mags, and hit it again. Nonhits or failing to change magazines properly or not safely reholstering his M9 result in time added.

The final station is a nearby training barricade where the shooter will transition back to his M4 and engage yet another metal head-and-shoulders silhouette at fifty meters. He must first shoot from a cramped prone position that will make him roll on his side to shoot from under the barricade, as if he were shooting from under a car. Then he will transition to a knee, shooting strong hand and offhand over the barricade. Finally, he shoots around a barricade corner while standing, both strong hand and offhand. He has two rounds to get a single hit on a fifty-meter metal silhouette from any of these five positions. When changing positions, the weapon has to be on safe. Nonhits and unsafe position movements result in added time.

Raw running times average between 250 and 290 seconds. Then the misses and safety penalties are added in. The scores are not revealed to the student shooters. The winner will get the class top-gun honor, and that will not be made known until graduation. Several in the class have been shooting well, but even the top shooters are unsure as to how much penalty time they picked up during the stress shoot. There's a lot of speculation who will win, but most students simply want to be among the graduates. After the last man is through the course, Sergeant Allen calls them into a group circle.

"Take a knee, men, and listen up," he begins. "See how quickly the mechanics can break down even with a little bit of stress?"

"ROGER THAT, SERGEANT!"

"Now, this was not a terribly stressful course; this was a shooting-station course, but you saw and felt what happens to some of your rounds when you're breathing hard and you're on the move. You missed targets you would have never missed on previous drills. We do this so you can see just how quickly the fundamentals of shooting can desert you if you don't practice. Combat shooting requires practice. Live fire and dry firing. Okay, imagine being on target at night, carrying twice as much weight, running farther, and the other guys are shooting back. Men, this is what Rangers do for a living. During this week we just covered the basics; we wanted you to see what right looks like. When you get to your battalion, get to the range as much as you can. We're gunfighters—this is what we do. Most of us belong to shooting clubs, and we shoot on the weekends so our skills are up to standard when we go to the fight. We're in a business where we can't just be accurate. We have to shoot on the move, we have to know where our Ranger buddies are at all times, *and* we have to put the rounds on target. Your life and your Ranger buddy's life depend on it. We good with that?"

"ROGER THAT, SERGEANT."

"Okay, it's been good shooting with you. Good luck to all of you. This is my last class; I'm headed out to 2/75 and back to the fight. Maybe the next time we shoot together it will be on target. Class leader?"

"Right here, Sergeant." Sergeant Sadler is at his elbow.

"Let's get the targets put away and get this brass policed up."

"Roger that, Sergeant."

For the Ns through Zs, the end of the marksmanship week is the end of week seven. The same for the As through Ms out on the breaching range. One week from today, Class 09-10 will graduate. Those who graduate will be awarded their Tan Berets and the Scroll that will mark them as Rangers in the 75th Ranger Regiment. Most know they will graduate. Others are not so sure. None of them are taking anything for granted. Next week, there will be the final PT test and the RASP 1 Commander's Board. For some, this board will determine whether or not they will graduate with Class 09-10.

I watched Private Kevin Seiple during the week of marksmanship training, and he was shooting very well. Private Seiple is a young infantryman on a mission. His family moved often so he's really from no one place. His last two years in high school were split between Missouri and Florida. He joined the Army right out of high school, two months after his daughter was born. Private Seiple is nineteen; his wife is eighteen.

"I was working summers and after school at odd jobs, mostly carpentry. Then the housing market went bust. I married my wife just before our daughter was born; it was the right thing to do. Neither of us wanted to move in with our parents, so we didn't have many options—I didn't have many options. The pay in the Army isn't that great, but the medical benefits and housing allowances are pretty good, so here I am."

His wife and daughter are currently in Florida with her grandparents while he's in training. As soon as he knows which battalion he'll be assigned to, he will begin making plans to bring them there to join him. Meanwhile, it's a long-distance relationship. It will be quite a while before Private Seiple can say he's had more days with his wife and daughter than away from them. Young Rangers spend a great deal of time on deployment or training away from home when they are not on deployment.

"So why Rangers?" I ask him. "Soldiers in the 3rd ID [infantry division] get the same medical benefits as Rangers. And you'd be with your family right now."

"When I decided to join the Army, I knew I wanted to be in a special unit. I had a high school teacher who was a Ranger. When he found out I was joining the Army, he said I should think about being a Ranger. And I was lucky. When I went down to the recruiting office and said this was what I wanted, they offered me a Ranger contract. I knew I was coming here when I signed up."

"Any problems with RASP, other than the separation?"

"I'm fine, but sometimes the downtime really gets to me. The training days go by quickly, especially now that we're learning something, but I hate the weekends. The weekend workouts aren't bad, but the rest of the time we clean the barracks or kill time with some other meaningless chore. I'd rather train during the weekends and get out of here sooner."

"So," I venture, "where would you be if you hadn't a wife and a baby?"

He gives me a wistful grin. "Not sure where I'd be, but I know what I'd like to be doing. I was a lead guitarist in a rock band. We were pretty good—not great, but good—and we were getting better. The music business isn't an easy one, so I'd probably be working a day job for pocket money and playing gigs at night—and probably sleeping in the back of my van."

"And now you're a soldier."

"That's right," he says with a firm smile. "I'm a daddy and a husband, and soon I'll be a Ranger. I've got no complaints; I'll do all right here."

Week eight—graduation week. For the weary candidates of Class 09-10, it's a week many felt would never come. There are forty-four of them, down a man from the previous week. The third of the class NCOs, a sergeant who was a Phase Two insert with Cory Sadler, left on emergency leave. His wife was hospitalized due to a traffic accident on Friday afternoon of the previous week. He was torn between staying or leaving, but the Phase Two cadre unhesitatingly made the decision for him: Go be with your wife. The accident took place Friday afternoon in New Orleans, where she was hospitalized, and there were no available flights out of Columbus to New Orleans that day. A cadre sergeant and a vehicle were immediately dispatched to drive him to New Orleans to be with his wife. Rangers take care of their own, even Ranger candidates.

Monday morning, the class forms up at 0600 for the Ranger Physical Fitness Test. Here again, the Ranger standard is 80 percent or better of the Army Physical Fitness Test maximums for push-ups, sit-ups, and pull-ups in two minutes, and for the two-mile run. Failing to achieve any of the minimum repetitions on the exercises or the minimum time on the run is to fail the Ranger PT test. All forty-four pass the two-mile run at the Stewart-Watson track, with the two-mile class best of eleven minutes and twenty seconds. The other top scores were 18 pull-ups, 98 sit-ups, and 87 push-ups. Eight candidates score over 300, which is considered outstanding. However, three men fail to meet the 80 percent standard in one of the exercises—one in push-ups, one in pull-ups, and one in sit-ups. They will be given a retest later in the week. If they fail that test, even by a single pull-up or push-up, they'll be dropped and/or made to appear before the board. Following the PT test, the class heads for the Peden classroom.

The first half of graduation week is punctuated by a series of lectures and presentations, including an ethics brief, a brief on antiterrorism, and an overview of the Ranger Family Support Group. They are also given the ImPACT. The ImPACT is a neuropsychological battery of tests designed to provide a baseline for concussion-related injuries. It was developed to track head injuries in sports and is now also used to track the violence visited on our Rangers in combat. There's also an in-depth service record review to ensure that those who graduate from RASP have up-to-date service and medical records. The only PT evolution is the end-of-RASP RAW assessment to evaluate the improvement, or degradation, of Ranger combat fitness that may have taken place during RASP. My personal assessment of these almost-Rangers is that they are all a great deal stronger than when they began RASP. Yet they may not have fully recovered from the daily grind that is RASP 1 for the RAW assessment to be a valid measure of their combat physical fitness. The only evolution of a training nature is the fast-rope orientation.

Fast-roping is a key Ranger skill that these warriors will use many times on deployment. It's a simple individual skill, but doing it proficiently with an assault team takes practice. The fast-rope is a three-inch cotton-composite line dropped from a hovering helicopter. The Rangers slide down the rope like a fireman's pole. When done properly, a team inserting by fast-rope are like multiple drops of oil sliding down a string. Operational insertion by fast-rope from a helicopter is a special-operations- and Ranger-centric skill. This fast-rope training for Class 09-10 is but an orientation, and is conducted from the climbing tower at Honor Field. In their Ranger squads, they will do this many times, both in training and on target when deployed. And they will do this at night with a weapon and full combat load.

Late Monday morning, the lead Phase Two cadre sergeants meet to discuss their recommendations for the all-important formal RASP 1 Review Board that will convene on Wednesday. This is an important meeting, as the recommendations that come from this meeting will be a primary input to this final review board. Most of those in Class 09-10 that have met standard are good to go. The RASP 1 Board will focus those marginal candidates who will appear before them per the recommendations that come from this cadre meeting. In addition to marginal candidates, all NCO candidates will appear before the board. In their review of these candidates, the RASP 1 Board will look at both phases of training. Their deliberations will serve as the final gate through which these candidates must pass beore they are allowed to move on to join the Regiment.

The meeting of the Phase Two cadre is informal but serious. Present are the senior instructors for each of the three weeks of Phase Two training—Staff Sergeant Simmons, Staff Sergeant David, and Staff Sergeant Diesing. The meeting is chaired by Staff Sergeant John Martinez, sitting in for the still-injured Sergeant First Class Sedwick. Sergeant Martinez is an experienced hand with a short period of broken service. He is a 2nd Battalion veteran with six combat rotations, three as a squad leader. He's something of a utility sergeant; he was in charge of Holdover when Class 09-10 was in the Pre-RASP section. He's also served as a cadre sergeant in Phase One.

It's a long meeting. Each candidate's training record and newly completed peer evaluation is reviewed and his performance is open for comment. Most are quickly approved as having met standard and are recommended for graduation. About fifteen records are reviewed in detail, and there is comment and spirited debate. These cadre sergeants have seen them at different times during the phase and, in some cases, have differing opinions. The ones that they collec-

tively surface for the attention of the RASP 1 Review Board are
those who had persistent issues throughout Phase Two. In the final
analysis, they recommend that seven candidates appear before the
final board. Two of those are the two remaining noncommissioned
officers who, by custom, must appear. All seven who will go before
the board will do so with a recommendation by the Phase Two cadre.
Of the five non-NCOs, three are recommended for dismissal, one
for an insertion/recycle to the next Phase Two class, and one for a
day-one, Phase-One recycle. An eighth candidate is considered for
the board, a soldier who's performing well, but is a little cocky. It is
felt that a board appearance might inject a little humility into this
otherwise strong candidate. Sergeant Martinez rejects this. "Let's
not take the board's time with this. I'll call him in for a formal ser-
geant-to-soldier chat to see if I can't get his feet back on solid ground."
This is good enough for the other cadre sergeants. By mutual agree-
ment, the seven candidates will appear before the Phase 1 Board.

For me, this meeting of the Phase Two cadre was both difficult
and telling. It was difficult, as I personally know and like the three
men who were recommended for dismissal. I know something of
their family backgrounds and why they joined the Army—why they
wanted to serve their country as Rangers. But the fact is that I'm not
a Ranger, and it's not my job to evaluate them. More to the point,
I'll not have to serve with them in combat. These cadre sergeants
are guided by the information in the training records, but what it
really comes down to is whether *they* would want to serve with this
soldier. Does this candidate have the maturity and temperament to
be an asset to his fire team in combat? Will he learn enough from
the veterans in his squad, before the next rotation, to stand with his
brother Rangers in the fight? These RASP graduates, at least the
Eleven Bravos, will soon see close combat—perhaps daily combat.
Sergeant Martinez and all of his cadre staff sergeants in Phase Two
are multitour combat veterans. All have been squad leaders in combat. They know what is needed to succeed in this environment. A

candidate's willingness to learn is more important than his intelligence. Humility is more important than talent. Will a soldier's graduation from RASP bring a sense of entitlement that will alienate his brother Rangers and cause him to fail? Among these cadre sergeants, there was unanimity on the process, if not on each individual candidate. As I observed this candidate review, I was very glad to be writing about them instead of making these difficult decisions.

Aside from their recommendations of boarded candidates, the Phase Two cadre also review and make their recommendations for the class honorees. There's the Physical Fitness Award, the Top Gun Award, and the Honor Graduate. The Physical Fitness and Top Gun awards are determined by the RPFT and the stress-test shooting scores. The Class Leader Award is given to the candidate peered highest by his classmates in both phases. The Honor Graduate is strictly a cadre decision. The Phase One and Two lead cadre sergeants determine who in the class consistently performed the best throughout RASP 1. Not all those to be honored at graduation are RASP 1 candidates. Along with the peer process, the candidates are also asked to cite the cadre member they felt was most professional and the best instructor. These cadre sergeants, one from Phase One and one from Phase Two, are honored as Cadre of the Cycle. The cadre themselves refer to this distinction as the candy-man award, meaning who was the easiest on the candidates. This is the source of some kidding by their fellow cadre sergeants. Yet those cadre members so recognized by Class 09-10 were, in my opinion, both hardworking and effective, and I sense they were quietly pleased by this recognition.

These honorees will be made known at graduation, with the exception of the Class Leader Award. Up to this point in RASP 1, the class leader has been selected by the phase cadre. For most of Phase One, that leadership was changed often. During Phase Two, it resided with the senior enlisted candidates—two class NCOs. With Class 09-10 in Phase Two, there have always been at least two

E-5 sergeants, and they served as class leaders. Now, for the final week of RASP 1 and for the graduation ceremony, the class chooses its own leader by way of the peer process. Many in the class, including Sergeant Mark Ikenboch, were peered high by their classmates. But the soldier who peered highest was Private First Class Alex Hammond, a quiet twenty-three-year-old infantryman from Pennsylvania. At six feet and a solid 175 pounds, he's one of the bigger men in the class.

Alex Hammond had first thought he wanted to be a Navy SEAL, but as high school graduation approached, he decided on the Army and was looking at special operations programs. He was on the verge of enlisting in the Army when he qualified for an Army ROTC scholarship. At his parents urging, he took the scholarship. This led him to the ROTC unit at the University of Colorado in Boulder.

"I liked college, but my heart wasn't really in it. My grades were just so-so and I was partying a lot. After two years, I decided that I wanted to be a serving soldier and that I wanted to be a soldier sooner rather than later. Neither my parents nor my ROTC unit were too happy when I left school, but it was my decision. Actually, my only option was to stay in school or enlist. I owe the Army service time for the two years of college."

To my question of why Rangers, he replied, "I came straight in as an Eleven Bravo infantryman. While I was in the AIT portion of OSUT, they ask for volunteers for Ranger training. There were actually more volunteers than there were places in RASP. A lot of guys volunteered just because you get to go to Airborne School before RASP. I'd done pretty well on the APFT, so I got one of the RASP slots in AIT. I was lucky to get here and lucky to finish, let alone be selected as the class leader."

"You weren't lucky; you earned it. Congratulations and good luck in the Regiment."

"Thank you, sir."

As the top peer, Private First Class Hammond will stand at the head of Class 09-10 for graduation. His selection by his peers was a surprise to me. We'd spoken a few times, and I knew Alex Hammond was a solid performer, but no more than that. I asked the cadre sergeants if this breakout by his peers surprised them, and they admitted that it did. Yet when his classmates were asked to "Write down the name of the best Soldier in the Phase (in both Phase One and Two), and why," his name came up more than any of the others. Here's what some of them had to say about him.

"PFC Hammond watches out for the guys beside him. He is always helpful, and I've never seen him lose his temper. He's very professional."

"Always does the right thing when no one is looking. He's a great soldier."

"He's always willing to help others. He's a good follower and a good leader."

"When we are given a task, he's always willing to help out. He will carry the load when one of his Ranger buddies is hurting."

"PFC Hammond always does what is right. He helped around the barracks, and did extra PT and studied the Ranger handbooks when others choose not to."

"It goes to show," Sergeant Martinez said of Hammond, "that we don't see everything. What goes on in the barracks is their world, and how they interact with each other is something over which we have no control. By the end of Phase Two, a candidate who is not a team player and refuses to help others will consistently and negatively light up the peer reviews. As for Hammond, good on him. I think this class chose a fine class leader."

On Wednesday morning, the formal RASP 1 Review Board convenes in a classroom at the Ranger Selection and Training Company headquarters. The board is chaired by Major Ned Matthews, the Selection and Training Company commander. Seated to his right is the RASP NCOIC, Sergeant First Class Tad Collier. Seated to his left is Company First Sergeant Jason Walker. Also present are Ser-

geant First Class Walt Iselin from Phase One and Staff Sergeant John
Martinez from Phase Two. Rounding out the board is Staff Sergeant
Jack Diesing, who will speak to the PT scores of the boarded candidates, and Staff Sergeant Jeff Walters, also with Phase Two, who will
brief their peer results. It's a formal setting with the seven board
members seated in a line at a series of tables in the front of the ROC
classroom. A single plastic chair sits before the board members. Outside the classroom-turned-boardroom, seven soldiers in a nervous
queue anxiously wait to be called in.

The process will begin with those candidates judged by the Phase
Two cadre to be the least likely to become Rangers or to remain with
the program. When directed, the first boarded candidate knocks on
the door and is told to enter. The soldier marches smartly to a position in front of Major Matthews, executes a right face, and salutes.

"Sir, Private Smith reporting to the board as ordered, sir."

Matthews returns his salute. "Very well, Private Smith. Stand at
ease. I'm Major Matthews. I believe you know the other cadre sergeants here at the table, is that correct?"

"Yes, Sergeant. I mean, yes, sir."

"Private, we are here to decide what comes next for you. There
are three courses of action that are open to us. You can be sent forward to the Regiment. You can be recycled, either to Phase Two or
back to day one of Phase One. Or you can be dropped from the program. Do you understand these alternatives?"

"Yes, sir."

"Very well, take a seat." Smith lowers himself in the chair but
sits at attention.

"Smith," Matthews continues, "we're going to ask you a series of
questions about your performance here at RASP, and we're going to
ask you to be open and honest with us in your answers, okay?"

"Roger that, sir."

Sergeant Walt Iselin begins the questioning. He asks open-ended
questions about Private Smith's difficulties and deficiencies during

Phase One, and why Smith failed to correct these shortcomings during Phase Two. Then Sergeant Diesing reviews his PT performance,
asking about his fitness to become a Ranger. Smith in fact failed the
final Ranger Physical Fitness Test as well as the retest. Next, Sergeant Walters asks Private Smith about his peer results—where he
thinks he ranked in the peer review. There's a pattern developing
here. Smith is first asked how *he* thinks he performed and was peered,
and then his answers are compared with his performance data and
his peer rankings. Following questions and comments from Sergeant
Martinez, Sergeant First Class Collier bores in. His remarks are more
statements than questions regarding Smith's deficiencies. Private
Smith tries to hold his ground, but it's not easy for him. He's twenty
years old, and he's been in the Army for a little more than six months.
Across the table for him are seven hard men with over three-quarters
of a century in uniform.

Smith is asked to leave the room while his future is discussed
and decided. It's decided that Smith will be dropped. There are a
number of performance issues, not the least of which is failure on
the RPFT. He also peered low. Smith is called back into the room
and reports as before.

"Private Smith, we have determined that you will be dropped
from the program," Major Matthews tells him. "You gave it a good
try, but we don't believe that you're a good fit for the Ranger Regiment. You'll be up for orders for another Army unit. I'm sorry it
didn't work out for you here. We hope what you learned here will
serve you well in your next assignment. You are dismissed."

Smith salutes crisply. "Rangers lead the way, sir."

"All the way," Matthews replies as he returns the salute.

The next two candidates, per the recommendation of the Phase
Two cadre, are also dropped from RASP. As with Smith, there were
issues of performance, unmet standards, range-safety violations, and/
or low peer evaluations that made the board's action rather clear-
cut. Nonetheless, in their deliberations, they looked for positive signs

in the candidate's performance or some reason that might indicate that a recycle could possibly correct the deficiencies. They could find none. Like Smith, these soldiers are sent away. In each case, the soldier is told to stand tall and to find another way to serve his country. Service in the Ranger Regiment is simply not for them.

The next two candidates are soldiers that the Phase Two cadre members recommended for recycle. One is a timid soldier who had problems on the shooting range, and while he passed the RPFT, his performance was marginal. He's a specialist with a college degree, but he's slow to pick up on military skills. The other is a candidate who performed to standard and had exceptionally high RPFT scores, but there is an issue with his attitude; he comes across as arrogant. With these two soldiers, the questions from the board are more detailed and probing, and the discussions that take place following the boarded soldier's initial appearance are far more spirited. In the end, the board follows the recommendations of the Phase Two cadre. The timid soldier will be a Phase Two insert, and given more time to attain proficiency. The second candidate, after a thorough dressing down by Sergeant Collier, becomes a Phase One, day-one recycle.

From Sergeant Collier regarding the day-one recycle: "You are being given a second chance. It's up to you to show these cadre sergeants that you have the humility to learn and the desire to be a team player—that it's not about you, but about those around you. You come before this board again and you're done, you understand?"

From First Sergeant Walker, "I don't think you have it in you to make the grade here; I don't think you can do it. Let's see if you can prove me wrong."

This candidate will have a full eight weeks to work on his attitude—and to prove the first sergeant wrong. The board, though far from being conciliatory, did take time with these two soldiers to ensure that each knew exactly why he was being recycled and exactly what changes he would have to make if he were to join the Ranger Regiment.

The two NCOs appear before the board by proscription. At first I thought their appearance was just a formality, but this is not the case. Their rank as E-5 sergeants will very quickly put them in a leadership position, perhaps as a fire-team leader on their second rotation. Both are Tabbed Rangers and both are Eleven Bravo infantrymen. They'll not have the time to grow into the job, as will the privates first class or even the specialists. They will be called on to lead in combat, and the questions put to them by the board are about leadership—their leadership during their time in RASP and their leadership going forward when they get to the Regiment.

"This is a different Regiment than the one you left a few years ago," they say to Sergeant Mark Ikenboch. "Do you think your time in the National Guard has prepared you for your new responsibilities?"

"The OPTEMPO [military speak for the high degree of operational activity of the deployed Ranger battalion and their supporting elements] has gone up dramatically, Sergeant Ikenboch. We go out and fight every night. Tell us why you will be a better leader now than when you were last here. Give us an example."

For Sergeant Cory Sadler: "You've had very little time with those stripes, and you've no time at all as a private or a specialist. What makes you think you can lead at this level?"

"Private Smith was in your platoon during Phase Two. He failed here. What did you do to help him become a better soldier?"

The grilling of the sergeant candidates was no less rigorous than it was for any of the candidates dropped or recycled. If anything, it was more aggressive. The board ultimately approved both for graduation and service in the Regiment. It was unanimous in the case of Sergeant Ikenboch, but not for Sergeant Sadler.

This RASP 1 Board took close to six hours with only a few short breaks. The members went about their business in an efficient and professional manner, and from the candid perspective of this outsider, rather coldly and dispassionately. The only softening or easing in the formality of the proceedings from them seemed to be reserved for those soldiers they dropped from the program. They took a few moments with each to try to ease the disappointment of their non-selection and to encourage them to continue to serve their nation and their Army. But no more than that. On balance, it was an inquisition. They knew what they were looking for in a young Ranger, and they moved straight to the core of what it takes to soldier in the 75th Ranger Regiment. That it was both emotional and probably a little terrifying for those who appeared before them was not part of their calculus.

The men who sat on the RASP 1 Board are charged with life and death responsibility—the lives of those they select and send forward and the lives of the serving Rangers who will have to depend on the courage and performance of these new men. There were five Purple Hearts among the seven members of the board. Between them, they had close to seventy combat rotations and literally thousands of combat operations. Who better qualified than these seasoned men to decide who is and who is not fit to join this warrior brotherhood? They did their duty—no more and certainly no less.

For this observer, it was high drama. I spoke to the two sergeant candidates afterward. "I've never been through something like that," Sergeant Ikenboch said of the ordeal. "And I've never been so nervous. It was like going into combat."

"I'm just glad it's behind me," said Sergeant Sadler. "I felt it could have gone either way. Thank God it went my way. I've wanted to be in this Regiment a long time. Now I'll get my chance."

Following the RASP 1 Board, the class is set for graduation. For Class 09-10, thirty-nine soldiers will don the Tan Berets of the 75th Ranger Regiment and wear the Ranger Scroll of their new battalion. Late on Wednesday afternoon, the candidates learn where in the Regiment they will serve. Eleven of these new Rangers will be heading for 1/75 at Hunter Army Airfield in Savannah, twenty-three will go to 3/75 right here at Fort Benning, and three, including Private

First Class Hayward, will join 2/75 at Fort Lewis, Washington. Two from 09-10 receive orders to the Regimental Special Troops Battalion at Fort Benning. The 2nd Ranger Battalion is the deployed battalion, and those going to 2/75 may or may not join them on deployment. This will depend on how 2/75 chooses to handle new Rangers who come to it while deployed. Those going to 3/75 will have their work cut out for them, as their Battalion is the next one out the door. The men are already in predeployment work-up, and will rotate overseas right after the first of the year. Those going to 1/75 have best hit the rotation cycle. The 1st Battalion is just now completing their postdeployment leave period. The new Rangers from Class 09-10 assigned to 1/75 will be joining their new squads and fire teams at the beginning of a deployment training cycle. I will be joining them at 1/75 as well in order to see how one battalion prepares its new Rangers for their first combat rotation.

Thursday is all about last-minute administration tasks, turning in equipment, and rehearsal for graduation. In anticipation of graduation, the families and friends of Class 09-10 are trickling into Columbus. The soon-to-be-Rangers are given time as their duties permit to help their families with their accommodations and arrangements.

Friday is graduation. The ceremony will take place at 0900 at Freedom Hall, a cavernous building on the edge of the Fort Benning airfield tarmac. When not being used for Ranger graduations or other Army graduation ceremonies, it is a staging area for mass parachute drops and for units deploying or redeploying from the battlespace. The graduation of Class 09-10 is a simple ceremony with high-tech, high-speed Ranger training videos being flashed on overhead projections. Sergeant First Class Tad Collier serves as the master of ceremonies. The commander of the Regimental Special Troops Battalion is the presiding senior officer, since all of RASP training is under his unit's command. Private First Class Alex Hammond marches Class 09-10 to front and center. They are in freshly pressed ACUs, and their freshly shaved heads glisten in the arc lighting of the hanger-like facility. Sergeant Collier welcomes the visitors, then introduces the graduation speaker, Command Sergeant Major William Acebes (Ret.). Acebes is a Vietnam-era Ranger with thirty years of active service. He has served as Command Sergeant Major for the 1st Battalion of the 64th Armor Regiment, the 1st Ranger Battalion, the 2nd Infantry Division, and U.S. Army Infantry Center. He is humorous, eloquent, and brief.

"They ask me to do this from time to time," he later confided in me, "probably because I make it a point to be brief. I do in fact try to keep it short. The longer I talk, the less time these kids have with their parents and sweethearts. But I love seeing 'em; they're all great kids. And serving as a graduation speaker now and then is about the only work left for a sixty-five-year-old Ranger."

Following Command Sergeant Major Acebes's remarks, Sergeant Collier steps in front of Class 09-10 and orders, "Don berets!" Each former candidate fishes into his left cargo pocket and pulls out a Tan Beret. It takes a few moments for them to complete the task. The setting of the Ranger headgear—with the Ranger flash set at a jaunty angle and the flat portion of the beret laid over the left ear just so—takes a little time. They'll get better at this; it's their first time. When they are finished, Sergeant Collier salutes them, and then he asks for family and friends to come forward to pin on their Ranger Scrolls. Actually, they stick on by way of Velcro. All Rangers wear the 75th Regimental Scroll, specific for their Ranger battalion, on their left shoulder. Once they have made a combat tour, they will wear the Ranger Battalion Scroll on their right shoulder. With berets and scrolls in place, Sergeant Collier returns to the podium. He then announces the class and cadre honorees.

"Specialist James Neuman, Private Kevin Seiple, Private First Class Brendan O'Connor, Private First Class Alex Hammond, Staff Sergeant Bill Bateman, and Staff Sergeant Edward David—front and center." Those named join Private First Class Hammond in front of the class.

Specialist Neuman, the quiet soldier from Missouri who served only briefly as 09-10's class leader just before its ordeal at Cole Range, is the Distinguished Honor Graduate. He was selected by the RASP 1 cadre for this award due to his overall performance and leadership. James Neuman, like Alex Hammond, was a solid performer who, while not being the best at any one thing, did everything well. More important, he helped those around him to do everything just a little better. These are the kind of new Rangers the squad and fire-team leaders hope they receive when they're assigned new men.

Private Kevin Seiple, the young guitarist-turned-Ranger, had the best marksmanship scores and is awarded the Class Top Gun Award. The popular Brendan O'Conner achieved the highest marks on the Ranger Physical Fitness Test to earn the Physical Fitness Award. Bateman and David were voted by the class as the most professional cadre sergeants from Phase One and Phase Two, respectively. All of the honorees, including Private First Class Hammond, receive a plaque presented by the RSTB commander.

After the honorees fall back into ranks, the audience rises while the class members recite the Ranger Creed, just as they have done each morning at morning chow formation for the last two months. Today, there is a special timbre in their voices and the final "Rangers lead the way" is deafening.

"This concludes the graduation ceremony for RASP Level One, Class 09-10," Sergeant Collier announces to the gathering. "In about fifteen minutes, we will begin a short presentation for the new Ranger families in the bleachers just behind this hall. There we will give you an overview of the deployment cycle of your Rangers, and some of what they will be doing in the months ahead. Thank you all for attending this graduation."

The new Rangers will not officially be released from RASP until the next week, but they are free until Monday morning. All that's left for them on this graduation Friday is to remove the last of their gear from the RASP barracks. They will be allowed to shift into civilian clothes for their final RASP muster. While they return to the RASP barracks, many of the families remain at Freedom Hall for the family briefing.

Sergeant Collier again conducts the proceedings with Major Matthews, the Ranger Selection and Training Company commander, standing nearby. He shows them a short video that addresses the current Ranger deployment cycle of four-to-five-month rotations to the battlespace and the seven-to-eight months in garrison. He also addresses the nature of Ranger operations overseas, but not in great detail.

"I want to thank you in advance," Sergeant Collier tells the families, "for the continued support of your loved ones as they carry out the Ranger mission. In many ways, your job is more difficult than our job. Typically, our Rangers will have a period of block leave just before they go on deployment and when they come back home. While they are back here in garrison, they will be training for the next deployment, so even when they're home they may not be released from duty every night. While your Ranger is on deployment, he'll be able to call you, but you will not be able to call him. E-mail is probably your best source of contact. We ask a lot of our deployed Rangers, but writing home is not something we can make them do, so it's on him to stay in touch." Collier quickly goes over a short list of Army and regimental support organizations and provides a website address for reference. "And finally, I want you to know that in the Regiment, we put great premium on leadership. Please know that the finest leaders in the United States Army will be leading and caring for your Rangers in the months ahead." During my time at RASP 2 at the 1st Ranger Battalion, I was to learn more about the close scrutiny and attention this Regiment gives to its leaders.

"Now I know you're anxious to be with your new Rangers," Collier concludes, "so I'll now open it up for questions. Please feel free to leave at any time. I know you're not here this day to listen to me, but know that myself, my company commander, and the rest of the cadre will be here as long as you have any questions for us." There are several questions, and many remain after the formal Q&A to speak with Sergeant Collier and the others.

The final formation of Class 09-10 takes place on the rocks shortly before noon. The newest Rangers are in civilian clothes, but they are clearly soldiers masquerading as civilians. They stand in ranks amid duffel bags and a scattering of personal gear. Again, it's Sergeant Collier before them.

"All right, men, take a knee." They fold in around him and drop to one knee. "You've worked hard, and you've earned the right to call yourselves Rangers. Don't go out this weekend and get in trouble and blow all that hard work. It's easy to be disciplined when you have no freedoms. We've kept you focused here in RASP and on a tight leash. Now you can do as you please, but remember who you are now. You're a Ranger, and we hold each other to Ranger standards. If you're out drinking, and you all deserve a beer or two if that's what you choose, but just remember to be responsible." He then gives them their reporting times and locations for the following week. "Good luck, be safe, and I look forward to serving with you in Regiment."

The former candidates from Class 09-10 scatter with their gear to join their families, friends, and ladies. I watch them disperse with Staff Sergeant Martinez. "Sergeant Collier had it right," he comments. "It's easy to stay straight and not get in trouble when you're not allowed to drink, drive, smoke, use a cell phone, and you're restricted to the post. We have a saying for that. 'It's easier to get to Regiment than to stay in Regiment.' But these are a good bunch of kids. I don't think we'll have any problems. I'd have any one of them in my squad."

The books are now closed on RASP Level One Class 09-10. They now belong to the 75th Ranger Regiment. Breaking them down by

MOS, thirty-two are Eleven Bravo infantrymen, four are combat medics, two are communicators, and one is a forward observer. Thirty-five of the thirty-nine new Rangers will go straight to their assigned battalions. Ten of these new Rangers, including the two communicators and one forward observer, will attend the three-week basic Radio Telephone Operator (RTO) course at Fort Benning before joining their battalions. The four class medics will initially be assigned to the Ranger Medical Section located in one end of the RASP building here at Fort Benning.

The RTO course is conducted by the Ranger Communications Company, Ranger Special Troops Battalion. This course is in high demand, as every squad leader in the Regiment wants to have as many men qualified to operate a radio as possible. The seats in each ten-man RTO class are first allocated to the communicators and forward observers. Then they're opened up for Eleven Bravos. In the RTO course, the students get theory and hands-on training on how to set up frequencies and call signs for Ranger tactical operations, and how to operate standard military radios and those radios used only by Rangers. Most of the Eleven Bravos in this RTO class are new 3/75 Rangers.

The four combat medics will follow a much different path from their fellow Ranger classmates. While they await a class assignment to the next six-month Special Operations Combat Medic Course, they will be assigned clinical duties at the Ranger Medical Section. The Special Operations Combat Medic Course is the gold standard for combat medical care. A great many Rangers owe their lives to the skill of their SOCM-trained Ranger medics. In addition to taking sick-call rotations, they will also attend specially arranged classes on anatomy, physiology, and medical terminology at Columbus State University. Once they complete their SOCM training, they will then head off to their Ranger battalions. For some of these Ranger medics, it could be nine months to a year before they join their battalions.

On September 6, 2010, there were 159 souls on the original roster of Class 09-10. The official "class-up" number, including the four soldiers who joined the class after the class left the Holdover barracks, was 147. Of those soldiers, thirty-six were able to don a Tan Beret on November 5, 2010. Three who graduated with this class were Phase Two inserts who completed Phase One with another class. As many as two dozen others who began with 09-10 recycled for injuries or other reasons. Some of those, perhaps as many as half of them, will graduate with a future RASP 1 class. Of the sixteen college graduates who began with Class 09-10, only four earned their Tan Beret. Of the fourteen married soldiers who began, just five are Rangers. There were four soldiers who were naturalized U.S. citizens, and only one of those graduated. Close to a dozen African American soldiers began with Class 09-10; only one is now a Ranger.

Class 09-10 roughly conforms to the 26 to 28 percent graduation rate of previous RASP 1 classes. And these figures roughly conform to the graduation rate for the four-week Ranger Indoctrination Program (RIP) that preceded RASP 1. Only time will tell just how well the RASP process will better serve the Regiment than its predecessor, the Ranger Indoctrination Course. The RIP graduates I speak with, including Sergeant Mark Ikenboch, who is a graduate of both programs, say that RIP was basically a physical screening. They maintain that RIP was a cruder version of Phase One of RASP 1—an assessment for heart with very little training. I'm told that new Rangers who arrive at their battalions with training in marksmanship, breaching, driving, and combatives are more easily integrated into their squads and fire teams than their predecessors, who had none of this training. I will learn more about this when I get to my battalion.

As an outsider, but someone familiar with other SOF training venues, I'm often asked by the RASP cadre and others in the Regiment about the RASP 1 process. How does this assessment and selection process compare with other SOF entry-level programs? What do I think of the physical standards imposed during Phase

One? Of the instruction being given during Phase Two? It's clear to me that the assessment and selection cadres and those up the chain of command are proud and optimistic about the relatively new RASP 1 process. It may be a little presumptive of me to weigh in on this, and, indeed, I may never be in that position. Yet there is one aspect of this process in which I do claim the experience of observation and can comment with some confidence. The cadre sergeants in Phase One and Phase Two are superb Rangers and role models—they are the equal, and then some, of any I've encountered in other SOF training venues. They embody a personal standard that is more important than any individual skill set. The longer these Ranger candidates are allowed to be in the close company of these role models, the better for all concerned. I've said and written a great deal about the issues and, yes, the deficiencies, of the Millennial generation. The transformation of a me-generation individual into a warrior is difficult and challenging for all concerned. Yet among the attributes of the Millennials is brand identification. These young, and in many cases not-so-young, soldiers are looking for a brand—an association. At this point in their Ranger journey, that brand is embodied in the assessment and selection cadres. The effects of this imprinting are more telling in Phase Two than Phase One simply because of the ratio of pain to teaching in the two phases. But it's ongoing, start to finish. The more these new men are able to look back on their RASP experience and say, "I want to be like Sergeant Bateman," or "I want to be like Sergeant David"—or like Sergeant Iselin, Sergeant Martinez, and Sergeant Collier—the better served is the new Ranger and the 75th Ranger Regiment.

As these new Rangers move on to their new assignments in their battalions, so do I. My next duty station for this work will be 1/75—the 1st Ranger Battalion at Hunter Army Airfield in Savannah. I can't wait. It's the next stage of their journey, and mine.

CHAPTER FIVE

RASP TWO, SURT, AND THE SCHOOL

RASP Two

RASP 2 appears, on first glance, to be a shortened version of RASP 1. The subject matter, including the physical testing and some of the basic professional requirements, are similar and are individually tested in the same way. A few of the critical events are much the same. Other professional and leadership requirements are different and designed around the specific roles and duties of these senior Ranger candidates. One important difference is the attention that is given to the psych evaluations and the rigorous ordeal of the RASP 2 Board. And there is the issue of expectations. In RASP 1, the emphasis is on assessing the heart of the soldier and his potential to master the skill set he'll need to serve in a Ranger squad. Is he tough enough and smart enough to be a Ranger? Can he grow into the job? Will he listen to the veteran Rangers he will be serving with? The focus of RASP 2 is the selection of leaders—men with proven track records who have the potential to assume positions of increased responsibility in the Regiment. The RASP 2 Board will carefully review the experience and prior service of an officer or a senior NCO, as well as how he comports himself during the RASP 2 selection and assessment process. Their job is to determine this individual's potential to serve as a leader in the Regiment. To call it a condensed version of RASP 1 is only partly valid. To characterize it as an executive or gentlemen's course would not be right. RASP 2 candidates are given a much narrower window in which to hit their assessment gates, and, as in RASP 1, they must perform to standard.

There are two kinds of soldiers who come through RASP 2: those who are new to the Regiment and those who are not. Those regimental veterans include virtually every infantry (11A, or Eleven Alpha) officer who is a senior captain or above and every Eleven Bravo infantryman who is a staff sergeant or senior. These Infantry Branch officers are generally bound for senior billets in the Regiment, such as company commander or senior staff positions. They have previously served in the Regiment and are returning for a second or even third tour. The senior enlisted leaders are usually NCOs currently serving in the Regiment and are now assuming duties as a platoon sergeant, company first sergeant, or higher. Occasionally, there will be a senior noncommissioned officer returning to the Regiment after a tour of duty outside the 75th or a senior sergeant with broken service returning to the fold. However, most senior Eleven Bravos now coming through RASP 2 are prospective platoon sergeants and company first sergeants. The roles of platoon sergeant and first sergeant are key leadership positions in the Regiment, and these veteran Ranger NCOs are made to leave their battalions to successfully complete RASP 2 prior to assuming these new responsibilities in their platoons and companies. The recent inclusion of these senior Ranger NCO candidates signals the recognition of the importance of their leadership position.

The other variety of RASP 2 candidates are those joining the Regiment for the first time. In the officer ranks, there are the Infantry Branch junior officers—the young Eleven Alphas. These are the prospective Ranger platoon leaders—first lieutenants and junior captains who have successfully led platoons in a line infantry company. Many will return to the Regiment in more senior positions as they gain rank and experience. Others will take what they learn during this tour as a junior Ranger leader as a foundation for an Infantry Branch career in the conventional Army. Occasionally, there are first or even second lieutenants in RASP 2 who are returning to the Regiment. Former enlisted men with prior enlisted regimental service reenter the Regiment as junior officers by way of RASP 2. If they made staff sergeant, or E-6, before they were commissioned, they may return to the Regiment as freshly minted second lieutenants. Those being commissioned from the ranks who were buck sergeants or junior will first serve as infantry leaders in another unit before returning to the Regiment. Other first-timers, both officers and senior enlisted soldiers, represent the specialties without which the Regiment could not function: medical, logistics, intelligence, administration, and communications. The chaplains and the doctors enter the Regiment by way of RASP 2, as do the cooks, combat medics, and truck drivers over in RASP 1. New noncommissioned officers, staff sergeants and above with select specialty MOSs such as cryptologists, information technology (IT) specialists, or veterinary technicians, will enter the Regiment through RASP 2. And all who are to remain with the Regiment, if they have not already done so, are expected to successfully complete Ranger School. In most cases, these senior noncoms, if they don't have a Tab, will attend Ranger School once they have successfully been assessed in RASP 2. On occasion, an NCO or officer will have to complete both Airborne School and Ranger School. Both the Scroll and the Ranger Tab, along with the Airborne Badge, are symbols of leadership in the unique warrior culture that is the 75th Ranger Regiment. Yet for all RASP candidates, the Scroll is the immediate goal and the prize.

As with RASP 1, there is no "typical" RASP 2 class. The classes usually range in size from twenty to twenty-eight candidates. Leadership within a RASP 2 class is administrative in nature and falls primarily to the senior NCO. I was able to observe RASP 2 Class 10-10 and selected portions of Class 01-11. Class 10-10 began with twenty-four candidates. Twenty-two met the physical testing minimums, and nineteen were selected to serve in the Regiment. In 01-11, twenty-two began, twenty tested out, and eighteen were selected by the RASP 2 Board, consisting of senior leaders from the Regiment. These numbers are representative, if not typical.

Shortly after the convening of a RASP 2 class, the men are briefed by the Regimental Commanding Officer or the Regimental Deputy Commanding Officer. Usually, one or the other of these two senior leaders is overseas. For Class 10-10, it was the deputy commander who briefed the class.

"Welcome to RASP Two," he told this class. "For those of you returning to us, welcome back. The Regimental Commander is currently with the forward-deployed units, but he sends his regards. First of all, thank you for volunteering to serve or to again serve with the Seventy-fifth Ranger Regiment. You've all distinguished yourselves at your previous commands, and you've been highly screened just to be in this RASP Two class. We here at Regiment are both pleased and blessed to have you with us. You are the future leaders of the Regiment, and this course has been designed with great care to help you in assuming those leadership duties. The cadre sergeants who will be working with you are our best; they've been carefully selected to assist you during this course. But with due deference to your performance at your current command and your professional credentials aside, this is an assessment and selection course. Over the next three weeks, you will have to show us that you have prepared yourself to be here and that you are willing and capable to shoulder these new responsibilities. You have to demonstrate that you are deserving of a position of leadership and trust in this Regiment. Those brave young Rangers we are all privileged to lead demand nothing less."

The deputy commanding officer briefly talked about the unprecedented level of OPTEMPO. In 2010, he tells them, Rangers have enjoyed a great deal of operational success. Yet these successes on the battlefield have not been without cost.

"During the first eight months of this year, we have conducted close to fifteen hundred combat operations. Those operations have led to many hundreds of hard-core enemy fighters being killed or captured. We've also lost fourteen young Rangers and sixty more have been wounded, many seriously. The surge in Afghanistan has caused us to deploy some units early and to hold others longer on deployment. Yet, as far as closing with the enemy, no one in the battlespace does it more often or better than the Seventy-fifth Ranger Regiment. So, as you can see, we are a regiment at war on a wartime footing." He pauses to survey the twenty-four members of Class 10-10. "Again, welcome to the Seventy-fifth. Show the selection and assessment cadre that you belong here and we have a job for you. Good luck to all of you."

Following the briefing of the regimental deputy commander, the Ranger Selection and Training Company commander and his company first sergeant gave the candidates an overview of their RASP course: what they can expect, what is expected of them, and a litany of the procedure, rules, and conventions that will govern their time at RASP. The S&T commander also spoke to the specific roles of his cadre sergeants in the RASP 2 selection process. The bulk of this assessment and selection course for regimental officers and senior NCOs will be carried out by S&T senior enlisted sergeants.

The physical standards of RASP 2 are addressed on a "pay-to-play basis." Candidates are expected to arrive at RASP 2 prepared for assessment; this is a proving ground, not a training ground. Within the first three days, they must pass the minimums on the Ranger Physical Fitness Test, run 5 miles in under 40 minutes, and complete a 12-mile ruck march in under 3 hours. There is no cadre-led preparation; they must stand and deliver. Of the twenty-four candidates in RASP 2 Class 10-10, two men fail to meet these minimum standards and are dismissed from selection. A number of the others are moving about on sore legs the next day, much like the RASP 1 candidates after Cole Range, but they have made standard. For the record, the best RPFT score (age adjusted) was 334. Top scores were 90 push-ups, 97 sit-ups, 22 pull-ups, and a 2-mile run time of just under 12 minutes. The best 5-mile run time was 31 minutes and 39 seconds. The first candidate in on the 12-mile ruck march, over a hilly course on a very hot day, did it in 2 hours and 28 minutes.

Other critical events during their first week of RASP 2 are much the same as for the RASP 1 critical events. There is Ranger First Responder training and qualification and the Ranger standards/history written exam. The RFR training and practical application is the same, but the material is delivered in a one-day window rather than the two days given for RASP 1 candidates. All these officers and NCOs have had first-aid training, and many have had this same RFR course. Due to the smaller number of candidates, they are able to get through the classroom material and move on to the practical application more quickly. The Ranger standards/history exam, like other RASP 2 critical events, is a onetime, go or no-go evaluation. By the end of the final evolution on Friday, the candidates must have completed and turned in their psychological evaluation questionnaires. Between the graded events, there are classes on breaching, Ranger-specific weapons, and operational fire support.

Week two of RASP 2 has no critical events or tests, other than the continuous observation and assessment by the ever-watchful RASP 2 cadre sergeants. Week two will cover marksmanship and combat shooting. The candidates are expected to display proficiency on the range with the standard M9 Beretta 9-millimeter pistol and the M4 rifle. As in RASP 1, marksmanship training and qualification is based on the safe handling of weapons in combat-shooting scenarios. Here again, the instruction parallels that of RASP 1. With the M9, the focus is on range safety, shooting mechanics, and putting the weapon into action from the holster. There is barrier-shooting training and the El Presidente shooting event. With the M4, they zero their weapons and shoot a series of timed drills at multiple targets. Time permitting, there is a stress shoot for the RASP 2 candidates. All the while, the RASP 2 candidates are being assessed on their ability to take instruction and how they comport themselves on the shooting ranges. Which of them works to improve his shooting? Which of them is the first to help a fellow candidate? Many of them shoot very well, but how do they take to the coaching and corrections of the cadre shooting instructors? Which of them is the first on his feet from a break and hustles to prepare for the next evolution?

In the being-trained-while-assessed category are the fast-rope drills and the time in the shoot house. While several candidates in Class 10-10 have fast-roped, this is the first time for many in the class. The twenty-two candidates meet well before dawn on Honor Field and are briefed on fast-roping. They make four passes down a fast-rope suspended from the fifty-foot tower, once Hollywood, or without combat kit in the lighted area, and once with kit. Then the cadre turn out the lights, and they do it again in the dark. Again, fast-roping is a key Ranger skill, and these future Ranger leaders will do this again as their regimental duties allow or dictate. For the future platoon leaders and platoon sergeants, they will do this often under operational conditions.

The shoot-house evolution is a repeat for some, a first-time experience for others. This shooting evolution is scheduled for RASP 2, but not RASP 1. The shoot house at Fort Benning is a maze of rooms defined by specially formed concrete barriers that can both absorb and not ricochet live rounds, including the high-velocity 5.56-millimeter rounds from the M4 rifle. The "house" itself is an open-air, shed-roofed complex served by a gantry system that can move, replace, and reconfigure the concrete partitions. The RASP 2 candidates conduct room-clearing drills in teams of four-shooter stacks, first with blank ammunition, then with live rounds. In the rooms are silhouettes of armed bad guys and bad guys holding hostages in front of them—targets to be engaged quickly and targets to be engaged carefully. This is precision combat shooting. All shooting is red-dot shooting, during which the targets are engaged with the M4-mounted LA-5 visual lasers. After each round of shooting, the candidate shooters receive coaching and instruction—and assessment. Following the live-fire drills, silhouette targets are scored, hits to the bad guys are counted, and stray rounds that may have found a hostage or a noncombatant are noted.

"Here again," the lead cadre sergeant tells me, "not all of these candidates have been in a shoot house, and they need to see this at least once." We are standing on one of the catwalks where the room-clearing drills can be viewed and critiqued. "The platoon-leader and platoon-sergeant candidates have all done this, and depending on their previous unit or previous assignment in the Regiment, they may have a lot of time in the shoot house. Yet few of the officers will be doing this kind of operational shooting." He grins. "Oh, a few of them will put themselves in the stack from time to time, but it's not their job. Their job is to manage the overall fight and stay with the big picture; they'll be on the radio coordinating the support assets. The platoon sergeants will be closer to the fight than the officer platoon leaders, but more often than not, they'll find themselves coordinating the fight. This kind of shooting is for the squads and fire teams. We want all of them to experience this, and for the Eleven Alphas and senior Eleven Bravos, it's a review of their close-quarter shooting mechanics. For the rising platoon sergeants and first sergeants, the cadre assess their ability to train the other candidates in the course, as they are all masters of close-quarter combat from their years of experience in the Regiment. During their battalion workups, they'll be up here on the catwalk observing and critiquing the shooting of their squads and fire teams, or at least they should be. This is the work of the Ranger assault teams."

Thursday and Friday of the RASP 2, week two, are given over to the field-training exercise with the RASP 1 class. This FTX, including the morning team PT session, the parachute jump, and the beginning of the Cole Range portion of the exercise, has been touched on earlier in this book. The RASP 2 candidates are assessed throughout the exercise, but particularly so during their time at Cole Range. Cole Range activity is designed to push the RASP 2 candidates and to assess their decision making when they're tired. One such drill requires each candidate, after a round of Cole Range PT, to complete a simple task, such as moving several wooden pallets over a barrier. But there are constraints to this seemingly simple task, so it's no easy chore. To accomplish his mission, the candidate must come up with a plan, then organize and lead his assigned RASP 1 soldiers to get the job done. His problem-solving and organizational skills are on display.

Just before dark, the senior candidates take to the woods with a rucksack, a combat kit, a rifle, and two or three enlisted Ranger candidates from RASP 1. They are further armed with map and compass, a light, a radio, and a set of night-vision devices (NVDs). The RASP 2 candidates enter the woods on a navigation course that will take them to a number of stations, where they'll be presented with mini-mission scenarios. At each station they'll be asked to accomplish a mission or tasking. These taskings relate to, but are not limited to, instruction they may have received since they came to Ranger assessment and selection. It will take the candidates most of the night. I'm being a little vague here by design; I've been asked by the S&T cadre to keep the specifics of this part of RASP 2 assessment confidential. I can, however, say that the stations were challenging, realistic, and well thought out. How the candidates respond to and resolve these taskings will become a part of their assessment package.

The FTX is also the only time the RASP 2 candidates are observed actually leading troops, and their leadership and interpersonal skills are carefully noted. In many cases, the RASP 1 candidates are asked for their impressions of how well they were led or how well they interacted with their RASP 2 team leaders.

The final week of RASP 2 is a busy one—physically, professionally, and, most of all, emotionally. There is a RAW assessment, a body-fat measurement, briefings on the Regiment, and administrative matters such as equipment turn-in and course critiques. But the key event of this third and final week, the one that will determine the immediate professional future for these officers and senior NCOs, is the RASP 2 Assessment and Selection Board. All that has taken place since they entered the assessment and selection process comes down to their appearance before this board. They all know the deal. They will stand before this board of senior Ranger officers and enlisted leaders, and they will be grilled on their physical, professional, personal, and psychological suitability to serve in the 75th Ranger Regiment. Information from each candidate's Army career and the RASP 2 assessment process are organized, formatted, and assembled for the RASP 2 Board—electronically and on hard copy.

In preparation for this final week of their assessment, the RASP 2 candidates will have completed the standard battery of personality and psychological exams in preparation for their one-on-one psych interviews. These include the standard Minnesota Multiphasic Personality Inventory, the Shipley IQ test, the Jackson Personality Inventory, and a pre-lie-detector test. Unlike the RASP 1 candidates during their psych evaluations, each RASP 2 candidate—at least those who have no apparent psychological issues—meets for an hour or two with a PhD psychologist. This is done over the weekend before the final week of RASP 2.

"Our primary task here," one of the psychologists told me, "is to take the information derived from these tests and what we learn during the interviews, and make it available to the RASP 2 Board in the format they require. We provide a psychological assessment and evaluation, and that becomes a part of each candidate's board package. As a secondary task, we provide feedback and individual assessment to the individual candidates. We tell the soldiers what characteristics we find that are positive or complimentary to his military duties and where we think he might be weak. Depending on the individual, we may get into some personal and private issues. These are very successful and motivated officers and senior NCOs. They generally know themselves pretty well. And this is not the first time they've been assessed or had their personality critiqued, though perhaps not in this detail. Most find this feedback helpful, and it usually doesn't conflict with their own perceptions of themselves. At this stage of their military careers, most candidates have a good idea of their strengths and weaknesses. For the most part, it's a validation, but often we're able to shed some light on a trait or perception of which they're not aware. And they get a chance to ask questions. Within our time constraints, we answer them as best we can and give them as much honest feedback as we can.

"We do this for other SOF units," he said. "Each special operations component is different—culturally and professionally. Yet aside from weeding out pathologies which are exceptionally rare, all SOF units have similar requirements in what they're looking for in their troops as well as their senior leaders. Few of these candidates are normal in the civilian context or in even the context of other military personnel. These are type A individuals who want to excel— need to excel. All of them are risk takers, yet with proscribed boundaries and qualifications on the risks they take. Special operations components in general are looking for smart people, and they're looking for stability, reliability, and team play. But there are differences. Some SOF units will put more of a premium on specific traits like creativity and problem solving. Others look for adaptability. We find the Rangers to be more structured and more demanding of an adherence to a standard. I think they're looking for predictability—men who will stay in their lanes and leaders who will insist on a high standard of performance in themselves and those they lead. They want men who will perform in their assigned roles and who will continue to work to improve their professional skill sets. On balance, the Ranger Regiment is looking for smart, fit, disciplined, adaptive leaders that will push themselves and the units to accomplish their assigned special operations taskings."

"I found the whole process fascinating," a young first lieutenant—a West Pointer—told me, "and useful. I've never had this type of screening before, and I learned a lot. The psych eval confirmed much of what I knew of myself, but it helped me to focus on other aspects of my personality. Some of those aspects were not positive," he admits with an easy smile, "but they were spot on, and it made me aware of some of the areas where I need to improve. I found it very worthwhile and informative, and more than a little humbling."

This from another first lieutenant: "I think the interview was primarily to confirm that we weren't trying to game the psych tests—that we were honest and forthcoming in our answers and that the information that comes out of these tests represents who we really are."

"Did you learn anything new?" I asked.

He considers this for a moment. "I did. For example, the psychologist suggested that I needed to expand my vocabulary—that I don't always express myself as well as I might. Actually, I've always been told that I speak and write well. I'm going to do some thinking about that one. Perhaps he was right; perhaps that's an area where I can improve."

The only physical evolution for the RASP 2 candidates during their third and final week of RASP is the Ranger Physical Assessment Test (RPAT). For these candidates, it will not be graded as a critical event, but is an introduction to what one cadre sergeant called the mother of all PT tests. The RPAT is designed to be a Ranger squad event and can be run as a team-building exercise. It can be run in Ranger-buddy pairs or as an individual competition to see who's fit and who's *really* fit. Each Ranger runs the RPAT course in full combat kit, body armor, and Kevlar helmet, which together weigh between 40 and 50 pounds, depending on plates and ammunition load. The course begins with a 2-mile run, followed by a 20-foot rope climb and controlled descent. Next, the Ranger competitors must drag a 160-pound sled for 100 yards. Then they climb up and down a 20-foot caving ladder, sprint 100 yards, climb an 8-foot wall, and sprint another 100 yards. The final event is a 1-mile run.

"It was hard," one of the Eleven Bravo NCOs said to me, "but not as hard as I thought it might be, as we did it as a group and I'm in pretty good shape. I did drink about a gallon of water. I'm sure I lost several pounds, and I'm glad it's October and not August."

The final requirement prior to the candidates' appearance before the RASP 2 Board is their board essay. The candidates are given a topic and an hour to complete the essay. No computers or word processors are allowed. The board wants to see how they write in longhand and whether they can spell and punctuate without word-processor help. This is an exercise I personally would not care for. The essay is designed to see how the candidates cogently express their thoughts in a short period of time. The essay topics are probative and revealing, and may ask the candidate to be candid about his personal life. It's yet another means of finding out more about the candidate in preparation for the board.

Another important input to the board is the peer review. Even among a contingent as carefully screened as these RASP 2 candidates, there are varying levels of skill, leadership, and ability to work with others, and these candidates are forced to rank and rate those they would most and least like to serve with, and why. This is never easy, especially in a group like this, but always useful and revealing.

Like the RASP 1 candidates, they will comment on the top and bottom two individuals, but they must also rank their entire class from top to bottom.

Then there is the collective assessment of the RASP 2 cadre sergeants. Unlike in RASP 1, especially the Phase One portion of RASP 1, there has been no harassment and certainly no "corrective training." The cadre sergeants in RASP 2 teach, demonstrate, mentor, test, and assess. On occasion I hear, "Hey, sir, you better step it up here," or "Sergeant, you need a better grasp on how this is done," but at all times the interaction is professional, courteous, and measured.

"You'd be surprised," the senior cadre sergeant told me, "just how closely the peer reviews, the psych evaluations, and our cadre assessments are aligned. These are all good men, but some simply break out better by comparison, or their personal traits are more in keeping with the kind of soldiering we do here in the Regiment."

Tucked in and around the candidate appearances before the RASP 2 Board during this final week of RASP 2 are operational and regimental briefings. There are briefings on advanced communications and the technical intelligence-collection apparatus that serve the deployed Ranger elements. There is an ethics brief. And there is a series of briefings and presentations on the diverse and enabling capabilities of the Regimental Special Troops Battalion. Many of these were well above my security classification, but one that was not was the Duties and Responsibilities briefing given by Major Ned Matthews, the Ranger Selection and Training Company commander.

"This briefing will get a little heavy on the duties and responsibilities on the operations side of the house, so it may be a little off point for those of you with technical or support-related responsibilities. Yet the tone of this will apply to all of you—all of us. It's been said many times that the Army is an officer-led, NCO-run organization. That's certainly true here in the Regiment, but I think it goes deeper than that. There are many reasons for this, not the least of which is that we officers come and go; the NCOs don't. So we ask our Ranger NCOs to not only run the Regiment, but to take on expanded leadership roles, especially on the operational side of the house. It's something that we officers have to understand, and while it affects how this Regiment conducts its business, it's especially important in our combat operations."

Twenty-two RASP 2 candidates from Class 10-10 are scheduled to appear before the RASP 2 Board. They know that there is little that will not be available to this board, from the evaluations that have taken place over the past two weeks to their entire service record. The details of their professional and personal history will be under close review. The candidates also know and understand that the RASP 2 Board will be formal and candid, and that there is nothing off-limits. Their performance—their strengths as well as shortcomings—will be addressed in detail. Each will be made to speak to any negative aspect of the current RASP evaluation or to any point in time during their previous military service. They know it will be an emotional and perhaps uncomfortable ordeal. They also know it will be a tribunal of sorts, one to which they have voluntarily submitted themselves and which will determine the immediate direction of their military career. Nothing from my experience with the RASP 1 Board, or other SOF selection boards I've been privileged to observe, prepared me for the in-depth screening that awaited these RASP 2 candidates.

The RASP 2 Board is composed of voting and nonvoting members. The nonvoting members include the psychologists, the senior RASP 2 cadre sergeant, the regimental administrative assistant, and, at times, a subject-matter expert. The administrative assistant briefs the candidate's package, providing an overview of his background and military career and any omissions from the packet. The subject-matter expert is there to provide an evaluation of those candidates who bring a technical skill or specific military specialty. For example, the regimental fire support officer was present to question and advise the board on a candidate artillery officer whose duties at the Regiment will entail mortar, artillery, and air support for Ranger missions. The regimental veterinarian was there for the boarding of an NCO vet tech. No additional subject-matter expertise was required for the Eleven Alpha infantry officers or Eleven Bravo infantry NCOs. The five voting members of the RASP 2 Board are senior Ranger infantrymen.

I was allowed to sit in on the Rasp 2 Board for Class 10-10, but was asked to reveal no specifics, in deference to a process that will continue to select future leaders of the Regiment. I can say that it was formal and probative. Candidates were asked to make a short presentation on a preassigned topic so the board could assess their knowledge and presentation skills. They were questioned on their military specialties and asked to respond to hypothetical situations that involved leadership and moral dilemmas. There were questions that examined their personal motivations, their perceptions of themselves, and their perceptions of others.

The waiting candidates were then asked to reenter the conference room and to formally report again to the president of the board. The finding of the board, or verdict, is that a candidate is selected, non-selected, or conditionally selected—this latter finding usually in the case of an NCO with a technical MOS who has yet to attend Ranger School. Of the twenty-two candidates from RASP 2 Class 10-10 who were boarded, the board selected nineteen, with one of those being conditional pending his successful completion of Ranger School.

This was not the first time I've witnessed the selection of SOF component leaders, yet it was one of the most thorough. It was formal, direct, and emotionally charged—high drama, indeed. The board proceedings drained me physically, and I can only imagine what it must have been like for the candidates.

"I clearly remember when I was on the other side of the table," a board member told me, "and it's an experience like no other. It's a rare chance to learn something of yourself, but it's still a terrifying ordeal."

"I was here as a lieutenant," one of the newly assessed captains told me, "and prior experience makes it no less emotional, nor easier. If anything, I think it was harder as I kind of knew what to expect, and the anticipation was hell. But once I was in there and responding to questions, I settled down and felt a little more comfortable."

From one first lieutenant: "I haven't been gone over like that since I was a Rat at VMI [an entering freshman at Virginia Military Institute]."

When an officer or NCO is told by the president of the board that he has been selected, the relief is tangible. Each board member rises and shakes hands with the newly selected, or reselected, Ranger.

"Welcome to the Regiment."

"I look forward to serving with you."

"Great to have you with us."

"Congratulations."

But not all the selections by the board are unanimous, nor were they for Class 10-10. This means that some members of the voting board will serve with officers and NCOs whose selection they voted against. Yet I could detect no reservation or lack of warmth on the part of a dissenting voter when he welcomed a new selectee. Both the selectee and the selectors are bound by the will of the selection board.

It is the policy of the current 75th Ranger Regimental Commanding Officer to personally welcome each newly assessed Ranger leader to the Regiment. When this is not possible, which is frequently, it's done remotely by a video teleconference link. For Class 10-10, the OPTEMPO in the battlespace made even this remote welcome impossible. In the RCO's place, the Regimental Special Troops Battalion commander and his command sergeant major stepped in. The battalion commander is a tall, spare man who moves with both an ease and a sense of purpose. He was a voting member of the board, as was his Command Sergeant Major.

"Once again, gentlemen, congratulations on your selection," the RSTB commander says to the selectees. "This has been quite a process you just underwent. Maybe an ordeal might be a better word, am I right?" Nods all around. "So what are some of the takeaways from this experience? Someone? Anyone?"

"A review of our suitability," offers one new Ranger.

"A validation of our skill sets."

"A commitment to the standards of the Regiment."

"All valid," the battalion commander replies, "but I would suggest that what you've just been through is also a valuable and learning tool. Now that it's over and you're not standing in the arena, anticipating the next question, take a moment later today or this evening and seriously reflect on what just took place. You may never have a more honest and candid evaluation of yourselves. Think about what was said to you and how you may have responded. We listened to you and we selected you. Now it's time for you to think about what happened, and to take what you've learned and use it to make yourselves better soldiers and better leaders.

"I'd ask you to take special note of your peer reviews. You will be given your peer reviews as they were given to the RASP Two cadre by your classmates. If someone says, for example, that you are quick to judge others, it's a data point. If two of your peers say that, it's cause for concern. When three or more say it, you have to admit that it's a personality trait. Take this information on board, think about it, and decide what you might do to address this shortcoming. Okay?" Again, nods all around. "We all have shortcomings and negative traits. It's what we do about them that will help us to excel, here in the Regiment or elsewhere.

"Looking ahead, you'll probably never serve in a regiment, or any other unit, at a time of greater operational activity. We are in a fight with a very nasty and determined enemy. We are finding him increasingly competent in the field, and technically and tactically sophisti-cated. He's trying to kill or maim our Rangers and we're trying to kill or capture him. He's willing to die fighting, especially if he can take one or two of us along with him. In September, just this last month, we conducted a hundred ninety-six combat operations. In roughly half of them, we came off target having successfully killed or captured the target individual or individuals. Before 9/11, any one of those operations would have been regarded as a milestone engagement—something that would have been discussed at length throughout the Regiment. Now we do this a half-dozen times a night. It would be commonplace except for the fact that each time a Ranger steps off the ramp of a 47 [MH-47 Chinook helicopter] or sprints from the rear of Stryker [the eight-wheeled armored personnel carrier], he never knows for sure just how much resistance he will face or what kind.

"That fifty percent hit rate did not come without cost. We lost four Rangers in August alone and thirteen were wounded. So as you reflect on these past weeks here at RASP, give some thought to what's ahead and the kind of leadership and attention to duty our Rangers deserve. Again, welcome to the Regiment, and thank you for volun-teering to serve with us. Never forget that each of us earns our Scroll every day. Command Sergeant Major?"

The RSTB Command Sergeant Major is a shorter, older, thicker, and perhaps less-refined version of his battalion commander. Like many Army and infantry sergeant majors, he often punctuates his speech with the invective *hooah* (pronounced "who-ah", with emphasis on the "who"). It can mean just about anything, depend-ing on its usage and how it's spoken—like certain words in the Thai language that are inflection dependent. The RSTB CSM uses the term as a Canadian might use "eh?" or a New Yorker might say "right?" without having asked a direct question. The CSM pushes through a litany of dos and don'ts for between now and when these leaders assume their new regimental responsibilities. Then he moves on to more weighty matters.

"The battlespace is always changing, gents, and we have to be prepared to anticipate and deal with those changes, hooah. I've made twenty-seven deployments in my long career, seven to Afghanistan alone since 9/11. They're all different, and yet they're not different. It's still the basics that make us who we are, hooah. We don't do anything that the regular Army doesn't do. We just do it better. We pride ourselves on our standards. Our standards are no different from Army standards; we just choose to rigidly enforce them, hooah. A great deal of our success on the battlefield comes from this rigid enforcement of standards. Never forget that, and never let your personal standards or those of anyone in the Regiment slip. We are all about Army standards and the pride and professionalism with which we execute the Ranger mission, hooah. Good luck and welcome to the Regiment."

SURT

Perhaps the most overlooked course conducted by the Ranger Selection and Training Company is Small Unit Ranger Tactics, known simply as SURT. Most Rangers and former Rangers will recognize this course by its previous name, the Pre-Ranger Course. This is a three-week course of instruction designed to prepare Rangers in the Regiment for the sixty-one days of Ranger School. The Ranger Regiment currently enjoys sixty slots for each Ranger School class. Ranger School classes, like SURT classes, convene monthly, or nearly so. There are eleven per year. SURT classes are scheduled so the Regimental Ranger School candidates finish SURT on a Friday, take Saturday off, and are delivered by the SURT cadre to Ranger School on Sunday morning. Again, and by design, SURT prepares enlisted Regimental Rangers to successfully complete Army Ranger School. In order to become a noncommissioned officer in the Regiment, a young Ranger must first earn his Ranger Tab. Most enlisted Rangers attend SURT and Ranger School after twelve to eighteen months in their battalion, completing one to two combat rotations. SURT has a secondary mission of preparing personnel from other SOF components for Ranger School. These few nonregimental SURT candidates usually come from other Army SOF units, though there may be an occasional Navy SEAL, marine, or SOF airman in SURT.

The Small Unit Ranger Tactics curriculum can handle up to eighty students, but there is seldom that many in a beginning class. The goal is to have sixty SURT graduates ready to enroll in every convening Ranger School class, but that, too, does not happen often. The Regiment has priority for placing students in a SURT class; any soldier, sailor, marine, or airman must first successfully complete SURT before he can take one of the allotted Regimental Ranger School vacancies. Just as RASP is the gateway to the Regiment, SURT is the gateway to Ranger School for non-Tabbed Rangers in the Regiment.

"We'd like to put sixty of our Rangers in every Ranger School class," Sergeant First Class Don Bowden tells me, "but that hasn't happened in a while." Sergeant Bowden is the SURT NCOIC. "And with the current battalion deployment rotations, it may not happen for a while. There's just too much work overseas and too little time back here. But the guys we do send do pretty well. Typically, seventy-five to eighty percent of the students who come to us will leave here SURT-qualified for Ranger School. A few will report here out of shape, and we immediately send them back to their battalions. Occasionally, someone will get hurt—sprain an ankle or become sick—and we will try to hold them over for the next class. And sometimes we get guys here who are just not mentally ready for Ranger School. For some reason, they think it's owed to them or that we have nothing to teach them here in SURT, or they just lack motivation. We usually pick up on this early on or it's caught in the peer process. If we become aware of it early on, sometimes we can have a talk with the individual and get them on track. If it surfaces later on or they get peered really low, then we offer them a day-one recycle.

"Three things have to happen while they're here," Sergeant Bowden says of his course, "not counting the swim test, which is basically the same as for RASP One. First of all, a guy has to be physically fit, which means he has to score eighty percent on the Army Physical Fitness Test, run five miles in under forty minutes, and complete the twelve-mile ruck march in less than three hours. And our rucks are heavier than RASP rucks. There may be some slippage on these standards at the beginning, but a candidate will have to test out before we let him move on to the school from SURT. Then he has to show us he can learn the basics of land navigation and demonstrate proficiency in small-unit tactics during our field-training exercise. Yet probably the most important thing he has to do is to show us that he can and wants to be a leader, and that he will go to Ranger School, do his best, and not embarrass the Regiment. If a guy falls short on any of these things, we'll recycle him or send him back to his battalion."

I was aware that other Army units at the division level conduct pre-Ranger courses. "How do you stack up against other Ranger School prep courses?"

"It's not something we track all that closely, but we do better than most. Our Ranger School candidates have a high rate of success. That would stand to reason as we *are* Rangers and our guys have to succeed to stay with the Regiment. The success rate for all candidates at Ranger School is about fifty-five percent—sometimes more and sometimes less. The success rate for our Rangers from SURT is between seventy-five and eighty percent. So, overall, about three out of every four Rangers we receive here at SURT will put on a Ranger Tab within a candidate cycle or recycle."

"And if they don't?" I ask. "I mean, make it through Ranger School?"

"They go back to their battalion for further disposition. It will depend if he's an Eleven Bravo or a specialty MOS. It will also depend on the circumstances that caused him to be disqualified from the school. Sometimes they will be afforded another chance, and sometimes they will be released from the Regiment and sent elsewhere in the Army. A soldier has to get through RASP to get to Regiment, and with few exceptions, he has to get through Ranger School to stay in Regiment. He certainly has to complete Ranger School to achieve any leadership position in the Regiment. No enlisted Eleven Bravo will be advanced from specialist to sergeant unless he has a Tab. Our job here at SURT is to do what we can to help them get that Tab."

The Small Unit Ranger Tactics course is conducted at Cole Range with SURT candidates returning to the Ranger Selection and Training Company for certain classroom work and to the Fort Benning Main Post pool for the swim test. SURT candidates are physically at Cole Range for approximately two of the three weeks they are in the course. Classes in essential Ranger School skills such as operational planning, patrolling, reacting to contact, and small-unit tactics are taught at the open-air bays at Cole Range. "Ranger School is one big outdoor classroom," one of the SURT cadre instructors says of the process, "so our course here is built around keeping our students outside as much as possible to condition them for this.

"We want them to get used to moving under a ruck and living out of a ruck. This takes a little time and some adjustment. It can be very different from their operational training and combat deployment cycle in their Ranger battalions. There are issues of foot care and hydration and hygiene while in field conditions that have to be worked out and practiced. And there's the issue of sleep. We don't sleep-deprive them like they're going to be sleep-deprived at Ranger School, but we seldom let them get more than six hours a night, and during the FTX it can be as little as two hours. Functioning without sleep is a knack, a rhythm if you will, and we want them to see a little of it so it won't be such a shock when they're up two or three nights in a row at Ranger School."

I also notice that the SURT cadre very professionally and firmly reestablishes the student and cadre-sergeant relationship to prepare these Regimental Rangers for their dealings with the the Ranger School Instructors (known as RIs). And this is not an easy thing. Currently, most if not all of the SURT students have been in combat. Some have only one tour, a few have three, but most have two combat rotations behind them. These are men who have been to war; they've been in close combat, taken life, and seen close friends killed or wounded. Now they're back in school. They have to submit to the artificialities of a training environment and even to the corrective-training attentions of the SURT cadre. Most fall into this student role with little trouble. There's a lot of military-training muscle memory in every Army soldier and every Regimental Ranger. A few struggle with it, resulting in a cynical attitude and a less-than-wholehearted effort on the part of the SURT candidate.

Another issue that has to be dealt with by the SURT cadre is the issue of basic small-unit tactics. "Those of us who have been around a while," says Sergeant Bowden, "can see the relationship between basic infantry tactics and the tactics we use on deployment today. It's there, and if you're a student of tactics, you can see it. But sometimes they younger guys can't. They're used to executing the advanced tactics that have made us successful in Iraq and Afghanistan. Our current overseas operations are very high-speed—driven by precise tactical intelligence and our own well-developed TTPs [tactics, techniques, and procedures]. And at this stage of the game, we are very proficient assaulters. Sometimes, there is a perceived disconnect between basic infantry tactics and the tactis we use on deployment. The older guys get it, but not all the younger ones do. So we have to slow it down and get them in the mind-set of those tried-and-true infantry tactics that are in the *Ranger Handbook*—the foundation of all of the tactics we use on a nightly basis in raids across Afghanistan.

These are the tactics they will use in Ranger School. More importantly, they'll have to demonstrate field leadership using these tactics or they'll not get their Tab."

He pauses to frame his words. "It's like this. These Rangers have been doing high-speed assault operations and doing them well. But they've only had to play their individual part—they've been filling a role on a Ranger fire team. They've been told what to do and where to be and how to conduct themselves on target. In many ways, they've become talented actors in a dangerous but well-choreographed skit. Now *they* have to move the pieces on the chessboard. *They* have to lead in this slow-speed, woodland tactical setting or some mock village or some simulated terrorist target. They have to grasp the tactical situation, give the orders, and get a squad or even a platoon of weary and sleep-deprived Ranger School candidates to do what they're supposed to do. It's not easy for a specialist or a PFC, no matter how much combat experience he has."

Small-unit tactics as practiced in the Army and as detailed in the small-unit-tactics bible, the *Ranger Handbook*, are a proscribed and highly formatted approach to small-unit or Ranger-type operations. It's how squads and platoons fight independently but within the context of a larger battle plan. Specifically, it's a cookbook approach to operational planning, patrolling, ambushes, assaults, and reconnaissance missions. It also proscribes how these same small units go about the business of living and sustaining themselves in hostile field conditions.

The heart of the SURT course is the five-day field-training exercise. Friday afternoon of their second week in the course, the student platoon receives an operational tasking from "higher" to conduct a road ambush of an enemy squad at a given location within a given time window. The platoon leader receives the order, makes assignments of responsibilities, and the platoon begins a collective planning effort for the operation. This sets in motion a formatted gathering of detailed information that will include unit organization, weather data, friendly and enemy forces in the area, logistics, available supporting elements, command and signal requirements, and the like. The student platoon leader will also issue a warning order to his men to alert them as to what kind of mission they must prepare for, the equipment needed for the mission, and the time of the mission operational briefing or operations order.

The planning for this first SURT field-training mission comes together on a Saturday morning when the platoon leader, who will also serve as patrol leader, gives his operations order for the platoon-ambush mission. The operations order (OPORD) is a detailed briefing of the mission, the objective or target, the enemy order of battle, the infiltration to and egress from the objective area, the actions on objective, and the host of details that will affect and support the mission. This briefing may take from one to two hours. That portion which deals with the actions on target is supported by a sand-table terrain-model mock-up of the target area so the platoon has a visual reference for the tactical flow of the proposed action. After the briefing, the platoon will conduct rehearsals for key portions of the operation, specifically the actions on target. By noon on Saturday, the platoon is kitted up and patrolling from the Cole Range base area into the woods on the way to their objective. At any time during the planning, patrolling, or execution of the mission, the cadre can and do replace leadership within the student platoon.

Periodically, depending on the patrol's movements, and after every major phase of the operation, the SURT cadre will stop the exercise play for a review of what has taken place thus far in the operation. This is called an after-action review (AAR). It's a simple critique of what just took place—during a briefing or during a tactical evolution. The cadre sergeant will tell the students what they did right, what they did wrong, and even some variations of how they might do it differently. It's a chance for the SURT students to ask questions. Then they pick up the exercise play and move on.

"We let them go for a while, then we change leaders," one of the

Left: Ranger Assessment and Selection, Phase One, Day One. Soldiers from RASP Class 09-10 lay out their personal gear for inspection on the first formal day of their Ranger training.

Right: "The first stanza of the Ranger Creed is . . ." Phase 1 Ranger candidates recite, verbatim and from memory, the six stanzas of the Ranger Creed. Then they move out for morning chow—on the run.

Introduction to Ranger Standards. Class 09-10 receives their class on Ranger Standards. All Ranger candidates are expected to conduct themselves in keeping with the standards of the U.S. Army and the 75th Ranger Regiment.

Photos courtesy of Dick Couch

RASP Pool Drill. Ranger candidates from Class 09-10 warm up for the Ranger Swim Assessment and Evaluation by doing pushups at pool side, faces in the water on the down count. All candidates must pass the RSAE to stay in RASP.

Rucksack Press. The class pushes their rucks toward the sky to warm up for their first rucksack march. They carry fifty-five pounds for six miles wearing shorts and T-shirts. Future ruck marches will be longer and in heavier kit.

The Cole Range Crucible. Candidates arrive at Cole Range after an eight-mile ruck march in full training kit. Here they again heft their rucks to start the four days of misery that will cut RASP Class 09-10 by half.

Left: Medical Inspection–Feet. A Ranger medic checks the condition of candidates' feet at Cole Range–one of the many mandatory medical inspections conducted daily. Of concern are blisters and that they are treated before they become infected.

Combatives at Cole Range. A cadre sergeant demonstrates a take-down during combatives training. Later in the drills, the class will extend into the beef circle, and the candidates of Class 9-10 will vent any grievances they may have with a fellow Ranger candidate.

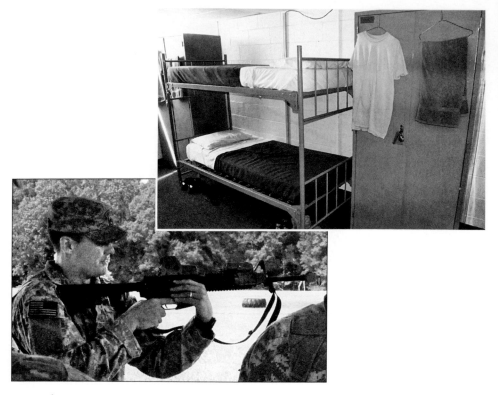

Top Right: Home Sweet Home. Ranger candidates live in four-man to twelve-man rooms in the RASP barracks. Standards extend to the condition of rooms and exactly what each candidate may and may not keep in his locker.

Above: The Weapon of Choice. A Phase One cadre sergeant introduces the candidates of Class 09-10 to their battlefield companion, the M4 rifle. This Ranger M4 is fitted with an EOTech holographic sight, the LA-5 target pointer/illuminator/aiming device, and a high-intensity light.

Physical Training: A Way of Life. Here a RASP 2 candidate leads a member of RASP 1, Class 09-10 through an obstacle during the joint RASP1/RASP2 training. In training and in the Regiment, Rangering means physical training.

Explosives Calculations. For each breaching charge, the net explosive weight, minimum safe distance, and safe fragmentation distance has to be calculated and marked on the charge. One Ranger buddy makes the calculations and the other checks his math.

Get Close, Get Low. The student breachers of Class 09-10 crowd close to the door they've just set to blow. There are any number of ways to make an entry; explosive breaching is just one of them. Ranger candidates spend a full week in Phase Two learning breaching technique.

Fire in the Hole. With the student breachers just a few feet away, the charge defeats the door as intended. In combat, a Ranger fire team would follow the blast through the breached door.

Right: .12 Gauge Breach. The twenty-four-inch Remington M870 .12 gauge magnum breaching shotgun is yet another tool in the breacher's arsenal. Here, a Ranger candidate from Class 9-10 attacks the three hinges of a metal training door.

Below: Before. Training doors on the explosive breaching range, 0700.

After. Training doors on the explosive breaching range, 1400.

Left: Secondary Weapons System. For Rangers, it's the Beretta 9-millimeter pistol. Pistols are no longer taught at Army Basic Combat Training. More than half of the Rangers coming to RASP 1 have never fired a pistol. They will now!

Right: Rounds on Target. A Ranger candidate from Class 09-10 shows tight groups at close range, which is the Beretta's specialty. The target squares are two inches on a side; front sight focus and break the shot.

Primary Weapons System. RASP 1 Class 09-10 and the Special Operations M4 rifle. It's with the M4 that Rangers bring the pain to the bad guys. Sergeant Ed David, one of the Regiment's premier shooters, shows Ranger candidates the basics of combat shooting.

Above: Combat Shooting. Candidates shoot from behind a barricade. In combat, it will be over the hood of a car.

Right: More Combat Shooting. Candidates shoot from under a barricade. In combat, it will be from under a car.

Top: Shooting on the Move. A Ranger candidate from RASP Class 09-10 takes his turn at the combat stress course. He's on the clock with time added for misses and violations of safety protocol.

Right: Fastest Way to the Fight. For most in Class 09-10, this was their first experience with fast roping. This is one of the few times they will do this without fifty pounds of equipment and/or in the daylight.

RASP One Class 09-10. Specialist Alex Hammond stands before thirty-eight of his classmates as new Rangers. Moments earlier, they donned their tan berets for the first time. Whatever else may lie in their future, they have earned the right to call themselves Rangers.

After-Action Review. Sergeant Jon Jackson, Platoon Sergeant for the Second Platoon, Bravo Company, 1st Ranger Battalion, reviews the finer points of taking an enemy bunker during Two-Bravo's predeployment training.

Ranger School and the Tab. A Ranger School instructor, or RI, gives an impromptu field critique at the Army's Ranger School. Ranger School, also at Fort Benning, awards the coveted Ranger Tab. For all in RASP 1 Class 09-10, Ranger School is in their future—after combat rotation.

Leadership Call, Airfield Seizure. A 1st Battalion officer briefs the MLAT—multilateral aviation training, i.e., a battalion-sized operation to seize an enemy airfield. On-call, airfield seizure is a standing requirement for the 75th Ranger Regiment.

Elevator Drills. A part of MLAT training is fast roping, full kit, day and night from various rotary-wing platforms—up and down. Here, 1st Battalion Rangers drop from an MH-60 from the 160th Special Operations Aviation Regiment—the famous "Nightstalkers."

Air-Land Infiltration. Rangers from the 1st Battalion queue up for a night equipment jump at Hunter Army Airfield in Savannah, Georgia. After the C-17 drops the jumpers, it will land with a complement of vehicles.

Special Operations Ospreys. VS-22 Ospreys land Rangers from Delta Company, 1st Ranger Battalion during a live-fire exercise at Fort Campbell. The company live-fire is a component of the task-force training in the predeployment workup.

Hardworking Grenadier. Rangers new to the Regiment are often assigned the role of grenadier. Here a Ranger wields the newer grenade launcher, the M320, while his Ranger buddy covers him.

Support by Fire. An M240 Gunner from the 1st Ranger Battalion lays down a base of fire during a live-fire exercise at Fort Campbell. His brother Rangers will assault while this gunner directs his fire in the path of their advance.

Ranger Sniper. Precision shooting by Ranger snipers is an important part of the Ranger assault package. Snipers, among other roles, provide sniper over-watch for the assault teams.

Combat Assault. This is job one for Rangers of the 75th Ranger Regiment. Here, Rangers from the 1st Ranger Battalion seize a bunker during a live-fire exercise. Bunker busting involves rockets, hand grenades, and heavy volumes of fire.

Above Right: MOUT Training. Military Operations in Urban Terrain, or simply MOUT, involves moving and fighting house to house. Here, Rangers from Delta Company of the 1st Battalion train at the MOUT site at Fort Benning.

Above Left: Entering the Compound. Seizure of an enemy compound is something Rangers do routinely on deployment. Here, a fire team from Alpha Company, 1st Battalion trains at a MOUT site at Fort Campbell. Note the sniper in over-watch position.

Fire Team Entry. Rangers from Two-Delta, 1st Battalion rehearse their room-entry mechanics at the Fransworth shoot house at Fort Benning. Rangers conduct these drills with and without kit, day and night, blank fire and live fire–over and over.

Pieing It Out. Room-entry, room-clearance is a precise business. Each shooter has a sector for which he is responsible. Here, Rangers practice covering their assigned sectors.

Room Clearing, Full Kit, Blank Fire. RASP 2 candidates rehearse clearance procedures at the Booker Range shoot house at Fort Benning. They will then move on to live-fire drills and night live-fire drills.

More Shoot-House Drill. Only RASP 2 candidates spend time in the shoot house. RASP 1 Ranger graduates will not enter the shoot house until they get to their Ranger battalion.

For Our Fallen Brothers. 1st Battalion Rangers honor their fallen comrades. A special table at the Ranger DFAC/dining facility, Hunter Army Airfield, is always set for those forever absent, complete with a fresh flower, folded napkin, and tan beret.

cadre sergeants says. "Over the course of the next few days, we'll do what we can to give everyone a chance to lead. Usually, we begin by having the stronger leaders go first so the others can see how they conduct the patrol and learn from them. Then we put some of the weaker ones in charge. If they don't handle it well, we may pull them out for a while, counsel them, and put them back into a leadership position at a later time. This is all to simulate what will be asked of them in Ranger School. Ranger School has a reputation for a pass-fail approach to tactical leadership, and that's true. Also, the RIs have a reputation for being mean and sadistic, but that's not entirely true. A lot of teaching goes on at Ranger School. The RIs, while they can be demanding, are terrific instructors. We do what we can here so when they see it again at Ranger School, it'll be for the second time. Ranger School classes are big, and they often go over the material very quickly. We also know what they're teaching in Ranger School, as every few classes or so, one of us will go over and walk with the RIs and their squads or platoons for a phase of the course. This little FTX we run here at Cole Range is a condensation of some of what they will be asked to do in each of the three phases of Ranger School."

The SURT platoon ranges out into the woodlands on a compass bearing toward their objective. They patrol in an extended formation, pausing periodically for a security halt and to conduct SLLS (pronounced "sills"—short for "stop, look, listen, smell"). All wear the standard ACUs with soft caps. The backs of their caps and the flaps of their rucks have two squares of reflective tape sewed on, what Rangers call cat eyes. This helps a Ranger to follow the soldier in front of him at night. They move under monster rucksacks that weigh upwards of seventy pounds. The weapons-team Rangers are particularly heavy with the extra ammo, the M240 medium machine gun, and the 240 steel tripod. En route, commands are exchanged with hand and arm signals. Roads that must be crossed are called linear danger areas and are traversed in a proscribed manner. Twice during their patrol to the objective, they receive artillery fire in the form of artillery simulators tossed by one of the two cadre sergeants walking with the SURT platoon.

"Incoming," cries the patrol leader at the whistle of the whistle-bang simulator, and the platoon drops to the forest floor. Then they sprint from the area, inasmuch as they can run through the under-growth with seventy-pound packs. On crossing one road, they are ambushed by an enemy patrol and have to react to contact, again in the proscribed manner. The enemy patrol is a squad of opposition role players from the Holdover barracks, mostly soldiers in the World-wide section. The SURT patrol soldiers dump their rucks and the fight is on. Commands from the platoon leader and his squad leaders echo through the forest as one squad tries to lay down a base of blank fire while the other tries to maneuver to flank the attackers. Then one of the cadre sergeants calls, "Endex" (for "end of exercise"), and the platoon gathers at the point of attack, for an AAR of what just took place. After recovering their rucks, they sit on them to form a classroom in the woods.

"Okay," one of the cadre sergeants tells them, "you got caught by the enemy just as you were crossing the road, right? One squad had already crossed the road and was on the other side. So what do you do? You eventually have to cross the road with the rest of the pla-toon to join the other squad. You guys in the lead squad did the right thing; you tried to flank the enemy from your position, but you had no supporting fire. You"—he directs his words to the patrol leader—"had no choice but to turn and burn—lay down a base of fire and get the rest of your platoon across the road, right?"

"Roger that, Sergeant."

"And it took you a while to start giving commands. You knew immediately where you were taking fire from. And since you're already compromised, start barking orders—get a base of fire down and get your people moving. Once contact is made, you have to dic-tate the fight. You guys see that?"

"ROGER THAT, SERGEANT!"

"Okay, let's get back into patrol formation and press on with the mission."

After continuing on for close to an hour, the patrol is again attacked by artillery and two men are wounded. The patrol must now move quickly from the artillery barrage carrying two men, two extra rucks, two ammo vests, and two weapons. The patrol finally gets within four hundred yards of the objective and goes into a security halt, which, due to its proximity to the objective, becomes the operational readiness position (ORP). The patrol leader sets in his security elements, taking time to position each Ranger pair on the perimeter of the ORP. It's at this time in the ORP that the SURT cadre sergeants relieve the patrol leader, squad leaders, and platoon sergeant, and appoint new ones. Then, from the ORP, the new platoon-patrol leader takes a few men forward to do his patrol leader's reconnaissance. Once the new patrol leader has eyes on the objective and selects a good position to conduct his ambush, he sets in a security element and brings up the other members of the patrol to the ambush site. Several hundred yards to either flank, he has security elements on the road to warn of the approach of the enemy to their ambush site. With security in place, the rest of the patrol members crawl up on line to position themselves for the ambush. The patrol leader sets his M240 machine-gun team to best advantage and situates each member of the platoon for the ambush. With everyone in place, they wait for the enemy.

As if on cue, the enemy comes down the road, but from the opposite direction than which they were expected. The enemy consists of the SURT Humvee and six enemy soldiers—Holdover soldiers again, dressed in Arab garb and carrying AK-47s and rocket-propelled grenade (RPG) launchers.

"Allahu Akbar," they chant, and "Death to Americans." The holdovers are into their roles.

The patrol leader initiates the ambush with a simulated claymore mine detonation, but well before the Humvee is in the kill zone. The patrol opens fire and rakes the Holdover enemy with heavy automatic-weapons fire. After a running battle with the enemy, a few of whom seem to have miraculous longevity, the ambush site is secured. At Ranger School, they will face a more disciplined and professional enemy force, as there is a company of soldiers at the school whose sole job is to role-play as opposing forces. The SURT patrol leader directs the on-target procedures while his first sergeant calls out time hacks. The longer they stay in the area, the more vulnerable they are to an enemy quick-reaction force. With the vehicle and the enemy KIAs searched, the patrol leader calls in his security elements and prepares to move out.

My description of the planning, the conduct of the patrol, and the careful approach to the objective do not do justice to the detailed mechanics that must accompany each step of the mission. Even a simple patrol to a road-ambush site is a complex, formatted undertaking as proscribed in the *Ranger Handbook*. I've made it far simpler than it is. The same applies to the actions on the objective—before, during, and after the initiation of contact. There are established procedures for dealing with the dead and wounded—their own and the enemy's—and any items of intelligence that are recovered from vehicles or enemy personnel. In SURT, the Regimental Rangers practice this over and over under the critical eye of the cadre sergeants. In a few weeks, the actions of these SURT Rangers must stand up to the scrutiny of the Ranger School instructors.

Following this road ambush, the cadre sergeants call for endex and an AAR. They were not terribly pleased with the conduct of the ambush, so the role players and the Humvee are sent back up the road and the patrol is made to execute the ambush again. The second iteration is better, but not perfect.

"On that last ambush, you may have received a go from the RIs or maybe not," a SURT cadre sergeant tells them. In each phase of Ranger School, each student must get a "go" from the Ranger instructors while he's in a leadership position. "The first ambush was a definite no-go. I still see too many of you guys not putting out or doing your best when you're away from the action or not in a leadership position. You have to do your part. Support the current student leadership and anticipate what might be coming next. Be ready to move; be ready to react. You will get your Ranger buddy his go, and he will get you yours. So pay attention and give a hundred percent start to finish, okay?"

"ROGER THAT, SERGEANT!"

After another leadership change, the SURT platoon patrols off back into the woods and heads for a location where it will set up its patrol base. Shortly before midnight, the men make their way into the base. The patrol base is the Ranger element's home away from home, and not simply a patch of woods where the men dump their rucks, roll up in their poncho liners, and get some sleep. A patrol base must be carefully sited for concealment and away from high-traffic areas. It must be secure, or as secure as it can be made to be with the weapons and materials available. Comfort is a consideration but well down on the list from the tactical requirements. Once into the patrol base, the platoon leader will set in his gun teams and each rifle position so they establish interlocking fields of fire. Then he will develop plans for security rotation, weapons cleaning, sleep, hygiene, and eating. They will remain in the patrol base until they are tasked with their next mission or called in from the field. The cadre sergeants may elect for the opposing forces to probe the security of the patrol base, or if the base is well sited, well defended, and the platoon is into good routine, they may leave them alone for the few remaining hours that night.

The next morning, the platoon is tasked with a mission by a fragmentation order (FRAGO) sent by radio. The new platoon leader marshals his men and makes planning assignments for the operation. He gives a quick warning order, and later that morning he gives his operations order. There are no terrain-modeling tools available, so he draws the plan up in the dirt. Someone thought to bring some chalk and a length of yarn, and with the help of rocks and pinecones, the objective—another platoon ambush—is depicted with some relief. After a walk-through rehearsal near the patrol base, the platoon moves out in extended patrol formation. After the platoon ambush and yet another patrol base, there will be more FRAGOs that will task the platoon with two raids and one more platoon ambush.

Following the FTX, the SURT class returns to the Selection and Training Company barracks for two days of equipment overhaul, equipment inventory, and administration. There is also the peer process, which in SURT is different and somewhat unique. The peering takes place in squad increments, with twelve to fourteen Rangers per squad. They rate one another one to fourteen, or however many are in the squad, with one being the worst. For their worst two squad mates, the peer grader is asked to comment on those Rangers' dependability, teamwork, attention to detail, tactical knowledge, and physical stamina. Then, in a classroom, the two or three lowest peering members in the squad are made to sit in chairs and face the rest of their squad. Each squad member who peered one or more of these Rangers low will then tell his Ranger buddy, face-to-face, why he peered him low. The SURT cadre sits off to one side and listens to the comments of the squad and the responses of the men in the hot seats facing their squad mates. Following this mini inquisition, the SURT cadre will meet to discuss the peer results and the cadre input from the whole three-week SURT process. During this informal board, the SURT cadre will make its final determination of who will go on to Ranger School, who needs more time at SURT, and who may need to return to their battalion, perhaps to return to SURT for another try in the future.

Sometimes I can't help but to project this kind of peer review in a corporate, academic, or government setting. How would the individuals in these organizations respond to such a candid and personal evaluation by their coworkers? Can you imagine this within an entrenched group of civil service employees, with their continued employment on the line? Those who work for corporations or are in government service or academia don't have to submit to this kind of review. They have unions and civil representation to prevent this kind of scrutiny. They also don't have to successfully complete Ranger School to keep their jobs or to become combat leaders in an elite regiment. Yet it is an interesting thought.

Following the cadre review, there is administration time. This is important, as the men headed for Ranger School must have their orders and medical records up to date. Ranger School in-processes a great many soldiers on a monthly basis, and anyone who arrives without the proper documentation will be turned away.

The SURT graduates bound for Ranger School will have only Saturday off to get their equipment lists flushed out and their affairs in order. On Sunday morning, they form up at 1000 behind the S&T Company headquarters for the bus ride across Fort Benning to the Ranger Training Brigade. A SURT cadre sergeant is there to see that their paperwork is in order and that they are in the proper uniform—ACUs with only U.S. Army and name tabs. As during SURT, rank will not be used in Ranger School. The bus ride from the S&T Company to Ranger School is fifteen minutes. Yet these Rangers from the Regiment know they are entering another world. As they wrestle their gear from the bus and form up away from the other Ranger School candidates, I can tell they are anxious, even nervous. Few of the other four-hundred-plus candidates have the background, preparation, or motivation as these candidates, yet for these Rangers from the 75th Ranger Regiment, it's still a step into the unknown.

The formations and administrative details that attend day one of Ranger School are like a massive grade-school enrollment. There are no parents, except for a few pre–Ranger School sergeants like the attending SURT cadre sergeant, and the students are better behaved. They quietly stand in their disjointed formations or queue up with their orders and medical records, which they will exchange for their school assignments in this Ranger School class.

"I think this group will do well," says the cadre sergeant who accompanied the thirty-some candidates from the Regiment. "They were a motivated SURT class. They'll be on their own from here on, but we keep tabs on them. We have access to the Ranger School student-tracking system so we can see how our guys are doing. There will always be a few who will be rolled back and have to repeat one or more phases of Ranger School—some for injury, some from deficiencies in their performance. There's a Holdover section here at the Ranger Training Brigade just like in RASP One. We track them in school and in Holdover. We don't close the books on them until they come back to us from the school, with or without a Tab."

The waiting soldiers, including the Ranger School candidates from the 75th Ranger Regiment, exude a collective, underlying current of anticipation. They've heard all the stories. They all know it will be hard. As a group, those from the 75th know their chances of finishing with a Ranger Tab are better than those of the other candidates. Still, I sense their apprehension. They all know a serious ordeal awaits them.

RANGER SCHOOL

The U.S. Army Ranger School at Fort Benning is a unique military training venue and a unique military training experience. There is nothing else like it in this man's Army or any other. Calling it a school seems inadequate. It's more of an ordeal. Few military training programs can rival Ranger School for its complexity, transformative effects, and culture imprinting. It is at once a training course, a testing platform, and a leadership laboratory. I may get resistance in some quarters for saying this, but it is one of the last serious, openly male rites of passage in our military. Ranger School is a keeper of our nation's warrior values and warrior cultural standards. It trains Army leaders for war and serves to keep them warrior-ready in times of peace.

Ranger School came into being in 1950 to train soldiers in the Ranger companies for service in Korea. In 1951, the school began to conduct Ranger-type training for all combat units in the Army. Today, the school is structured as a brigade-sized organization with three training battalions and a headquarters element. Its sole mission is to conduct training classes and to award the coveted Ranger Tab. As previously mentioned, the Ranger Training Brigade/Ranger School and the 75th Ranger Regiment are two separate and distinct commands with different missions. The school is the nation's premier combat leadership school. The Regiment is the nation's premier direct-action-raid force. The school operates under the direction of the Army Training and Doctrine Command. The Regiment is a component of the U.S. Army Special Operations Command. Yet they share a common passion and lineage for both the warrior profession and a standard of excellence in tactical proficiency. Graduates of RASP call themselves Rangers. Graduates of Ranger School are referred to as "Ranger Qualified," but the Tab they proudly wear on their shoulder does not say "Ranger Qualified." It says "Ranger."

There is no way that I can do justice to Ranger School in these few pages. *Sua Sponte* is the story of the forging of young Rangers who deploy and fight with the 75th Ranger Regiment. Ranger School trains combat leaders for the Army. In the balance of this chapter, I'll do my best provide an overview of Ranger School. Both the Regiment and the school share a cultural heritage, and both put a premium on combat leadership. Again, no Eleven Bravo Ranger infantryman in the Regiment will be promoted to E-5 sergeant without a Ranger Tab. The Regiment expects a great deal from its leaders, and just one of those expectations is the Ranger Tab. With that understanding, let's take a closer look at Ranger School.

The school is a sixty-one-day course with approximately three weeks of instruction in each of the three phases: the Benning Phase, the Mountain Phase, and the Florida Phase. All three phases pit the collective armed combat force of the Ranger Training Brigade against an enemy force known as the Aragon Liberation Front, a notional narcoterrorist organization. This enemy will be pursued through difficult wooded, mountainous, and wetland terrain. The brigade is organized into three battalions with a fixed cadre of Ranger instructors in each phase. Student Rangers fill the ranks of the training battalions as they progress through the phases of training. The 4th Ranger Training Battalion fights the Aragon Liberation Front in the Georgia woodlands, the 5th Battalion in the Georgia mountains, and the 6th in the Florida swamps. The student force engaged in this war-in-progress begins at Fort Benning with anywhere from three hundred to five hundred Ranger School candidates. Due to attrition, considerably fewer will carry this fight to the mountains and the wetlands.

Phase One begins at the Ranger Training Brigade headquarters at Camp Rogers on Fort Benning with brigade organization, land navigation, a terrain run, combatives, and the Army Physical Fitness Test. Candidates who don't achieve the Ranger minimums are summarily disenrolled. The personal restrictions are RASP-like: no supplements, no snacks, no tobacco, no cell phones, no field civilian equipment, and only authorized prescription medications. Ranger candidates bring to the school a very proscribed set of personal gear and are issued their operational equipment and training weapons with blank adapters. On Wednesday, the class conducts a foot march from Camp Rogers to Camp Darby, where the heavy lifting of the Phase One of Ranger School will take place. The first six days are devoted to candidate training in small-unit tactics and physical conditioning. The candidates are given classes in Ranger tactics, then tactical demonstrations with a series of cadre-led and cadre-assisted ambushes and reconnaissance missions. The heart of Phase One is the six days of graded missions.

My experience at Ranger School included one such mission. The day begins at about 0530 with a mission tasking for my Ranger squad—2nd Squad, 1st Platoon, A Company, 4th Ranger Training Battalion. The squad is tasked with a reconnaissance mission of an enemy base-camp facility. On receipt of the mission tasking, the squad begins the operational-planning and gear-preparation process for this mission. The student squad leader who will lead the patrol gives his warning order at 0630, which alerts the squad as to the type of mission, the equipment that needs to be prepped for the mission, and the squad assignments for both the planning and execution of the mission.

It's almost surreal, watching these Ranger candidates go about their chores in the morning chill. They move with purpose, but none are moving too quickly. There are fourteen of them. They are all moving in and around the squad bay, an open-air, three-sided post-and-pier shed with chalkboards, bench seating, and a dirt-filled terrain-model box. They are dressed in gray knit watch caps, Army windbreakers, ACU trousers, and boots. In the immediate area around the squad bay, each man's entire allotment of personal and operational equipment and his personal weapon are laid out on his poncho liner. Everything is bathed in fluorescent lighting from the bay. This is their eleventh day of Ranger School and the second day of graded missions. They returned from the field and their first day of grading at 0300 that morning. On average, they've had about an hour and a half of sleep per man.

After the warning order and an AAR of the warning order by their Ranger instructor, the squad sets about planning and prepping for the mission. This routine of one to two hours of sleep, squad mission tasking, mission planning and preparation, and mission execution is very similar to the routine I watched unfold at SURT, only the sleep portion is greatly reduced. At Phase One of Ranger School, they return each night to the squad planning bays to rest, refit, receive new operational tasking, and prepare to go back out. They are allowed two MREs per day—one when they come in from a mission sometime after midnight, and one when they begin their day, about 0500. The candidates sleep in and around the squad bay so they are never far from each other.

"What happens if it rains?" I ask one of the candidates.

He considers this. "I don't know, sir. It hasn't rained on us yet."

There are two Rangers in this squad from the 75th Regiment, both from 3/75. One graduated from RASP only last April and has been assigned to the 3rd Battalion Armory since his RASP graduation. He's one of the very few RASP graduates who will attend Ranger School before making a combat deployment. The second 3/75 Ranger has had three combat rotations. Both are here for their Tab. Both are capable soldiers, but there's a maturity and air of quiet confidence in the Ranger specialist with the three combat tours.

"It really is a lot like SURT," one of them tells me. "I had no idea about patrol orders and warning orders and security halts, at least as we're expected to do them here, before I went to SURT. Now we're seeing it again, and it's starting to fall into place. Except for these rucks, it would be almost fun. So it's not easy, but it's doable."

"It's a grind," says the other, "and it's just beginning. I've yet to cycle through a graded-leadership position. That'll probably happen today. I can get through this; I just hope I can pull it together and do well when I have to lead the patrol."

At 0930, the squad leader begins his operations order as proscribed in the *Ranger Handbook*. His squad members seated at the benches in the bay take notes and follow the briefing in their own *Ranger Handbooks*. He roams from chalkboard to whiteboard and often refers to the terrain model, which now has miniature hills, ravines, streams, and an Aragon Liberation Front base camp. One of the squad members, a Ranger candidate in the squad's senior-sergeant role, moves behind his fellow squad mates, occasionally nudging them to keep them awake or having them stand. In the back, the Ranger instructor makes notes on the OPORD; it's a graded event. The briefing takes just over two hours, followed by an in-depth AAR by the Ranger instructor. This RI is a sergeant first class and a multitour combat veteran from the 82nd Airborne. During his critique, the RI refers to each of them as "Ranger," rather than by name.

"When you give them the mission concept, Ranger," he tells the student patrol leader, "don't read it from your operational tasking—give it to them in your own words. Tell them straight up, soldier to soldier, what they'll be doing and how they'll be doing it."

"Roger that, Sergeant."

On balance, I thought it was a detailed and well-delivered operational order, and I suspect he's probably an officer, but Ranger School candidates wear no rank. I later ask the RI about the background of this patrol leader. "I really don't know," he tells me. "Most of us make it a point not to know or ask. That keeps our grading fair and not dependent on rank." I ask him about the issue of giving a student a no-go for an evolution. "We usually don't tell them if they passed of failed so they don't let up after they've rotated through a leadership position. Periodically, we let them know, especially if they're doing poorly. Sometimes if a student fails twice, we may send him to another squad so another instructor can grade him. We insist on a standard here, but we go to some lengths to make it an impartial standard." Later that day, I had a chance to chat with the squad leader who gave the OPORD and will begin this mission as the patrol leader. He's a West Pointer, a new second lieutenant infantry officer.

Following the operations order and AAR, the squad sanitizes the boards, destroys their carefully constructed terrain model, and prepares to move out. Everything of an accountable nature—weapons, radios, training grenades, mock claymore mines, NVDs, binoculars, lasers, etc.—are inventoried and accounted for. All personal gear and operational gear needed for the mission is pushed into individual rucksacks. Operational gear that is carried or worn on their combat vests or racks is tied down with 550, or nylon parachute cord. Lost or stranded equipment is a big issue. When the squad leaves the squad bay for the rehearsal area, the men take everything and leave nothing. Personal and operational gear that is not needed on the mission is put in a duffel and cached in a storage facility near the A Company building.

Early afternoon finds the student squad, with me in tow and the RI walking off to one side with his grading sheets, patrolling across the woodlands near Camp Darby toward the objective. Here again, it's very similar to SURT, but the patrol formation seems a little more professional and better disciplined. A part of it could be that half of the men in the squad are officers, many of them West Pointers fresh from the Infantry Basic Officer Leadership Course. And a part of it could be that this patrol counts; the patrol leadership will get a go or no-go for the patrol, and those in a nonleadership role want to help them get that go. It's probably a little of both.

En route to the objective, the patrol is taken under fire by an enemy patrol, receives (simulated) artillery fire, and crosses a linear danger area, or road. After each of these, the RI calls them in for an AAR of what was right and what was wrong. Most glaring was the danger area crossing. "Ranger, you have to push out the security on your flanks at least a hundred yards in this kind of open terrain," he tells the patrol leader. "They do you no good as early warning positions if they are in as close as you had them." At a security halt, the RI calls for a leadership change. The patrol leader and the two fire-team leaders, A-team and B-team, are relieved. It takes a few minutes to trade out radios, NVDs, and associated equipment for the change of leadership. One of the 75th Rangers becomes the A-team leader. The team, under his direction, will continue with the patrol's land-navigation duties and lead the patrol to the enemy base camp.

"There's a great deal of artificiality in this, but we're grading them on procedure," our RI tells me as we press on to the objective. "Back in the squad bay, we grade them on planning and the warning and operations orders. Once out here in the field, it's about basics of managing a patrol, reacting to contact, and their conduct on target. Everything we do here is about the basics and the fundamentals of conducting a good patrol and a good assault. Phase One here at Darby is the crawl phase. Phase Two and Three will be the walk and run phases. Here we do squad patrols; at the other phases, they will conduct more complex platoon-sized operations. Yet even here at Darby, each graded patrol is a little more difficult and a little more demanding than the previous one."

The patrol and new leadership continue with the mission, crossing another road and going into a security halt, then on to an operational readiness position some three hundred yards from the objective. Then per the operations order and the *Ranger Handbook*, the patrol leader leads his recon element forward to put eyes on the objective and make sketches of the target area. This reconnaissance will take several hours, as they will observe the target well after dark. After the recon element rejoins the rest of the patrol, the squad rucks up and they begin to carefully exfil from the ORP. Periodically throughout the patrol, the RI calls a brief halt to conduct teaching, give correction, and sometimes point out a refinement of a tactic. He questions the patrol leadership, seeking clarity on their tactical decision making and often challenging them on the decisions they made. But he's now talking to a tired bunch of soldiers. As they take a knee for an AAR, one or two of them start to nod off.

"Hey, wake up!" he says in a firm but civil tone. "I didn't ask you to come here; you all volunteered for this. Being tired and hungry is no excuse for not getting the job done. If this is too much for you, you can volunteer out. And it's going to get a lot worse before it gets any better."

After the AAR, the men continue with the mission and the night-time patrol back to their squad bay.

"Tomorrow is going to be a good day," one of the candidates confides to me as we move away from the Aragon Liberation Front base camp.

"Why is that?"

"We have a parachute jump scheduled," he replies. "The rules say that you have to be given six hours of sleep before a drop. Six whole hours—talk about sweet!"

Phase Two, the Mountain Phase, is conducted by the 5th Ranger Training Battalion at Camp Merrill near Dahlonega, Georgia. There, the Ranger candidates receive mountaineering training, which covers knots, belays, rappels, and a whole range of rope work. Then they take to the mountainous terrain for ten days of mission planning and mission execution. Infiltration to their objectives can be by helicopter air assault, parachute, or a long foot march across the Tennessee Mountain divide. Here again, the missions become more complex in the planning and more physically demanding in the execution. As the Ranger candidates become mentally and physically drained, they have to soldier on, leading other tired and spent Ranger candidates when called on to do so. At the end of the Mountain Phase, the class parachutes into the third and final phase of Ranger School.

Phase Three is the home of the 6th Ranger Training Battalion and Camp Rudder at Eglin Air Force Base in the Florida Panhandle. Training is conducted in a coastal swamp environment and further extends these already-tired Ranger candidates. It's during Phase Three, perhaps more than the other two phases, when personal discipline and mental toughness come into play. A student Ranger will march close to two hundred miles during the sixty-one days of Ranger School. Much of that marching is under a heavy ruck. Now he will do some of that through mud and swamp. His body will quit on him unless he has the mental stamina to press on. After instruction in medical procedures, reptile management, and small-boat handling, along with an update on the enemy order of battle, the student Rangers are inserted by helo or parachuted into a ten-day FTX of ongoing day-and-night operations. All the while, the mental and physical stress continues to build—the pace never slackens. The FTX culminates in a complex raid on the island fortress of the

Aragon Liberation Front. Ranger candidates who have met standard spend two more days at Camp Rudder with peer evaluations, equipment overhaul, and counseling. For those marginal candidates, there is the Ranger School Board.

The successful survivors return to Fort Benning and Camp Rogers thinner, wiser, very tired, and terminally hungry. How much thinner? On average, a Ranger School graduate will weigh twenty pounds less than he did at the beginning of this ordeal—on average. The small men don't have that much to lose; for many of the larger men, it's a great deal more. In these few pages, I've not come close to doing justice to the physical and mental rendering that characterizes this important combat leadership school. It's not just a Tab; it's a personal and emotional transmutation. I asked one Ranger School graduate what he learned there. He said, "I learned that when I was cold, wet, hungry, and hadn't slept in a few days that I could still be a leader." Another answered without hesitation: "I learned a great deal about myself." As these Ranger-Qualified soldiers continue with their Army careers and beyond, these past weeks of struggle will serve as a template for physical and mental endurance, and a benchmark for future growth as a warrior. "Hey, it's hard," they will often say of a difficult or challenging situation, "but it's nothing compared to Ranger School."

Ranger School graduation is both a demonstration and a ceremony. The first is quite spectacular. It takes place at Victory Pond, near Camp Rogers, and is complete with Rangers patrolling, fast-roping from helicopters, and leaping from helicopters into the water. There are demolitions, combatives, and the slide for life—a carnival-like ride on which a Ranger descends an inclined wire from a two-hundred-foot tower while hanging from a pulley and T-bar, dropping into the water at the last second.

The graduation ceremony is straightforward and nearly identical to the RASP 1 graduation. Both are geared to the families of the graduating Rangers. I attended the graduation of Ranger School Class

11-10, notable in that this class graduated almost sixty years to the day after the graduation of the first Ranger class. Three hundred and forty-six soldiers began with this class; 148 are in ranks to be awarded their Ranger Tab. Just under half of them are commissioned officers. Of those 148, 30 are Rangers from the 75th Ranger Regiment.

Presiding at this graduation was the Ranger Training Brigade Command Sergeant Major, a former battalion CSM of the 75th Ranger Regiment. As at the RASP 1 graduation, the guest speaker was both impressive and brief. Command Sergeant Major Chuck Waters (Ret.) is the personification of a vigorous senior Ranger. He enlisted in the Marine Corps for World War II at the age of fourteen, fought on Guadalcanal, and was wounded on Bougainville just after his sixteenth birthday. Following the war, he left the Corps for the Army. His military and civilian accomplishments are too numerous to name. He graduated from that first Ranger class sixty years ago. Though he's well into his eighties, the Command Sergeant Major's remarks were humorous and on point as he cited the accomplishments of the graduating class. I've listened to a good number of military-graduation speakers; Command Sergeant Major Waters was perhaps the most impressive, both in his remarks and his person. There were awards for the Distinguished Graduate, the two Honor Graduates, and for leadership. After a recitation of the Ranger Creed, nearly identical to the one that took place at the RASP 1 graduation, the brigade CSM invited the family and friends of the new Ranger-Qualified Rangers to come down and award them their Ranger Tabs.

Following the graduation, I spoke briefly to an Army captain attached to the Ranger Training Brigade. He had come to the school after a tour as a platoon leader with the 75th Ranger Regiment and still wore his Tan Beret at a rakish angle.

"I didn't know much about the Regiment when I came through Ranger School as a young infantry second lieutenant," he told me. He still looked young, but infantry captains in today's Army are seasoned combat veterans. "I had three enlisted Rangers from Regiment in my squad, and they clearly stood out from the rest of us. They were tough, focused, and battle tested. I decided then and there that I wanted to lead men like these. It became my goal from that day on to serve in the Seventy-fifth Ranger Regiment."

"What are your goals now?" I ask.

"To do my best here at the school to train Rangers for the Army, then to command a line infantry company in combat. After that, my goal is to return to the Seventy-fifth Ranger Regiment as a company commander."

If Ranger School is a rite of passage, then those who wear that tiny strip of cloth called the Ranger Tab are of a warrior class. It crosses generations and rank structure. To call it a simple shared experience would be to shortchange a brotherhood that is forged at the edges of an individual's physical and mental limits. It binds noble warriors such as Command Sergeant Major Chuck Waters to General David Petraeus to the sergeant first class veterinary technician from the Regiment who just graduated with Ranger Class 11-10. On returning to their battalions, these Regimental Ranger School graduates will step into important leadership roles. The lives of other Rangers will depend on their leadership. Many will deploy into combat within weeks of their graduation. Ranger School is an important step in the grooming of warriors for service in that unique and special brotherhood called the 75th Ranger Regiment.

CHAPTER SIX

THE RANGER BATTALION

Rangers can be deployed overseas and into harm's way in any number of forms. The smallest would typically be a Ranger company, although a detached platoon or even a squad can function independently depending on the mission and how that platoon or squad is supported. Or, as was the case during the invasion of Panama in 1989, the entire Regiment can parachute into the fight. Since 9/11, the Ranger Regiment has been continually engaged in Iraq and/or Afghanistan. For most of that time, its presence has consisted of at least a single rifle battalion and one-third of the Regiment's combat power. Given the recent overlap of the forward-deployed rifle-battalion rotations and the ongoing augmentation of deployed rifle battalions by the Ranger Special Troops Battalion, the Ranger presence in the active theaters has been a battalion plus, equating to more than 40 percent of the Regiment at any given time. With the step-up, or "surge," of the operations in Afghanistan beginning in spring of 2010, this plus-up has been close to a battalion and a half.

So, that's four Ranger battalions with a battalion and a half overseas at any given time, augmented by a cadre of regimental staff officers and senior NCOs that are individually deployed close to half the time. In addition to their time overseas, Rangers are often training away from home when they're not on deployment. "Being home" is an elusive thing. During a predeployment training cycle, as you will see in this chapter, being home can amount to getting in well after midnight from a night-assault training evolution and being at a first-call/leaders huddle at 0600.

While he may not be home every night he is not deployed, a Ranger's life in battalion is measured in overseas rotation—since 9/11, combat rotation. Currently, the Ranger battalion rotations are about four months in duration, with a single company leaving as much as two months ahead of the battalion and another company remaining a month to six weeks after the battalion rotates home. So for half the battalion, a deployment is a little more than four months, counting transit time; for the other half, it's five to six months. The rifle battalions are not quite on an annual rotation cycle. The cycle is more like ten and a half to eleven months, so no single rifle battalion will miss every Christmas or every Thanksgiving. From my sketchpad calculations, Rangers of 75th Ranger Regiment are on deployment, in harm's way, an average of five months a year and away from home for about half of their time in the Regiment. For most Americans, our lives are punctuated by the seasons; for a Ranger in a battalion, it's the combat rotations.

Before we get to the mechanics and breakdown of the rifle battalions, let's take a moment with the Regimental Special Troops Battalion. The RSTB was provisionally activated in July 2006 and formally became part of the Regiment in October 2007. The mission of this battalion is to support the Regiment in areas of command and control, communications and data processing, operational intelligence, surveillance, and reconnaissance. These capabilities not only support the regimental rifle battalions, but also serve to integrate the Rangers into the deployed joint special operations task forces. In addition to these forward-deployed, battlefield-centric duties, the RSTB's Ranger Selection and Training Company, as we've seen in previous chapters, trains and assesses new Rangers and prepares Regimental Rangers for Ranger School.

In addition to the S&T Company, there are four other companies: the Headquarters and Headquarters Company, the Regimental Communications Company (RCC), the Military Intelligence Company (MICO), and the Regimental Reconnaissance Company (RRC). The Headquarters and Headquarters Company provides logistics, transportation, and tactical airborne/air-assault support for the RSTB staff. The Regimental Communications Company is responsible for a broad range of combat communications and worldwide automated communications/information systems. The RCC maintains and supports sophisticated, encrypted commo systems from the tactical level up through the task force level. These RCC communicators also conduct radio/commo training for the platoon- and company-level radio operators. The Military Intelligence Company provides multilevel, multidimensional intelligence support that ranges from detainee screening/interrogations to an extensive military technical-collection apparatus to liaison functions with other military and government agency intelligence organizations. The MICO is just one of the reasons that Ranger assault elements enjoy such precise targeting information.

The Ranger Reconnaissance Company is in the business of reconnaissance, surveillance, advance-force operations, and direct action in support of the regimental or special operations task force objectives worldwide. That said, reconnaissance is their specialty—tactical, technical, and special reconnaissance. By "special," I might well say "classified," as they gather information by some unique and diverse methods that carry the highest security classification. The RRC trains and supports five stand-alone operational teams that can be tasked with a variety of sensitive direct-action missions. These teams maintain expertise in the use of communications, weapons systems, infil/exfil capabilities, and tactical procedures—most of which are well beyond the scope of this book. This RRC is an agile force, one that might be tasked with a hostage recovery or the targeting of a high-value al-Qaeda leader.

The Ranger Special Troops Battalion, unlike the rifle battalions, deploys in individual and team elements from the home base at Fort Benning. And unlike the rifle battalions, there's no battalion-centric, predeployment work-up for overseas rotation. Rangers and Ranger teams from the RTSB train with the rifle companies and platoons, and they are constantly going to and coming from the battlespace as both attached and detached elements. This keeps these talented special Rangers deployed overseas *at least* a third of the time. And like their brothers in the rifle battalions, they are often away from home between deployments as they train and prepare for their next overseas rotation. Only those in the RSTB's Ranger Selection and Training Company are currently excused from combat deployment.

The three rifle battalions are geographically and even culturally different, but structurally they look the same. For this book, my duty assignment was the 1st Ranger Battalion at Hunter Army Airfield in Savannah, Georgia. Organizationally, 1/75 looks very much like its two sister battalions. Each rifle battalion has four rifle or light infantry companies (Alpha, Bravo, Charlie, and Delta) and a single support company (Echo). There's also a headquarters company that supports the battalion staff as well as the rifle companies and platoons. The four rifle companies in each battalion are the pointy end of the Ranger spear. Each rifle company has three rifle platoons and a headquarters platoon. Each rifle platoon has three rifle squads and a weapons squad. While I was with 1/75 during their predeployment work-up, I was embedded with a succession of these rifle platoons.

The Ranger rifle platoon, for training and deployment purposes, *is* the Ranger combat family. The men live, train, and fight together.

Within this extended family are the squads and fire teams that take the fight to the enemy. At the head of the family are the father and mother—the officer platoon leader and the enlisted platoon sergeant. The platoon leader is a junior captain or a senior first lieutenant, and the platoon sergeant is an E-7 sergeant first class. But keep in mind that this family is highly matriarchal, and the role of this platoon sergeant cannot be overstated. It is the most important combat leadership position in the 75th Ranger Regiment. Much of the balance of this chapter and book will deal with this miniculture called the Ranger rifle platoon and the duties and relationships of the Rangers who serve in these rifle platoons. Whenever possible, I will be focusing on the new platoon Rangers.

It's these rifle platoons that make up the companies that make up the battalions. When career Rangers talk of their days as a private, they'll say, "I grew up in 2nd Battalion," or "I grew up in 3/75." For the purposes of this book, I grew up in the 1st Ranger Battalion.

While my time in battalion was with 1/75, my first introduction to the battalions was with the 3/75 at Fort Benning. It was a chance encounter and, for me, a moving and important one. In telling the Ranger story, writers like myself are often caught up in the hierarchical issues such as the breakdown of the battalions, companies, platoons, and so forth. But these organizational mechanics often step past the intimacies and personal sacrifices that accompany each Ranger deployment. Shortly after I checked in with the Ranger Selection and Training Company in September 2010, I had my first meeting with Sergeant First Class Tad Collier, the RASP 1 NCOIC. After he showed me around the RASP compound and introduced me to his senior cadre sergeants, he invited me to a 3rd Battalion social function.

"Mister Couch, my old company at 3/75 is having a cookout this weekend. Why don't you join us? The company has just finished their postdeployment block-leave period, and this is their first gathering as a company since they returned from the fight." Battalion Rangers are granted two weeks of leave en masse before they rotate to the battlespace and two weeks when they return. It's called block leave. "I think," Sergeant Collier added, "you might find it interesting." And this became my introduction to a Ranger Company—specifically, Bravo Company, 3rd Ranger Battalion, or B-Co (pronounced "Bee-Ko") of the 3/75.

Bravo Company has a storied place in modern Ranger lore. Since the 3rd Ranger Battalion's reactivation in 1984, the company has participated in every American military combat engagement. No Ranger company or unit has more time in combat than Bravo Company of 3/75 and none, to my knowledge, has suffered more combat losses. I knew about Bravo Company from my reading on the Battle of Mogadishu. Six of the Rangers killed in that terrible struggle were from B-Co. I also knew they were among those Rangers who first entered into Afghanistan on one of the first combat missions in the Global War on Terrorism. And having spent time in Haditha, Iraq, I knew that during the invasion in 2003, B-Co Rangers had taken the important Haditha Dam and held it for several days against Republican Guard counterattacks. But I knew little of the extent of their ongoing and recent combat losses. Since 1984, twenty-two B-Co Rangers have been killed in combat. I was to learn a great deal more at this post-block-leave gathering. This particular function was a casual affair at Fort Benning, a pork barbecue with all the trimmings. It was funded by the Lead the Way Foundation. The Lead the Way Foundation is a nonprofit organization started by James P. Regan in honor of his son, Staff Sergeant James J. Regan, a 3/75 Ranger killed in action in 2007.

Again, this was the first time B-Co had been back together since its redeployment. In many ways, it was a bittersweet gathering; the end of a block-leave period means the beginning of the work-up for the next deployment. The B-Co Rangers were with their wives, sweethearts, and immediate family. Yet there were some absences. Bravo Company had suffered four killed and some twenty-five wounded during its five-month tour—many of them seriously and unable to return to duty. This was a casualty rate of close to 15 percent for this one company during a single combat rotation. But while the company was missing four Rangers, the families of the fallen men were present at this gathering.

I was speaking with the parents of one of those B-Co Rangers when we were joined by his platoon sergeant. He politely introduced himself and began to talk about their son. Transfixed, I listened as this platoon sergeant told a mother and father how their son died, what this sergeant and the Ranger medics did to try to save him, and that he was there beside their son at the aid station when he died of his wounds. The sergeant did not mince words or talk around it; he told it straight up, from the time their son was wounded until he expired. He was never in pain, he told these parents, but he omitted none of the details of the action. Their Ranger had died a hero and a patriot, he told them. The father remained stoic while the mother wept softly.

"If you have any questions about anything," he said to them, "now or in the future, you call me. You are still part of our family; you always will be. Your son will always be with us—here, back on deployment, wherever. He'll forever be a B-Co Ranger."

These words from the platoon sergeant were measured and from the heart, interrupted only by an occasional Ranger who came by to give the parents a hug. This is war and the aftermath of war, as experienced by few outside the military. I sense this is not an isolated occurrence in the 75th Ranger Regiment. There was little formality to this warrior gathering. The company first sergeant called for everyone's attention and spoke to the group for but a few moments. He asked for a toast to the fallen Rangers, and he thanked the families who had come to be with them this day.

"This last deployment, by any measure, was a rough one," he told them, "so I'll not go into it—you guys were there. We lost some very fine Rangers. Those men are still with us in spirit, and we will never forget them—never. They will always be a part of Bravo Company, just as you, their loved ones here today, will always be a part of Bravo Company. You are family." He then thanked the wives and sweethearts who stood by their Rangers while they were deployed and would again stand by their Rangers when they deployed again in just a few short months.

This was my introduction to an operational rifle company in a battalion of the 75th Ranger Regiment. As an outsider, I was made to feel welcome—accepted. Few of them knew who I was or how I happened to be with them that evening. The fact that I was an SOF operator, a generation or two removed, was enough. I felt it an honor to again be in the company of true warriors. Now, more than ever, I wanted this book to reflect credit on these fine soldiers and the sacrifice they continue to make for their country.

I began my time in-battalion with 1/75 at Hunter Army Airfield near Savannah in early January 2011. Hunter Army Airfield is a satellite base of nearby Fort Stewart, the home of the 3rd Infantry Division. Hunter is built around a massive (more than eleven thousand feet) runway and extensive, hard-stand tarmac areas. It's an aviation-centric installation—home to the 3rd Aviation Regiment, which supports the 3rd ID; the 117th Aerial Control Squadron; and the 224th Military Intelligence Battalion (Aerial Exploitation). In addition to the 1/75 Rangers, there's the 3rd Battalion of the 160th Special Operations Aviation Regiment (Airborne)—the famous Night Stalkers, who support special operations units in their training at Hunter and worldwide in the operational theaters. In comparison to the massive installations of Fort Benning and Fort Stewart, it's a much smaller and more intimate base. And, barring traffic, it's but a ten-minute drive to the historic district of downtown Savannah.

On Hunter proper, the 1st Ranger Battalion enjoys a modern compound similar to that of the 3/75 at Fort Benning. This modern military complex stands in contrast to the Spanish-moss-draped live oaks and palm trees that populate Hunter and nearby Savannah. There is a battalion headquarters building, complete with memorabilia and an array of captured small arms and crew-served weapons from current and previous wars. Adorning the walls is a rogues gallery of past Ranger targets, including Saddam Hussein and Manuel Noriega. Nearby is a large barracks complex, motor pool, Ranger gym, an always-superb Ranger dining facility chow hall, and a long brick building that is the home of the four 1/75 Ranger rifle companies. This company complex is the stateside home of the operational Rangers. Each company has its own admin spaces with adjacent offices for the company commander and the company first sergeant and a large conference room. Each platoon has an office shared by the platoon leader and the platoon sergeant that doubles as a small executive meeting room for those two leaders and their four squad leaders. The main portion of the company building is devoted to the squad bays. Each Ranger squad has its own caged area for personal lockers and equipment storage, and a space for prepping its operational gear. These squad bays are the training and social hub for the Rangers assigned to that squad. It's their operational home when they're not on deployment. Internal to each company is a supply section, a communications section, and an arms room.

The 1st Battatlion has recently returned from the fight. The post-deployment leave periods, depending on the individual company rotation schedule, ended in late November or early December. Some training activity took place before the Christmas holiday, but the entire battalion is back now to the serious business of preparing for the next deployment. My initial assignment at 1/75 is with Bravo Company, 2nd Platoon—or in Ranger-speak, Two-Bravo. A Ranger company is made up of some 140 souls, with 32 to 36 Rangers in each of the three rifle platoons and slightly more than that in the headquarters platoon. And, again, a Ranger rifle platoon has three rifle squads and a weapons squad.

This is a book about Rangers—specifically, new Rangers—and we'll soon get to them. But bear with me a while longer as we take a moment with the organization of a Ranger rifle squad and how that squad is supported in combat. A fully manned squad is made up of nine Rangers—a squad leader with two fire teams, each with four Rangers. The squad leader is an E-6 staff sergeant, but sometimes a senior E-5 will fill this role. The fire-team leaders are E-5 sergeants with an occasional experienced specialist or corporal as team leader. The Ranger rifle platoons, and by extension the rifle squads, can be augmented with "enablers" from the platoon, company, or battalion level, or from supporting conventional Army assets. From the platoon weapons squad, each rifle squad will have an attached gun team, and from the company fire-support section, an antiarmor team. We'll learn more about these two squad augmentees during the squad fire-and-movement drills. Other platoon/squad enablers, without getting into specific sourcing, can include medics, radio operators (RTOs), fire-support specialists, snipers, dogs and dog handlers, explosive ordnance disposal (EOD) technicians, hazardous-material specialists, interpreters, and intelligence specialists. The expanded capability provided by these enablers is mission dependent, and they are included on an as-needed basis to support the work of the basic Ranger squads and their fire teams.

Prior to my joining the platoon, Two-Bravo had just completed its week of ground-mobility training. For this mobility training, the Regiment maintains a complement of Strykers, the big eight-wheeled armored vehicles, and a complement of MRAPs—mine-resistant ambush-protected trucks. These armored vehicles are for predeployment training only, but they closely mirror those vehicles that await the deployed platoons when they rotate to the battlespace. Overseas, Strykers and MRAPs are used operationally for ground mobility and are crewed and driven by Rangers. The up-armored and unarmored Humvees now see limited use in current combat operations. The Ranger companies and platoons still have permanently assigned Hum-

vees for battalion training. Overseas, Rangers use vehicles for administrative transport and logistics, but seldom in combat. For airborne
mobility, the insertion platform of choice is still the special operations MH-47 Chinook helicopter, although Rangers may enter the
fight by way of the MH-60 Blackhawks or the MH-6 Little Birds.
In addition to their ground-mobility training, the Two-Bravo Rangers had spent a day on the shooting ranges with their work guns,
zeroing them in for the deployment training cycle.

Before I headed out for the current week's training with Two-
Bravo, I met briefly with the company commander, a major, and his
company first sergeant. "We begin live-fire training with fire-and-
movement drills and react-to-contact drills with the squads and fire
teams," they told me. "Then we work up from there to platoon-
centric training and company-sized coordinated drills. Sometimes,
it's not a linear progression from small units to larger units, but we
try. However it comes together, it all starts with the fire teams and
how they move and shoot as team elements. This starting small gets
the veterans back into form and allows the new men to settle into
their roles with their new fire teams." This was not unlike the deployment work-up as I understood it from the squads and fire teams at
3-75 at Fort Benning.

In looking at the company's roster, I saw only two familiar
names—new Rangers from Class 09-10. I ask about the new men
and how they are assigned within the company.

"I interview each new Ranger when he arrives," the B-Co first
sergeant told me, "and get some feel for who they are and where they
might best fit into the platoons. The platoon sergeants talk with
them as well. Then the platoon sergeants and I review personnel
needs and decide who goes where." I knew that one of the Rangers
from Class 09-10 assigned to B-Co was dealing with some family
problems. I was not surprised that the first sergeant knew all about
this soldier's issues and was working with him on them.

Two-Bravo began its week of range work with a day of gear prep-

aration, dry firing of weapons, and walk-throughs of tactical movements. For most range and live-fire shooting, the 1-75 Rangers must
travel from Hunter Army Airfield to nearby Fort Stewart. While
Hunter is small and convenient, the downside is that it's an hour's
drive to the Fort Stewart training areas. But Fort Stewart has the
ranges and the room—some 280,000 acres, which make it a third
again larger than Fort Benning. It's a huge base—the biggest military
installation east of the Mississippi. My platoon's initial range drills
at Fort Stewart parallel those of the RASP 1 marksmanship training
with barricade shooting, shooting at known distances, rifle-to-pistol
transition drills, and modifications of the El Presidente timed drills.
This first day of shooting focuses on drill with M4 rifles and the M9
Beretta pistols. New to me, and perhaps to the single new Ranger
in Two-Bravo, a soldier from RASP 1 Class 01-11, are the pop-up
targets. At 50, 100,150, 200, 250, and 300 meters, there are molded-
fiberglass, torso-silhouette targets that present themselves on a
hinged arm. When they are hit, they drop down; after a few seconds,
they pop back up. Instant feedback. About half of the Two-Bravo
shooters use the EOTech holographic sight on their M4s. The other
half use the Elcan Specter DR combat sight, an optic that features
a crosshair reticle and a quick 1X to 4X power adjustment. The better shooters are consistently toppling silhouettes at 300 meters from
the standing position. Everyone on the firing line works with M4s,
even those whose primary combat weapon is a SAW or one of the
heavier machine guns.

Two-Bravo's platoon sergeant briefs the men on the day's shooting and conducts a safety briefing, but the drills themselves are conducted under the direction of the squad leaders. Throughout the
day, the squad leaders work with their two fire-team leaders and
drill their Rangers. The platoon leader and the platoon sergeant, for
the most part, serve only as safety observers.

Two-Bravo's platoon leader is a captain who grew up in central
Florida and who says he's had a great tour with the 75th Rangers.

He's going back for his third combat deployment with 1/75, his second tour as a platoon leader. It's typical for a new officer to deploy once in a staff or support role before making a deployment as a platoon leader. Currently, this captain is looking for a way to extend his time with the battalion, but he's already overdue to attend the important Maneuver Captains Career Course and to move on to a tour with the conventional Army.

Two-Bravo's platoon sergeant is Sergeant First Class Jon Jackson. Jackson is from Wisconsin and was working as an apprentice pipe fitter when the first plane slammed into the World Trade Center. He immediately went down to the Army recruiting center and joined up.

"I'm one of the first of the GWOT [pronounced "gee-what"] platoon sergeants," he told me, meaning his entire service career has been during the Global War on Terrorism. "I got to Regiment as a private just after 9/11, and I've been in the mix ever since. This rotation will be my twelfth combat deployment." The Two-Bravo platoon sergeant is youthful-looking and a solid six feet one. He directs his platoon with equal measures of unquestioned authority, good humor, and a no-nonsense expectation of attention to detail and safety. As with all platoon leader and platoon sergeant teams, they complement each other. The platoon leader tends, for the most part, to issues of training and scheduling up the chain of command, while the platoon sergeant manages squad leaders and the training issues within the platoon. They easily stay in their lanes of responsibility, deferring to each other without consultation.

After a full day of shooting, the platoon breaks for hot chow that is ferried out from the battalion DFAC to the ranges on Fort Stewart by the company supply sergeant. Then Two-Bravo is back on the range. The same shooting drills that were conducted during the day are conducted at night with NVDs and IR targeting lasers.

Following the night-shooting evolution, the platoon moves by bus to another range for the next day's training. The platoon gets to their makeshift billet about 0200. In deference to the cold—the temperature is in the low twenties—Two-Bravo takes refuge on the concrete floor in one of the range-support buildings. Before they crawl into their sleeping bags, they clean, oil, and prepare their weapons for the next shooting evolution. After four hours of sleep and another round of hot chow delivered by the company supply team, the platoon is back out on the range. This time the drills are fire-and-movement and react-to-contact.

The training is conducted over a single drill lane or direction of movement that the Two-Bravo's squads will run over and over again. The drills are conducted in two-rifle-squad increments—first and second squads, then first and third squads, and finally second and third squads. This might be a good time to detail the role of the platoon's fourth squad, the weapons squad. The squad itself is comprised of a squad leader and three gun teams. Each gun team has a gunner and an assistant gunner. Their "gun" will be either the M240 medium machine gun, which can be employed with a bipod or with the new lightweight folding tripods, or the more-compact Mk-48 machine gun. Both weapon systems deliver the heavier link-belt-fed 7.62 NATO round. One gun team is attached to each squad. Most of the training I observed at 1/75 was with the M240. The weapons squad leader is usually the senior of the platoon's four squad leaders, and he serves as third in command within the platoon. With his gun teams embedded with the three rifle squads, he's in a position to assist his platoon sergeant with the tactical deployment of the platoon.

The drill lane for this exercise begins as two squads, with their attached gun teams, move in extended patrol formation through a sparsely wooded area of the range. All are in full combat kit and body armor, and carry a full ammunition load. The first station is a reaction-to-contact; here, two silhouettes pop up in front of the patrol and are engaged by the leading squad element. It then becomes a fire-and-maneuver drill as the lead squad leader directs his two fire teams in bounding maneuvers to assault the fiberglass enemy soldiers. The two enemy targets drop when they are hit and pop back up to be hit again. After moving past the two-man ambush, the patrol advances to a position where it must confront an enemy bunker. This is a serious target, and the lead squad leader brings both his fire teams on line to take the bunker under fire. He positions his two SAW gunners and his gun team, with tripod-mounted M240, to effectively bring suppressive fire to the bunker. But small-arms fire alone will not knock out an earthen bunker. The squad leader then brings his antitank (AT) team up to a position where he can engage the bunker.

The AT section is part of the B-Co headquarters platoon. The section trains with a variety of anti-armor weapons, including the LAAW and AT-4 shoulder-fired rockets, as well as the Javelin missile system, but the current weapon of choice is the 84-millimeter Carl Gustav recoilless rifle. The Gustav is a highly accurate and devastating weapon when used on armor, buildings, and bunkers. The "Goose" team, consisting of a gunner and his assistant, take the bunker under fire. The squad leader then sends one of his fire teams to flank the bunker. With one fire team engaging the bunker with steady suppressing fire, the other team starts its assault. The supporting fire team shifts its fire ahead of the assaulting team, then lifts fire (ceases fire), as the assaulting team closes on the bunker and attacks it with close-in fire and hand grenades. This bunker-assault completes the support-by-fire, fire-and-movement engagements by a single squad.

This support-by-fire assault is a standard fire-and-movement infantry tactic, but it's a potentially dangerous one. The supporting fire team is delivering live rounds ahead and in front of the flanking fire team's attack. Over the years, three 1-75 Rangers have been killed in live-fire training accidents, though none recently. The platoon leader, the platoon sergeant, and the B-Co first sergeant, who joined the platoon for this day of training, move up a little closer in their roles as safety observers to ensure the squad leader's shift-fire and lift-fire commands are executed smartly.

Moving through and past the cleared bunker to the edge of a tree line, the two-squad patrol is then engaged across an open ravine by a squad of enemy fiberglass pop-ups and a realistic-sounding, pneumatic automatic weapon. This time it's a fire-and-movement drill with one full squad providing a base of fire and the other squad racing through the cover of the woods to a flanking position. Then it's another support-by-fire assault by the flanking squad as they bound to and through the enemy squad position. Again, the shift-fire and lift-fire commands are closely supervised. The final engagement on this training lane is an enemy attack by yet another squad of fiberglass pop-ups and by a target vehicle some 150 meters away. This calls for another Gustav rocket to engage the vehicle.

Each movement through the drill lane, including a comprehensive after-action review, takes about an hour and a half. This day, Two-Bravo runs the same drill six times—three with blank ammunition and three with live fire, including the Carl Gustav training rockets. The squad leaders run the drills and conduct the training while the platoon leader, the platoon sergeant, and the company first sergeant follow close behind to observe. Sergeant Jackson, as the platoon sergeant, takes an active role when two squads are engaged, as he would in combat. He works through his squad leaders, physically moving between them or directing them on their tactical radio net. If two or more squads are engaged, the platoon sergeant coordinates the engagement. Once the shooting started, it was, for me, organized chaos. Lots of yelling, running, and shooting, and squad leaders moving from gun team to SAW gunners to riflemen to direct fire.

"A-team, on me, moving!"

"Gun team, move up!"

"Base of fire. Seven round bursts every fifteen seconds!"

"B-team moving to two o'clock!"

"Smith is down!" A Ranger drops to a knee, flushes his magazine, and replaces it with a fresh one. "Smith coming up!" He's back in the fight.

"Ammo status—give me a bullet count!"

"SAW gunner, pick up the pace!"

"Moving to eleven o'clock. On me!"

Throughout the drills there is constant attention to safety, especially during the shifting and lifting of fire as the flanking elements assault with the live-fire rounds moving in front of them. Yet safety is practiced at all times, even with those iterations using blank ammunition. And a great deal of respect is given the Gustav, both to the business end and the rocket backblast. Along with safety and sustaining rates of fire, an ongoing inventory of remaining ammunition is a continuing part of every drill. And the drills are exhausting. During the AARs, when the Rangers remove their helmets and gather around Sergeant Jackson for a critique, steam pours from them into the cool air.

During the AARs, Sergeant Jackson and the first sergeant go over each engagement in detail. When it comes to the actions on target and the final clearing of the bunker, the first sergeant weighs in.

"You can't assume that just because the bunker took a Gustav round that there's no one alive inside. Play the hand out! Make your approach expecting opposition. And remember, it's all about angles— watch your angles of fire and keep a steady volume of fire going into the openings until you can get a grenade in there. Even then, be very careful as you conduct your final clearing procedures. Look for enemy movement, but know where your Ranger buddies are at all times."

Following one of the AARs, I find Private George Dempsey reloading magazines for the next drill. "Learning anything?" I ask the only Ranger in Two-Bravo that has yet to make a combat rotation.

"You bet I am," he replies, "but there's so much to learn and know. The guys in my squad have been great in helping me get settled in, but I have to admit it's an intimidating process. And it's consuming.

I have to be thinking all the time—about what I'm doing now and what I might be doing next. It's physically and mentally exhausting. So, just like in RASP, I'm trying to work as hard as I can and take it one day at a time."

New Rangers in the rifle platoons are assigned one of three roles in their fire team. They will be a rifleman with an M4 rifle, an automatic-weapons (AW) man who will carry the Mk46 squad assault weapon or SAW, or the team grenadier. The grenadier carries an M4, so he can also serve as a rifleman, but his primary weapon is the Mk320 grenade launcher. This compact weapon weighs just over three pounds and is carried on the Rangers combat rack like a sidearm. It can quickly be put into action and accurately deliver 40-millimeter grenades out to two hundred meters. The 320 recently replaced the M203 grenade launcher, the same one *my grenadier* carried back in the day some forty years ago. Most new rifle-squad Rangers will serve their first rotation as a grenadier. Those new Rangers assigned to the weapons squad will serve as assistant gunners (AGs), primarily for the M240 medium machine gun.

Over chow that evening, I'm able to spend a few minutes with Sergeant Jackson. I bring up his new Ranger. "On balance, Dempsey is doing a good job," he says. "He's just about where he should be at this stage as a new private. I think he's going to do well in combat. His skills are average—maybe even a little below average—but he listens. That's very important. As long as he listens and stays focused, he'll do just fine. We can bring him up to standard."

"How many don't do well?" I ask. "By that, I mean how many come to battalion but prove to be unsuitable for duty in the Regiment?"

He gives this a moment's thought. "I'd have to say about one in four are just not up to the task. Some are capable, but their personal life is screwed up or they drink too much off duty and just don't make it here. These guys all have security clearances, so they can't be in any financial trouble. A few just don't have the situational awareness to be moving in close proximity with other Rangers at night with a gun—it's not in them. And some are just too timid, or they lack the ability to know when to dial it up. There's a time to be measured and careful, and there's a time when you have to be hyperaggressive and really on your game. That means charging into the fight, shooting bad guys again and again until they go down, and quickly moving onto the next target. This business is not for everyone. The new guys we're getting from RASP seem to be better screened and better prepared as compared to the Rangers we used to get from RIP, so maybe more of them will succeed here." Sergeant Jackson looks up as the rest of the platoon is starting to stir. "Excuse me, sir. Time to go back to work."

The platoon sergeant and the rest of his platoon are back out on the range. It's now full-on dark with a half-moon on the rise, and it's getting cold again. Everyone now has their night-vision devices in place. They run three more drill iterations with blank fire and another three with live fire. It's just after 0230 when they return to the cramped range building and begin to clean and oil their weapons. The final day of this range period will be spent at the Fort Stewart shoot house, an isolated facility that's a forty-minute truck ride from the fire-and-movement range.

Once at the Fort Stewart shoot house, the platoon immediately begins by setting up targets and prepping doors for breaching. This shoot house is a maze of walls and partitions constructed of hard-rubber composite blocks that can safely absorb the high-velocity 5.56 M4 rounds and the shrapnel from explosive breaching. It's also constructed so that both the external and internal doors can be breached mechanically, ballistically, or explosively. The breaching portion of the drills means that there's not only initial prep time in setting up for the training, but ongoing rehabilitation time. While half the platoon is moving through shooting drills with their weapons, the other half is standing by, armed with skill saws, hammers, and power screwdrivers. After each breaching/shooting evolution, the rehab crews attack the shattered doors and casings to get them ready for the next team of shooters. There are also target silhouettes that have to be repositioned and remarked.

The drills are set up for single-room clearing, then multiple-room clearings in which an assault team will clear one room and tactically flow into an adjoining room. These iterations are done by fire teams of three to four Rangers. A full drill will have a fire team entering the building with an explosive breach—usually done with a simple eighteen-inch explosive cutting charge. The team will then move tactically to an internal door, kick it open, and engage silhouette targets to clear that room. Then, using a holitool or the breaching shotgun, they force a second door to clear a second room. Often, a room clearing is preceded with a flash-bang grenade tossed in for good measure. For the daylight training, all shooting is done with the visible, red-dot lasers.

Up on the catwalk above the room partitions, the platoon leader, platoon sergeant, and squad leaders observe. All three participate in directing the drills, but the squad leaders are the primary supervisors; room clearing is a fight led by their fire-team leaders. The observers hold mini AARs after every evolution, running the same drill several times and often doing a walk-through to lock down the mechanics of movement. Again, they do this with blank fire, then live rounds. Then, after nightfall, everyone dons NVDs. The drills are again run in the dark—first with blanks and then with live rounds. After single fire-team entries, the squads move on to dual-team room clearings, with the squad leaders directing the action. At night in the shades-of-green world of the NVDs, the rooms are lit with the IR laser dots dancing on the silhouette targets and the occasional searing streak of a SAW tracer. As in actual combat, the fire-team leaders call out the action on the tactical net of their MBITR radios, which are tuned to their squad leaders.

"A-team, breaching complete, room secure, three enemy KIA."

"Roger, A-team leader, three enemy KIA."

"B-team reporting room secure, two enemy KIA. Preparing to breach second room."

"Copy, B-team. Have you breaching second room."

A lot is on these fire-team leaders; they must move, shoot, and communicate in fast-moving, dynamic situations. The final nighttime drills dial up the intensity with two fire teams conducting full-assault profiles together. The shoot house is surrounded by a six-foot wooden fence that simulates the stone or mud wall that often protects a courtyard compound in Iraq or Afghanistan. The fire teams approach in the dark with scaling ladders. They set up security positions while moving over the fence to the shoot house. Once in place, they conduct a coordinated breaching of two external doors and move into multiroom internal-clearing scenarios. Again, the squad leaders direct and coordinate their fire teams under the watchful eye of Sergeant Jon Jackson. In a real scenario, there could be three or more fire teams conducting simultaneous multiroom clearing operations. In this scenario, the platoon sergeant would be looking "inward" to assist his squad leaders with movement and activity, while the officer platoon leader would be glancing inward but looking "outward" to keep the ground-force commander informed and any supporting elements in a position to help the work of the squads and fire teams. The platoon leader, platoon sergeant, and squad leaders are on two radio nets: the tactical net, which directs the squads and fire teams; and the command net, which includes the ground-force commander and supporting elements. Each has a boom mike and a radio bud in each ear. The fire-team leaders monitor only the tactical net. There are operational scenarios that call for fire-team members to be on a third, personal radio net, but that is not the norm. "We don't need privates on radios," one squad leader tells me. "We need them looking for targets." In many engagements, the platoon leader will also be the ground-force commander. In these situations, he will make full use of his radio operator (RTO), who monitors the tactical and command nets in addition to maintaining a satellite link back to the

operations center. The platoon leader is also accompanied by a forward observer (FO), who may be a platoon Army FO or an Air Force
joint tactical air controller (JTAC). Two-Bravo has an Air Force
JTAC. In a Ranger platoon, the platoon officer carries an M4, but
his primary weapons system is his radios. The more senior the
Ranger, the more radios and radios nets.

In describing this one week of range work, I've made all this far
simpler than it is in the actual execution. Even at the squad/fire-
team level, this is complex and dangerous training in preparation for
life-and-death combat—combat engagements these Rangers will face
on a daily basis. One of the few benefits of a long war is that there's
a lot of muscle memory and experience in these Ranger assault elements. New men like Private Dempsey are drinking from a fire hose
as they go through these drills, but there are Rangers to his left and
right who have done this many times before—in the shoot house
and in Afghanistan, where the targets they will engage have guns
and shoot back. When the drills are run, the targets put away, and
the brass shell casings all policed up, it's 0300 on Friday morning.
The Rangers of Two-Bravo finally pile into the back of two LMTV
canvas-covered trucks for the cold ride back to Hunter Army Airfield. Friday is a relatively easy day in garrison, with weapons cleaning, gear overhaul, and a parachute jump for those who have not
jumped with the new T-11 chutes.

This is but one week in the life of a Ranger platoon preparing for
the fight—2nd Platoon, Bravo Company, 1st Ranger Battalion. In
some ways, it was a little more busy than most, but certainly not
unusual. Rangers are always busy. Working long hours in garrison,
being away from home, and performing with little sleep are all standard fare for Rangers in deployment preparation. The long days and
working halfway through the night reminded me of the week at Cole
Range during Phase One of RASP. Later on, Two-Bravo will be back
on the shooting ranges for training in company- and battalion-sized
engagements. These range periods in the larger formations will be

similar to these squad/platoon drills. There will be blank-fire drills followed by live-fire drills over dedicated range lanes with multiple repetitions. These fire-and-movement drills, with larger elements and additional fire-support components, will be more complex and require more attention to command and control. Common to all this range training are the long, exhausting days with little sleep. The Rangers typically run these drills during the daylight and again at night. If it's cold and rainy, as it was for much of Two-Bravos range drill, the work will go on. This is battle drill, one of the Ranger Big Five.

Bravo Company of 1/75 has only three Rangers who have not made a combat rotation. There may be a few more if and when other Rangers are posted to the battalion from RASP and are assigned to B-Co. "We'd like to get them here at the beginning of the work-up, but we'll take them as they're sent to us," the first sergeant tells me. "For the late arrivals, my squad and fire-team leaders will teach them what they can as fast as they can and give them operational responsibility as they show us they can handle it." Bravo Company's situation is a little more immediate than the other three rifle companies; its B-Co's turn to be the surge company. This means it will leave well ahead of the rest of the battalion, so its preparation time is constrained. For this one company, a few of their predeployment training evolutions will have to be shortened or eliminated.

One predeployment training component that is neither shortened nor eliminated is physical training. I ask one of the Two-Bravo Rangers about PT. "On the ranges or during airborne operations, we don't have the time for PT or we have to sandwich it around the training. Otherwise, we do it every day. Our squad leader leads PT and tries to mix it up. We always stretch and do light upper-body work. One day is a long run, another day we run the obstacle course, and we swim maybe once a week. If we're working on Saturdays, we come in early and play soccer. About once a week, usually on a run, our squad leader crushes us. He's an animal, and it's pure punishment—

there is no other word for it. Some of the guys can run with him, but I'm not one of them. Yet I'm not too far behind. Past the regular PT, we all try to get to the gym two or three times a week to lift."

Private Dempsey had this to say of the physical pace in general. "I hurt every day. Running on ranges uses muscles that you don't always use in the daily PT. And the daily PT sessions during the nonrange days are smokers. They told us in RASP that squad PT would be hard, and they were right. These guys are all in shape. Some of them don't necessarily look fit, but they can all run while kitted up and they can all do PT. It's just part of the life. I'm sure I'll get used to it in time, but every morning it seems like there's a new set of muscles that is sore."

Of the three new men to B-Co, only Private Dempsey is from RASP 1 Class 01-11. The other two are from my class, Class 09-10. Private First Class Don Howard is a rifleman with the first squad of Three-Bravo. And Private Kevin Seiple, the Top Gun awardee from Class 09-10, is a gun-team assistant gunner with the weapons squad of One-Bravo. I found him in his squad bay working on his kit.

"How's it going for you, Ranger?"

"Great—couldn't be better. I'm with a great squad and a great platoon. And we're all busting butt to get ready for deployment." I ask him about his duties. "I'm an AG, and there's a lot to learn as well as a lot to carry. I have a big ammo load. I not only have to be able to handle the tripod and extra gun barrel, but I have to be able to service both guns [the M240 and the MK48]. Since I have to be able to do everything at night, I practice these things blindfolded. Above all, I have to take care of my gunner, and I have to know his job so I can run the gun if he goes down."

"How's the squad PT?"

"I do okay with PT. We do PT together, but sometimes I think they pour it on to see if I can handle it. I know they're watching to see if I can keep up. And I won't say it's not a struggle sometimes, but I can stay up with my squad." This is good for me to hear and to write about; physical training is one of the Ranger Big Five, and the new RASP Rangers seem to be doing this well.

"How's your family?" I ask. Private Seiple not only has to prepare himself for combat rotation, he also has to ready a very young family for their first separation. Neither is easy.

"My wife and baby will be staying with her grandparents while I'm gone. That seems like the best thing for us. It's hard to believe," he says with a wistful smile. "My daughter is just starting to talk. When I get back, she'll be starting to walk. Things are happening fast."

Like other new Rangers I speak with, he's both anxious and apprehensive about his first combat rotation. From my own experience back when, the combat missions blur and seem to run together, but I certainly remember the anxiety of that first deployment and that first mission. Like all young men headed for the fight, they have to trust their equipment, their training, their leadership, and, most of all, the men on either side of them.

These three new B-Co 1/75 Rangers seem to be holding their own, and to a man, the B-Co Ranger veterans speak highly of the new men from RASP. There is collective concern that the new program, while delivering on quality, may not be keeping up with losses—those who elect to leave the military and those lost in combat. If the economy remains sluggish, more Rangers may elect to remain in uniform. If the quality of the new RASP Rangers is indeed higher, then perhaps fewer will be released for standards, and those one in four who, by Sergeant Jackson's estimate, don't make it in the Regiment could become one in five or one in six. And, of course, if there's ever a light at the end of this long tunnel, the OPTEMPO may slacken, and fewer Rangers will be killed or severely wounded in action. That would be my hope. Too many variables; only time will tell. At this single point in time, the new RASP-trained Rangers seem to be keeping up with regimental attrition and living up to the expectations of the new training program.

With this trickle of new men into the rifle companies, the average level of combat experience across the force at this point in time is growing and perhaps is at an all-time high. In Two-Bravo, the junior squad leader is a very capable E-5 sergeant going back on fifth rotation. The other squad leaders are returning with anywhere from seven to nine tours behind them. The junior fire-team leader is on his third rotation; the norm is four to six.

While with B-Co and Two-Bravo, I've noted that military courtesies seem to be observed much as they were in RASP and the Ranger Selection and Training Company. Privates and specialists address sergeants and corporals by their rank, and sergeants and corporals address privates and specialists by their title and last name. When a private addresses a sergeant, he comes to a position of parade rest. While moving from the assembly areas to the ranges, privates run, even with kit. On occasion, when there is inattention to detail, privates and even specialists are dropped for push-ups. But in the chow lines during training, privates are pushed to the front of the line; privates eat first. There's an ease and good humor that accompany these formalities and observances, up and down the ranks. Only twice during my time with 1-75 did I see an NCO physically put a private through an extended, remedial PT. Yet when something needs to be done, like policing brass on the range, everyone bends to the task. And when there's urgency to the task, like the rehabbing of targets and doors in the shoot house, everyone runs. These men are personally close, yet they are able to maintain structure and observe standard military courtesies in a relaxed and informal way. Other SOF units, in my experience, have less structure and more familiarity within their junior chains of command. I have no way to judge or compare this to the way it is in the conventional Army, but the military courtesies and junior-senior relationships in the Ranger platoons don't seem to dampen the sense of brotherhood that these men share. Yet they are continually observed.

During my second week with Two-Bravo, the platoon Rangers

busy themselves with admin chores and prepare for MLAT, which was to begin the following week. MLAT is shorthand for Multilateral Airborne Training—or, more to the point, airfield-seizure training. There are skills that have to be rehearsed and certified before this training begins in earnest. MLAT evolutions and the pre-MLAT drills will be addressed later in this chapter when I join Alpha Company for its complete MLAT cycle. B-Co's MLAT will be modified around a compressed schedule due to their advanced rotation date.

On January 21, 2011, even as the 1st Battalion of the 75th Rangers prepare for the next rotation, they take time to honor and remember those Rangers who perished during the last rotation. There were seven of them:

Sergeant Jonathon Peney
Specialist Joseph Dimock
Sergeant Justin Allen
Sergeant Martin Lugo
Specialist Christopher Wright
Sergeant First Class Lance Vogeler
Staff Sergeant Kevin Pape

The ceremony itself was, for this non-Ranger and his wife, who were privileged to attend, both poignant and telling. Between them, these seven fallen Rangers had a total of *thirty-eight* combat rotations. This experience is irreplaceable, and the personal loss to their friends, family, and brother Rangers is unfathomable. Yet, as with the B-Co 3/75 Rangers who perished in the service of their nation and their Regiment, these Rangers will remain forever young in the hearts of those who knew them and fought with them.

Following the memorial service and a luncheon at the Ranger dining facility for the families of the Ranger dead, an awards ceremony was held. Among the numerous honors for valor presented were forty-two Purple Hearts, which included the seven awarded posthumously. For the 1st Ranger Battalion, this was close to a 10 percent casualty rate among the rifle-platoon Rangers for a single combat rotation.

The following Monday, I move to Alpha Company, 1st Platoon for the MLAT portion of the deployment work-up. Multilateral Airborne Training is again, military-speak for the training program that prepares Rangers to seize airfields—a critical mission set for the 75th Ranger Regiment. For A-Co and my 1st Platoon, or One-Alpha, this will occupy three weeks of their precious predeployment time. Before we get to this block of training, let's first talk about my new company and platoon. A-Co is organizationally a mirror image of B-Co, but with slightly fewer Rangers currently assigned to it. Yet with several months of training before deployment, A-Co will in all probability receive some new RASP graduates before it rotates into the battlespace. But at this point in time, there are *no* Rangers in A-Co who have not made a combat deployment—zero. Few company-sized units in this or any other regiment can make that claim.

"We have two Rangers who are in their first deployment training cycle," the A-Co first sergeant tells me. "They came to us just as we were going out the door on the last rotation, but no new guys. That will probably change, but none so far."

I made it a point to find one of those new Rangers—Rangers who had deployed without the benefit of the predeployment training cycle. Private First Class Chad Garcia is also a One-Alpha Ranger. He began with the first RASP class, 01-10, and graduated with 02-10. I caught him during one of the breaks during MLAT. I wanted to know how it had been to deploy within a few weeks of graduating from RASP. Garcia is a short man, Hispanic, serious, very fit, and he looks as if he's about fifteen. But he's a Ranger combat veteran. On meeting him, he stands at a stiff parade rest until I can get him to be at ease.

"I left to go to Afghanistan literally a week after I got here to 1/75," he tells me. "I'm an Eleven Bravo, and my first assignment was as an assistant gunner. I worked with other AGs and learned on the job. I even trained on the flight over. My gunner gave me hours and hours of one-on-one training. And I was always close to him when we went out on missions. We were usually in a static position in support of the assault teams. Then the second month there, when not with my gun team, I shadowed my squad leader and was with him as he directed the squad's two fire teams on missions. I learned a lot with him. All the while, I was participating in the rehearsals with one of our rifle squads before they went out on missions. By the third month, I was a rifleman in a fire team doing Ranger work. It helps a lot," he adds with a confident grin, "if everyone around you knows exactly what they're doing. And every step of the way, my Ranger buddies made sure I knew where I was supposed to be and what I was supposed to do. The preoperation rehearsals helped a great deal. And I was lucky to have such great guys around me. I still am."

"So how's your first MLAT going for you?" I ask.

"Great, so far. I'm on one of the gun trucks for the air-land portion of the MLAT. We did very little with GMVs (often shorthand for various modifications of Humvees) on deployment, so it's kind of a game to see how fast we can load and unload them on the aircraft. My platoon sergeant keeps a stopwatch on us, and we don't quit until we meet his standard. I can't wait until we get to the fly-aways. There's always something to learn or learn how to do better. It's all good."

The leadership of One-Alpha is an unusual mix of experience for a Ranger platoon. The officer platoon leader is a first lieutenant and a veteran of two combat deployments with a conventional combat unit. But he's new to the Regiment and 1/75, and new within only a few days of my joining the platoon. He was in RASP 2 Class 01-11 at Fort Benning while I was with Class 09-10 during Phase

Two of RASP 1. First Lieutenant Matt Kozart joined the platoon at the beginning of MLAT, which means he is assuming leadership of One-Alpha after a portion of their predeployment preparation is complete. The platoon sergeant is a quiet, competent veteran from Southern California. Sergeant First Class Seth Kline is returning on his thirteenth combat tour. He's five feet ten and weighs 180, and he has a very soft way about him. As with Two-Bravo, this platoon moves to the cadence of the platoon sergeant. Sergeant Kline runs One-Alpha's training and directs the platoon Rangers with a measured and undisputed authority. He never raises his voice; he seems not to have to. It's as if he has only to make suggestions to his squad and fire-team leaders. They comply immediately—if they haven't anticipated their platoon sergeant's intent and are already moving. It's my sense that this new first lieutenant is well thought of by his superiors at the company and battalion level, and that he probably broke out from his contemporaries during RASP 2. I also sense that there's a great deal of confidence in this platoon sergeant to give him a competent but inexperienced platoon leader at this stage of a deployment work-up. Probably both.

Airfield seizure is an important Ranger mission-essential task, one that can only be maintained with the recurring training and certification of all involved. This mission is a legacy of the failed Operation Eagle Claw, the disastrous attempt to free the fifty-two-member U.S. embassy legation taken prisoner in Iran in 1980. The mission failed largely because we had no standing, coordinated ability to mount a light-infantry, air-land assault into hostile territory. That has changed. If and when an enemy airfield or denied-area airfield has to be taken, there's every likelihood that the policy makers will want it done yesterday, and there will be little time for training or rehearsal. If airfield seizure is to be an off-the-shelf, on-call capability, then it has to be a front-loaded skill. Yet airfield seizure is a mission scenario the 1-75 Rangers will in all probability *not* execute on their next combat rotation. Rangers are not alone in this. Navy

SEALs routinely train for combat-swimmer attack and over-the-beach operations, then deploy to Afghanistan, where they will do neither. The 2nd Infantry Division in South Korea trains to respond to a North Korean incursion, a real but historically unlikely threat. So Rangers who know they will be conducting primarily platoon-sized assault operations in Afghanistan train for airfield seizure as a battalion—just in case. It's a stand-alone capability that only Rangers can do reliably and quickly, so they make time for it in their busy predeployment schedule.

An airfield seizure could be a company-sized operation, but more likely one that would involve a whole battalion—or two battalions or even the entire regiment. This makes it a complex action with extended command and control issues. On top of that, an airfield seizure is a daring and high-risk undertaking. It must be carefully rehearsed and worked up in stages from the simple to the composite. Airfield-seizure training takes place on two levels: the senior planning and execution level, and the on-the-ground, operational level. I'll not go into the multiple levels of command that accompany such an operation, as airfield seizure involves the invasion of another country with the chain of command going all the way to the president. At the company and battalion level, and by extension the regimental level, decisions have to be made and orders given quickly and responsibly, and in a very dynamic environment. Company, battalion, and regimental commanders, and their staffs, have to train to do this. They also have to train to manage the staggering amount of detail that accompanies the preparation and execution of a seizure operation. So MLAT is the training ground for those senior planners and leaders. Much as a private first class in Ranger School must learn to command a squad or a platoon and to "move the chess pieces" for a small-unit engagement, senior commanders must be trained in moving platoon- and company-sized elements during a larger raid. Since there are no simulators for this, commanders get this training during MLAT. Keeping in mind that a great deal of MLAT is for the senior company and battalion leadership, we will continue to track the platoons, squads, and the new Rangers in this training.

The first week of Multilateral Airborne Training has to do with simply getting onto the insertion platforms and offloading in a tactical manner. Once the mission is complete, the assault force must redeploy on those same platforms and tactically extract from the airfield. These insertions and extractions are practiced under combat conditions, first in the daylight, then at night. There is a very compressed crawl-walk-run approach to this insertion-extraction training.

At the beginning of the week, the platforms arrive, and one end of the big runway at Hunter Army Airfield is closed off for this training. From the U.S. Air Force there are five big C-17 transports. From the 1st Special Operations Wing (the Air Force SOF component) there are the MC-130 Combat Talons, the new CV-22s—the Air Force SOF version of the tilt-rotor Osprey—and a single AC-130 gunship. The SOF helicopters for this MLAT belong to the 3rd Battalion of the 160th Night Stalkers and include the big MH-47 Chinooks, the medium-sized MH-60 Blackhawks, and the MH-6 Little Birds. By my estimate, there is close to $2 billion worth of American airborne muscle parked at Hunter to support this training. This is training for the combat aircrews as well. Supporting an airfield seizure is as demanding and dangerous a mission as these aviators may ever be asked to fly.

At the platoon and company level, there are basic skills that have to be practiced and certified, on and off the aircraft. The first of these involves FRIES training. FRIES stands for fast-rope infil/exfil system. Put simply, it means fast-roping. This training begins at the battalion fast-roping tower. The Rangers then kit up and fast-rope from helicopters that have gone into a low hover. This is called an elevator drill. the Over and over, the Rangers perform this drill, both without kit (Hollywood) and with a full combat load, in the daylight and then again at night. The Chinooks can lift a platoon; the Blackhawks, a squad; and the Little Birds, a fire team.

The second basic MLAT skill set is the shackle drill. Rangers arrive on a denied airfield target in two ways. They can parachute or fast-rope onto the objective, which means they can fight with the equipment they carry in or with a limited amount of air-bundled/air-dropped support. Or they can land on or near the target airfield in transport aircraft and drive to the fight in GMVs and a host of other assault-support vehicles. Most integrated MLAT drills call for both—a combination of airborne and air-land infiltration. Usually, but not always, the airborne assault precedes the air-land operation in order to secure and clear the runways for the landing of fixed- and rotary-wing aircraft. Shackle drills are simply the practice of back-loading vehicles and Rangers onto aircraft and tying them down for takeoff, insertion, and recovery.

On the objective, the Rangers and their vehicles must tactically deploy and redeploy under simulated combat conditions. The Rangers practice these tie-down procedures on concrete mock-ups, then on the real aircraft sitting on the tarmac—day and night. These static drills precede flyaway drills, also done day and night, where seconds count. When a fixed-wing transport, a C-130, a C-17, or CV-22 Osprey is on the ground, it's vulnerable to small-arms fire. In well-rehearsed, procedural-driven scenarios, Rangers wearing NVDs quickly offload and set security to allow their aircraft to leave quickly. During the exfil, they reboard the aircraft in an orderly manner and execute their tie-down procedures for a quick getaway. Prior to conducting an MLAT mission profile, they run these drills over and over. Throughout this first week, amid the fast-rope and shackle drills, the Rangers of 1/75 all make a nighttime equipment jump and rehearse their initial drop-zone security and tactical procedures.

The amount of equipment and support that can be deployed in an airfield seizure is more than impressive. In addition to their kit and a combat load, the Rangers can parachute in with light motor-cycles and teams of dogs and dog handlers. The air-land package arrives with a mix of GMVs in the form of gun trucks, commo

trucks, towed heavy mortars, ambulances, and perhaps a complement of dismounted Rangers. The flow of assets from the fixed-wing
aircraft may vary depending on mission requirements—from Ranger
recon elements mounted on four-wheel ATVs to AH-6 Little Bird
helicopter gunships. All are landed, unloaded, and deployed in a
matter of minutes. Standing in the middle of this are the departure
aircraft control officers (DACOs). There is one for each aircraft,
usually a Ranger NCO. His only job is to supervise the loading and
unloading during infiltration and exfiltration, and to account for
every soul who leaves his aircraft. Rangers, vehicles, and equipment
may deploy/parachute on one platform and leave on another. The
DACOs are responsible for seeing that everyone who goes in comes
out. Priority one is that no one is left behind. Priority two is that all
weapons, radios, and sensitive equipment are accounted for.

The MLAT cycle is conducted in multiplatoon, company-sized
iterations and then as a battalion operation with multiple companies
in play. These are full mission profiles with warning orders, operations orders, airfield terrain models, rehearsals, and all the inspections and safety briefings that must accompany training and real-world
flyaway operations. In the battalion iterations, briefings and operations orders are delivered by the battalion staff and cascade from
the battalion level to the platoon level, where the platoon leaders
and platoon sergeants brief their squads and fire teams. The briefings are ongoing and exhaustive. At all levels, when the element
commander concludes his brief, be it the battalion commander or a
platoon leader, all present come to their feet and salute.

"Rangers Lead the Way."

"ALL THE WAY!"

At the airfield in the staging hangar, just prior to the aircraft
loading and boarding process, the full battalion gathers a final time
before commencing a nighttime seizure operation. The Rangers are
dressed in Ranger Combat Uniforms (RCUs), a muted dark-green,
woodland pattern of a custom design and material, with integral

pockets for elbow and kneepads. There are no names or ranks on the combat uniforms, only an American flag on one shoulder. All are in RCUs, from the new privates to the 1/75 battalion commander. All are a part of the airborne package or the air-land package. The command staff presents a quick intelligence overview and weather update to the assembled battalion. The battalion chaplain offers a prayer, asking God for safe and meaningful training. The Battalion Commander and Command Sergeant Major each offer a final comment, then a closing:

"Rangers Lead the Way."

The full battalion replies, "ALL THE WAY!"

In this particular exercise scenario, a fictitious nation is experiencing a rapid onset of insurgent/terrorist unrest. The airports are closed and American embassy personnel are at risk. The president has ordered an airfield seizure to rescue the trapped Americans. While executing their on-the-ground mission, the Rangers meet opposing forces with blank fire, which sets into motion reaction-to-contact and fire-and-movement drills. Exercise play may involve aircraft malfunctions that cause adjustments in the airfield exfiltration and/or extraction plans. The MLAT drills, like all Ranger exercises, have men notionally wounded that call for casualty care and casualty evacuation. And since this is Georgia and January, there are real-world weather delays and schedule slippages. As in real airfield seizure operations, there are Rangers in full combat kit, on vehicles and in parachute harness, patiently waiting for the order to board their insertion aircraft, or, once boarded, made to wait during weather holds. I expected some grousing and complaining that can accompany these uncomfortable and inevitable delays in full kit, but there were none. Even the privates and specialists seem to understand that much of MLAT is for the mission planners and command groups, and they accept it. Or perhaps tactical patience is a Ranger skill set as well.

For the new Rangers from RASP, every evolution, drill, and practice is a learning experience. At this stage of their battle preparation, it matters little that MLAT missions may have little real-world relevance to their upcoming deployment. Every time they kit up, they're building muscle memory and carrying their load a little better. One squad leader put it this way.

"Every drill that involves reacting-to-contact, bounding assault, or assault-by-fire serves to lock in skills that they *will* use on the upcoming deployment. Even moving in the shades-of-green world of NVDs, searching for targets with their IR sights, and working with their kit and weapons at night help to get the new Rangers in the rhythm of moving efficiently with their fire teams. The new guys simply can't spend enough time with their night-vision devices. Neither can the veterans, for that matter. Good as our NVDs are, and the new ones we just received are the best, it takes a lot of time to get used to moving at night in the green world. You see veterans running across broken terrain at night, vaulting over fences, like it was broad daylight. It takes the new guys a while to move like that. And there's fighting at night. The night-fight is all about situational awareness—where you are, where the enemy is, and where your Ranger buddies are. It's a very unique skill set—for the new Rangers, for all of us. For the veterans, this tactical drill at the squad and fire-team level is the same every time, but has to be done. We know and accept this repetition as part of the job—part of battle drill."

For three successive nights, this same scenario is run, and the same airfield at a small base in northern Georgia is seized and secured. This is like the squad live-fire drills conducted over the same training-range lane again and again, only it's all blank fire. With each iteration, the planners improve the plan. Rangers jump in via T-11 parachutes, and rally and tactically deploy a little better. The vehicles disperse from the transport aircraft a little quicker, and the assault force redeploys a little more orderly. Again, it's a series of battle drills—practice and certification for a real-world contingency that, should it occur, will be executed a long way from home, on contested ground, at night, and on short notice.

The MLAT series is just one block of training in the predeployment preparation cycle. With every training evolution there is planning, training support, scheduling, range and airfield clearance, gear preparation, briefings, coordination, safety and supervisory inspections, more briefings, documentation, after-action reviews, and gear rehab. Some nights, a platoon is out supporting the training of sister platoons, role-playing as enemy forces or serving as jumpmasters or safety observers. Throughout this training, there are individual needs and individual training requirements. There is sick call for training injuries, counseling issues, administrative issues, and the occasional personal or family emergency. A few of these Rangers are coming and going from schools: jumpmaster school, sniper school, and master-breacher school, to name a few. One-Alpha alone has two Rangers at Ranger School. And still, the training and certifications have to be conducted and met. Everyone, at all levels, is working long hours, but for the senior platoon leadership—the squad leaders, the platoon sergeants, and the platoon leaders—the burden is particularly demanding. As One-Alpha moves into almost exclusively night work, which they call vampire hours, the platoon leader and platoon senior sergeants come in midmorning and seldom leave before 0300 the following morning—night after night. On occasion, they are in for planning meetings as early as 0600, which means little or no sleep.

There is not the time here to walk through an entire MLAT mission at the company or the battalion level, but I hope you, the reader, get the idea: This is very complex, time-consuming, demanding, and dangerous training. On a multiple-moving-parts scale, it reminds me of Navy night carrier operations—the launching and recovering of aircraft at sea in the dark. The 1/75 MLAT for 2011, like other previous annual MLATs, is not focused on preparation for the upcoming combat rotation to Afghanistan. But the real-world aspect of all

this changed in the middle of this MLAT. While the battalion recer-
tified itself in airfield seizure, events in Tunisia, Egypt, and Libya
put American civilians and embassy personnel in those nations at a
potential risk. Mobs in the streets of a large Arab nation are cause
for concern, but we were still a long way from the mini-military
incursion that is an airfield seizure. Still, with Libya then on the
brink of civil war and foreign nationals scrambling to flee that country, I found it all a little serendipitous.

At the squad level, the basics still apply. Rangers with combat kit
still have to move, shoot, and communicate—at night and in various
tactical conditions. There's a great deal to learn for the newer men
and to relearn for the veterans, even during MLATs. During a break
in that training, I ask Staff Sergeant Tim Donaldson, One-Alpha's
weapons-squad leader, how he goes about breaking in his new Rangers. Donaldson is preparing for his eighth combat rotation, his third
as a squad leader. He's led both rifle and weapons squads.

"New men typically fall into two categories: the ones who catch
on relatively quickly, and those who struggle. The ones who struggle are usually young privates who are timid and unsure of themselves. They want to fit in, but they have a hard time relaxing around
the veterans. They're the guys who stand around their squad bays
at parade rest; they don't quite know what to do with themselves.
But we can work with them because they are anxious to learn—to
be a Ranger. They pay attention, and they don't mind the repetition
of the drills. The repetition gives them confidence, and they grow
into the job. So I like these new guys who may lack confidence, but
are willing to learn. We can make them good Rangers.

"The ones that catch on quickly are sometimes a cause for concern. Since the squad movements and the shooting come more easily to them, they may become impatient. Repetitious battle drill is
a way of life with us. When we run multiple fire-and-movement
drills or multiple repetitions in the shoot house, or even during these
MLAT drills, the more talented new men can lose their focus—they

don't give it their full attention. Since they get it quickly, they get bored—or, worse yet, complacent. Combat drill requires total concentration. If they don't lock in a total-focus approach with close attention to detail during training, they'll not do it in combat. And that's dangerous. But so far, the few new guys we're getting from RASP are focused and seem to want to learn."

"How was it for you?" I ask. I know something of Sergeant Donaldson's history. He's a Princeton graduate and was a nationally ranked squash player in college. In the late 1990s, he was working as a financial analyst at an investment advisory firm in New York. He was there before and after 9/11, and was in the subway on his way to work when the first airliner hit the first tower. In 2003, he decided that Wall Street was not really where he belonged and began to look for a way he could serve his country and make a contribution. As an analyst, he conducted a methodical cost-benefit approach to the issue of service, which led him to the Army.

"RIP (Ranger Indoctrination Program) was not a problem for me," he said of his initial Ranger training. Donaldson is short, compact, thirty-nine, and bald, yet he comes across as youthful and fit. "I was older, though I didn't look it, and I was in very good condition. A RIP cadre sergeant who knew my background gave me some very good advice. He told me to just be a private—to be a good private, but not to try to be more. So for twenty-one months and two rotations, I was that good private. It was good advice then and good advice now. It's the same advice I give to the new Rangers who come to us, and especially to the older or more accomplished new Rangers."

As a national-caliber athlete, I ask him about how he physically conditions his squad for combat rotation. "I do it a little differently than some of the other squad leaders. I spend time in the gym, and I know the other guys put in time there as well. So I don't worry about the upper-body conditioning. The demand is on the lower body. You have to carry your load, sometimes a long way and often for short distances at a dead run. We stretch and do some light upper-body exercise every day. Then, we run one day, fast walk with a ruck the next, and then a day of fast walking with kit and wind sprints with kit. Prior to deployment, I move the workouts to early after-noon to get ready for the Afghan summer heat."

"And in Afghanistan, what do you do?"

"On deployment, we work out on the days, or nights, we don't go out on missions. We're usually at altitude, sometimes over seven thousand feet, so we run on the off days, and the guys lift on their own. Every two weeks, we do the RPFT and a timed five-mile run. On occasion, a guy will let himself go, usually because he's eating too much. If he falls out of standard, he knows it and I know it. If it persists, then I'll step in, but that doesn't happen. We all know what needs to be done, and there's the loss of pride if you can't per-form to standard."

Toward the end of the MLAT cycle, I was able to spend a few minutes with One-Alpha's newest Ranger, First Lieutenant Matt Kozart. Kozart was a collegiate wrestler at Minnesota and has the physique and cauliflowered ears to prove it. He's five feet nine and a very solid two hundred pounds. The day after he assumed com-mand of One-Alpha, he was on an MLAT exercise and in a (blank-ammo) firefight on a notional enemy airfield. I ask him about being in battalion for only a few weeks and being a platoon leader on the eve of deployment.

"To be in the Ranger Regiment is the dream of every infantry officer. I've been working toward this ever since I was in Army ROTC. And to be a PL [platoon leader] on my first rotation is unbelievable. I'm very fortunate."

"So how's it going with One-Alpha?"

"It's great, but there's a lot for me to learn. PLs have a pretty good administrative load, so I have to learn how this command does things. Tactically, it's very different. On my previous deployments, I was up front and directing traffic. I'd send a fire team here or place a machine gun there; I had great soldiers, but I made most of the decisions. I don't do that here. If I see something developing before I can say anything or give direction, which I'm quickly learning is not my role, the fire teams are moving on their own. They know what to do and they do it. They're so professional. And smart. I've never been around a group of soldiers this talented."

I make a passing comment that you don't see too many squad leaders with degrees from Princeton, referring to Sergeant Donaldson's academic credentials, and he replies, "And what about Sergeant Kline?"

"Sergeant Kline?" I ask. Kline is One-Alpha's platoon sergeant. "What about him?"

Kozart grins. "I'm a fitness junkie, and I have a degree in nutrition. I have a passion for nutritional science, and I'm proud of that degree. Yet in my Ranger platoon, my senior squad leader has a degree in history and finance from Princeton and my platoon sergeant has a degree in mathematical physics from the University of California. It's a little humbling—impressive, but still humbling. And academic credentials aside, they're both terrific soldiers and terrific leaders."

With MLAT behind it, the battalion begins preparation for the Task Force Training (TFT) block of the deployment work-up. For TFT, I will be assigned to Delta Company of 1/75. Just prior to my leaving A-Co and One-Alpha, the battalion receives eleven new Rangers from RASP Class 02-11. Since Alpha Company's manning is low, seven of those new Rangers are assigned to A-Co. This means that the company must distribute these new men to fill the platoon needs and immediately begin to prepare them for combat. My platoon at A-Co receives three of the new Rangers. Two of them will go to the weapons squad and become assistant gunners, while the third will be assigned to a rifle squad. I assumed that all three would be immersed in the TFT exercise, but I was wrong.

"Two of our new soldiers are married," Sargent Kline told me, "and as important as the TFT portion of the work-up is, family comes first. I want these men focused on their squad and fire-team duties, and that's hard to do if you have a young family that's new to the Army and in transit. So the married guys will remain here and get their families settled, and we'll take the one single Ranger with us on the TFT. He'll be a grenadier. But the new AGs will get plenty of work with the guns, probably more than they would at TFT."

It seems that One-Alpha's weapons squad leader, Staff Sergeant Tim Donaldson, will also remain at Hunter Army Airfield during the TFT. His wife is about to deliver twins, so he, too, will be excused from this block of training. Between trips to the hospital and tending to his new family, he will train and drill his new assistant gunners in their duties. For the new Ranger grenadier, his learning curve with his new fire team will be steep indeed.

Task Force Training is a two-week block of training with close to a week on either side of this period devoted to associated training, preparation, and recovery. It will occupy the latter part of February and the first part of March. The term *task force* is used because a Ranger battalion approximates the size of deployed special operations task force, and TFT is a battalion training evolution. The 2011 TFT for 1/75 is a minideployment to the training ranges and facilities at Fort Campbell, Kentucky. This segment of the predeployment work-up is done at various Army installations and is moved around depending on range availability and base-resident unit activity, and to provide for a variety in training venues. In recent years, TFTs have been conducted at Fort Bragg, Fort Collins, and Fort Irwin. These bases, like most large Army posts, have MOUT training sites. MOUT stands for "military operations in urban terrain," and these training sites have buildings and compounds that look a great deal like those real-world targets in Iraq and Afghanistan. These installations have great utility for the Rangers and their mission. Fort Campbell has one of the more extensive Army MOUT training facilities. It's a huge modern complex that replicates what soldiers see when operating in urban environments in the Mideast, Southwest Asia, or parts of Africa. There are two formatted training evolutions scheduled for this TFT: a company live-fire exercise (LFX) and platoon full-mission profile (FMP) training. Between and during these two training evolutions, the individual companies and platoons will get in some general range work and be tasked with duties in support of the live-fire and full-mission profile training for other platoons.

For the initial portion of the TFT period, I'm assigned to 2nd Platoon of Delta Company, or Two-Delta. As with Two-Bravo of B-Co and One-Alpha of A-Co, Two-Delta has a very experienced platoon sergeant and a very capable platoon leader. Staff Sergeant Del Prather is from Michigan and is the only staff sergeant at 1/75 serving as a rifle-platoon sergeant. "I'd been an E-6 for a while when I decided to get out of the Army and become a cop," he explains. "I failed miserably, and when my marriage failed as well, I came back in. But those nine months out of uniform put me at the bottom of the promotion list." Sergeant Prather will be taking Two-Delta back on his fourteenth deployment. Prather is short and compact, with intelligent green eyes and just a touch of grey at his temples. I found him both wise and street smart, and with a wry sense of humor.

Sergeant Prather's platoon leader is Captain John Melton, a Pennsylvanian who came to the Army by way of ROTC at the University of Colorado. This will be his third deployment with 1/75 and his second as a platoon leader. "My timing was perfect," he says. "We deployed right as I arrived here at Hunter and that was, for me, a staff deployment. Now it looks as if I may get in another rotation as a PL after this one. Few junior officers are able to get in four rotations with the Seventy-fifth, and I just might make it."

Two-Delta also has some familiar faces. Among the hardworking veterans are three Rangers from Class 09-10 who are preparing for their first combat rotation. First, there's Private First Class Garth Palco, the youngest graduate from Class 09-10. Palco, the high school track star who decided against college and competitive running to join the Army, is a grenadier in the second squad of Two-Delta. Also in Two-Delta is Private First Class Gary Galdorisi. Galdorisi, the former D.C. policeman turned Ranger, is now a SAW gunner with first squad. And, finally, there is Private First Class Jason Bush in the third squad. Bush is the platoon clown. He's a serious and competent Ranger, but he's also ready with a good joke or a prank in garrison. Bush is his squad's grenadier. All are Eleven Bravo infantrymen. Delta Company received the bulk of the new Rangers from Class 09-10. There are five other 09-10 Rangers scattered throughout the company—four Eleven Bravos and one RTO. In addition to Palco, Galdorisi, and Bush, there is another Ranger who is new to Two-Delta. Specialist Ron Stone from RASP Class 04-10 arrived at 1/75 and D-Co a few weeks ahead of those from Class 09-10. Stone is a big man, six feet two and perhaps 240 pounds. He played rugby at the University of Massachusetts, where he graduated with a degree in communications. After working several years as an executive recruiter, he decided to join the Army and become a Ranger. Following his graduation at the top of Class 04-10, he went immediately to SURT and on to Ranger School.

"It was a struggle for me from start to finish, and I lost close to thirty pounds at Ranger School. Yet I was able to go straight through with no phase rollbacks. I'm very proud of that. It's a tribute to just how well the instructors at SURT prepared us. But it's been a long grind—OSUT, Airborne, RASP, SURT, and Ranger School. I was in one school or another for close to a year. It's really great to finally be in the Regiment and especially 1/75. The Two-Delta is an awesome platoon, and Sergeant Prather is the best. You never stop learning, and he's a great teacher."

"How was it going to Ranger School straight from RASP with essentially no time in an active, line Army unit?"

"It was hard, but I was a good student in college, and I know how to apply myself. I took it very seriously, knowing that I'd have to give

it my all if I was going to get my Tab. I'm twenty-four, and there's
no way I could have done that if I were eighteen or twenty. Ranger
School's tough, and it took everything I had. I'm very proud of that
Tab and that I went straight through. Now I'm looking forward
to finally going on deployment and to putting all that training to
good use."

It was current policy during the early days of the RASP Level
One program to send one or two of the top graduates directly to
SURT and on to Ranger School following their RASP graduation.
While no Rangers from Class 09-10 went directly to SURT and Ran-
ger School, the practice remains under review.

Task Force Training begins well before the battalion arrives at
Fort Campbell. The battalion Rangers pack out for this training very
much as they will when they rotate overseas. This will include their
weapons, personal kit, combat kit, and all the sensitive equipment
they will take into combat, such as their night-vision devices and
encrypted radios. Everything has to be laid out, inspected, inventoried, and loaded onto pallets. For weapons and sensitive items, there
is a proscribed chain of custody. For an individual fire-team Ranger,
his personal equipment inventory has over 130 separate items. On
actual deployment, the pallets and Rangers will be loaded onto C-17s
for the trip overseas. For the journey to Fort Campbell, the gear will
go by truck and the Rangers in a convoy of buses. The ride to Campbell by bus is just under the flying time it takes to get from Hunter
Army Airfield to Kandahar by C-17—about eleven hours.

"The TFT is an important block of training for us," one of the
Two-Delta squad leaders told me during the preparations. "It's also
a difficult time in some ways. We're away from home for two weeks.
During the MLAT, the days are long but we're never far from home.
It's the same during the squad live-fire training—when we're out for
a few days running. TFT is a short deployment. On the positive side,
we *are* away from home and can focus on training. There are no dis-
tractions. Nobody has one eye on the door, trying to decide if he can

get home for a few hours with the family. The negative is that in
only a few months, we'll be on deployment and gone for an extended
time. And this is two more weeks that we don't get to be with our
families. But we're Rangers—we take the good with the bad."

The company live-fire exercise has a great many moving parts.
The best way to describe a company LFX is to compare it to the
squad/platoon live-fire training at Fort Stewart with Two-Bravo.
During that exercise, there were two squads involved in the movement through the exercise training lane and perhaps sixteen or eighteen Rangers in the mix. The "enemy" presented themselves in twos
and threes as pop-up silhouettes, as a target bunker, or as a squad
of pop-up targets. As the reader may recall, Two-Bravo moved
through the training lane with fire teams, then entire squads, bounding forward using fire-and-movement and support-by-fire tactics.
The company live-fire exercise simply has more Rangers—140 plus—
and a much bigger support package. An entire platoon is responsible
for the supporting fire, with two platoons moving in squad-assault
elements and/or setting up intermediate support-by-fire positions.
My platoon, Two-Delta, is one of the assault elements.

The company commander, along with his platoon and squad leaders, first walks the training lane before the actual training begins.
Then platoons walk their individual lanes to acquaint themselves
with the key nodes in the flow of the exercise. The exercise itself is
a company-sized assault on an insurgent training base in a remote
area of our notional, fictitious nation—a nation that, by the way,
looks a great deal like a real-world candidate nation. This scenario
follows a logical progression of insurgent-force activity from the
MLAT airfield seizure and embassy-personnel rescue. Insurgent elements in this unnamed country nation have retreated and reorga-
nized to what they feel is a safe area to train and reconstitute their
forces. The base camp itself is a series of fourteen makeshift plywood
buildings protected by a bunker and a line of barbed wire laid over
a linear minefield. There are a series of automated targets that pres-

ent pop-up fiberglass enemy soldiers across the training lane. The LFX will begin with an airborne insertion by MH-60 helicopters and CV-22 Ospreys, followed by an assault-by-fire of the enemy camp by Delta Company. Generally speaking, a Ranger assault of this kind—one or two platoons or a full company, as in this LFX— follows a pattern: infiltration, containment, assault, isolation, exploit- ation, and exfiltration. The mechanics of an assault, airborne or otherwise, often follows these steps, including the assault and take- down of Osama bin Laden's compound in the Pakistan raid. As with the squad/platoon live-fire exercises, the company evolutions are conducted in the daylight with blank fire, then again at night with blanks. The following day, there's daylight live fire, then nighttime live fire—crawl, walk, run.

The action begins with the support package prepping the tar- get prior to the infil. Battalion 81-millimeter and 120-millimeter mortars begin to work the targeted base camp along with attack helicopters—AH-6 Little Birds and the more heavily gunned MH-60L Direct Action Penetrators. The MH-60Ls are awesome platforms with a mix of rockets, 7.62-millimeter miniguns, and 30-millimeter cannon. The mission of the mortars and air strikes is to engage the enemy fighters and pin them down. These attack air- craft, along with manned and unmanned airborne ISR (intelligence, surveillance, reconnaissance) platforms, also help to establish and maintain containment of the area. Containment is important. In his training scenario, as with real-world operations in Afghanistan, the enemy will either fight or run, and the high-value individuals will almost always run. The containment function is to not let these "squirters" run and escape from the objective area. The mission is to capture or kill them. Chances are, when an insurgent and/or ter- rorist leader bolts from the back door to avoid the attentions of a Ranger assault team coming in the front door, he is going to be tracked by more than one eye in the sky as he tries to make good his escape.

With the enemy camp under fire, the support-by-fire platoon lands in two MH-60s and moves quickly to their support positions. They take the camp under fire with Carl Gustav 84-millimeter rockets, 60-millimeter portable mortars, six M240 machine guns, and an assortment of SAW and sniper fire. The enemy base camp is now under a serious air-land pounding. This allows for the two assault platoons to infil on three CV-22 Ospreys. The Ospreys are vulnerable to ground fire, so the preparatory fire on the enemy position reaches a crescendo when the Ospreys appear over a nearby tree line. The assault platoons land and move into position. From these preassault positions, they detach squads to breach the barbed-wire and land-mine barrier, clear the bunker, and establish intermediate support-by-fire positions. The breach through the wire and minefield is done with bangalore torpedoes, just like in World War II and Vietnam. Then the assault teams begin to clear, secure, and search the fourteen buildings—the single-walled plywood constructions now well ventilated by the supporting fire. With the objective secure, the gun barrels turn outward to isolate the target and prevent an enemy counterattack. Following the assault and isolation phases, and a thorough search of the buildings, there is the orderly withdrawal of the assault elements from the target. As with MLAT training, there are notional Ranger casualties and casualty evacuations, and all personnel are carefully accounted for coming off target. The assault platoons are once again supported by fire as the gun teams carefully follow them back from the buildings and through the breach in the barbed wire and minefield. The art, as well as the danger, of this company-sized assault, as with the squad live-fire drills, is the shifting of fire just ahead of the assaulting elements during the attack and following them out with covering fire as they withdraw.

"This is serious business with support-by-fire teams shooting in front of our advance," Sergeant Del Prather said of the exercise. Two-Delta was tasked with one of the intermediate support-by-fire positions and with clearing the initial cluster of enemy buildings. "It requires a lot of command and control, and a lot of trust." I watched one iteration of the exercise from the main support-by-fire positions, and the weapons squad leaders were all over their gun teams, ensuring that they properly shifted their fire in front of the assault teams' advances and lifted (ceased) fire when the attack helicopters swooped in low for their attack. Support-by-fire is a deadly dance with the friendly forces moving close to moving friendly live fire.

The final iteration of the LFX is the night live-fire assault and an infrared light show of a proportion I've never before experienced. It's a black night with no moon and a partial cloud cover. Without NVDs, there's just a lot of noise and a few scarlet 7.62-millimeter tracers flying about. With NVDs, it's a dynamic, fast-moving shades-of-green stage presentation. It's like a rock concert with a bigger cast and more light. In addition to tracer fire that all but flares out the night-vision goggles, there are the IR targeting lasers from the individual Rangers, the attack helos, and the orbiting reconnaissance aircraft. The IR light, noise, and firepower aside, there's also an immense amount of discipline and professionalism on display.

On the night blank-fire iteration, I was able to follow the Delta Company commander on the ground. He manages the company combat assault through his command and mission-support radio nets and his mobile staff, which includes his RTO operator, his fire-support officer, his joint tactical air controller (JTAC), and his senior medic. This command post runs along with the company commander as he follows the assault teams in and precedes them out. But for the most part, the mission progressed with little or no micromanagement on his part.

"The reason we can do this mission this well," the Delta Company commander tells me, "speaks to the quality and ability of the squad and fire-team leaders. The fight is in their hands and they know what to do. I'm here to monitor the flow of action and redirect the ground force as necessary and to help manage contingencies.

I also coordinate the air-battle efforts and keep the battalion commander informed. But the fight is in the hands of my sergeants.

"This engagement is not beyond the ability of a conventional infantry company, but they couldn't do it this well nor this fast. They simply don't have the light-infantry background, talent, or experience. From the drop of the first mortar round until we come off target is less than two hours. No infantry company anywhere can do it that well and certainly not that fast. This is a very special capability that we offer the battlespace commanders in the active theaters and, along with the airfield-seizure package, to the national command authority. Other special operations units can do this at the platoon troop level, but only the Rangers can do this at the company or battalion level. We're special operations light infantry."

Light-infantry airborne assault is indeed a versatile capability. In the past, Ranger companies have been moved on short notice between theaters to provide policy makers an on-call, light-infantry assault option. Additionally, Delta Company is currently the Immediate-Reaction Company, or IRC, which means that this company, while it prepares for combat rotation, can go out the door at any time. Company and platoon leaders are on a one-hour on-call standby, 24/7, and they are never without their cell phones. Platoon and squad Rangers have to be reachable by cell phone so they can be in the company area within two hours of notification. The entire company must at any time be able to go wheels up, fully mission capable, bound for any contingency anywhere in the world, within nine hours of notification. The rest of the battalion is on an eighteen-hour fly-away standby. All this means that the 1st Ranger Battalion will go to war *no later than* this May. All except Bravo Company. They'll be in combat well before the end of March.

The duties of new Rangers in the company live-fire exercise are much as they were during squad live-fire drills, with the added dimension of their individual fire team's room- and building-clearing duties. "As a SAW gunner with a short run to the target," Private

First Class Gary Galdorisi recalled of the LFX, "I went in heavy—maybe a thousand rounds. My first job was to help provide a base of fire from an intermediate support-by-fire position. We provided cover for the squad breaching the minefield. Then my fire team was the first through the breach, and we cleared the initial series of buildings. After that, we held security and searched the cleared buildings while Second Platoon moved on to clear their buildings up the line."

"I was one of the 320s [referring to M320 grenade launchers] covering the breaching teams," said Garth Palco of his role, "and then I covered the bunker-clearing teams. I fired most of my grenades at the bunker, then became a rifleman for room clearing. Since we cleared the first buildings, I got to set security and watch the rest of the show." Like me, Private First Class Palco is having his first experience of watching a company-sized LFX at night through NVDs. "It was like nothing I've ever seen before." Like all the new Rangers I spoke with, he was amazed by the contrast of the full-on blackout experienced with the naked eye to the abundance of light with NVDs. This visual dichotomy is heightened by the sound-management headphones worn by Rangers. One of the marvels of the modern battlefield is the sound-canceling earphones/ear protectors that all Rangers wear. Made by the Peltor Manufacturing Company, these "Peltors" cancel out or block loud and sharp noises, and allow other sounds to come through with amplification. In the middle of a firefight, you can talk to a Ranger beside you, and the Rangers can hear the commands of their fire-team leaders. The next time these new Rangers see this kind of light show it will be in the battlespace, with real target buildings, real bad guys, and active opposition. A full-on, company-sized assault like this is rare in Afghanistan. Most actions are single-platoon operations and, on occasion, a platoon-plus or two-platoon operation.

Following Delta Company's final nighttime LFX and a lengthy AAR, the 1/75 battalion commander addresses the company's senior leaders. "This was a good exercise, and covering the few lessons you just learned, you guys did a great job. And now I want you to think about the kind of assault we just conducted. It's true that this evolution is larger than those you're likely to be doing on this next deployment, but you're all aware of the contagion that's spreading across North Africa and into the Middle East and Southwest Asia. A company-sized operation of this type is becoming more likely in light of these recent events; what we just did may very well be the rehearsal of what we might be called upon to do in the future. I'm privy to some of the classified, real-world contingencies, and it's not out of the question that we could do an operation like this for real." He comes to attention and salutes his Rangers. "Rangers Lead the Way."

"ALL THE WAY!"

The other exercise focus during TFT at Fort Campbell is the full-mission-profile (FMP) training. The FMPs are mock platoon-sized missions designed to lock in the mechanics, timelines, and the day/night rhythms of missions similar to the ones the platoons will plan and conduct on a routine basis in Afghanistan a few months from now. The first of these training missions comes to the platoon from "higher" on the initial day of the FMP at 1400 hours, much as it would on deployment. Like most real-world missions, this training mission is generated by sensitive and perishable intelligence, and must be acted upon quickly. Due to scheduling, I'm back with A-Co and One-Alpha for the FMP portion of the TFT. After Lieutenant Kozart and Sergeant Kline are assigned the mission, the planning begins. Following the warning order, the junior platoon Rangers set about prepping gear for the night's mission, and the senior platoon Rangers begin planning the mission. By 1800, the platoon is assembled in the briefing room for the operations order. The mission roughly tracks the extended scenario from the MLAT airfield seizure and the company live-fire exercise. A senior terrorist leader with a history of providing logistic assistance to the insurgents and of constructing IEDs, along with his personal security detachment, is expected to be in a remote compound in the foothills of our troubled notional nation.

Accompanying the One-Alpha Rangers are the platoon enablers who will help with the conduct of the mission. These enablers are not unlike the support elements that currently accompany Ranger assault platoons in Afghanistan. There are sniper teams, medics, explosive ordnance disposal (EOD) technicians, and an interpreter and a field interrogation team. In a real-world scenario, there may be Afghan National Army soldiers with them on such a mission.

Within Muslim culture, hospitality has a far different meaning and importance than in the West. In most cases, it cannot be withheld; and once it is offered, it levies an obligation on the host, who can be burdened with uninvited or unwanted guests. Thus, a Taliban leader or a group of fighters may impose themselves on an Afghan household; they cannot be turned away. When Rangers have to go after a Taliban leader who has been granted this sanctuary, collateral physical damage and cultural affront could follow an assault that has to be recognized and accommodated. The embedded Afghan army units help with this. They also help with what is called "battlespace handover." This is where the Ranger assault element leaves the area and the regional conventional forces—Afghan and/or American—move in and reassume control, restore order, and mitigate any damage. Our overall effort in Afghanistan is a counterinsurgency effort—a battle for the people—and the Ranger assault elements are only a kinetic piece of that overall effort. The Afghan police and army units are a key part of this effort to win the people. Winning the people begins with providing security, and security begins with the elimination of armed insurgent elements. The Regiment also partners with Afghan special operations units that support missions in these culturally sensitive conditions.

One enabler that is a battalion asset supporting the line rifle platoons are the Ranger dog teams, which consist of a Ranger handler and a Ranger dog. The dogs have been in combat rotation with the

Rangers for the last six years. The program has been highly successful, and there is now approximately one Ranger dog team per rifle
platoon. The dog teams train with the platoons and companies and
deploy with them. Their role and exactly how these dogs are used
is restricted information. I can, however, say that the dogs serve in
a number of capacities, and the term *general purpose* would apply to
their role in the Ranger assault package. The dog handlers are Ranger infantry sergeants, typically veteran Rangers, who have had Army
dog-handling training.

Task Force Training at Fort Campbell was the first I saw of these
Ranger dog teams. During the live-fire exercises, the dogs played no
role in the LFX, but walked behind and with the Rangers as they
moved through this assault training.

"We want them to be out there with the noise and the yelling
and the confusion so they get used to it," a dog handler said of training his dog, "so we can see how they react to the gunfire and the
night movements. They don't need NVDs, as they see pretty well
at night. For the dogs, it's mostly conditioning, much like a hunter
will want to shoot over his dogs in getting them ready for bird season. Even the veteran dogs need this exercise to get them ready for
deployment. For new dogs, like new Rangers, their first work-up is
important and very telling about their suitability for this job. Like
Rangers, some dogs pick up on this quickly, others not so quickly."

I noticed that during TFT the dogs lived in their portable kennels
and slept with the Ranger platoons in their tents. Being a dog lover,
I had to know about their deployment rotations and terms of enlistment. "My dog will be going back on his sixth deployment," one
handler told me. "I think we have one going back on his seventh. As
for what happens to them when they get too old or are no longer
capable of the overseas work, we adopt them out to police forces.
The police are pretty happy with our dogs. Like a lot of Rangers
who get out of the Army and go into law enforcement, so do our
dogs. A few of the guys take them home as pets, but the dogs want

to work, and there is no better life or work for a dog than police work."

"And I have to ask, what is the casualty rate for the dogs?"

"We've lost three dogs in battalion over the life of the program, and we've brought a few back with wounds. Some are able to return to the fight, others not. On balance, our dog casualties are about the same as the battalion Rangers, which, as you know, is pretty high. We're at war, and so are our dogs."

The objective of a typical full-mission-profile training is to combine mission planning and mission execution. Residential target compounds in play at the Fort Campbell MOUT site are like the ones these Rangers will see in Afghanistan. Battalion Ranger role players with kaffiyeh headgear and AK-47s patrol the compounds and await the Ranger assault teams. The mission flow is much like that of the live-fire exercise: infiltration, containment, assault, isolation, site exploitation, exfiltration. The objective is to get as close as possible without detection and to seal off the area so the targeted individual cannot squirt from the containment. Then it's breaching as necessary and an assault of the target compound. The Rangers quickly secure and isolate the buildings, thoroughly search the area, and then exfil from the area. This TFT allows for three of these FMPs per platoon. As the platoons rotate through the FMPs, the training goes on all night.

During these FMPs, I noticed a single One-Alpha Ranger getting some very special attention from his squad leader and his fire-team leader. Private First Class Will Hollings from RASP Class 02-11 has been with A-Co, 1/75, and his One-Alpha platoon fire team for a little over a week. In the few remaining weeks, he'll have to prepare as best as he can for this deployment. So during the breaks and after the AAR that follows every exercise, he's running drills with his fire team under the direction of his squad leader and his fire-team leader.

"It's coming at me pretty fast," Hollings said of his crash combat course. "I thought I did well at RASP, but now I realize just how much I don't know. And how much I have to learn. What's so amazing is that everyone has time for me—my fire team, my squad leader, everyone. When I make a mistake, they take the time to help me get it right. When the rest of the platoon is on a break, they're working with me, so I'm working hard and doing my best. I don't want to let them down."

"He's a good young Ranger," his fire-team leader told me. "He has plenty to learn before we take him on a real operation, but he's getting there. He's aggressive and he listens, and that counts for a lot."

One Ranger I see by Hollings's side a great deal of the time is Private First Class Chad Garcia, the Ranger who joined Alpha Company and One-Alpha on the eve of their last rotation. He's right there—helping, demonstrating, encouraging, and mentoring. "He'll do just fine," Garcia says of his new charge. "He's ahead of where I was when I went on deployment last year." Early mornings and before and after chow, I see the two of them, Private First Class Hollings and Private First Class Garcia, walking behind their guns and moving tactically around a chain-link fence, gate, or a nearby building corner with Garcia in the lead one time, Hollings the next. They're now Ranger buddies.

The time is getting short for the three rifle companies of 1/75 still at Hunter Army Airfield. Bravo Company is already on deployment and settling into combat routine, so the 1st Battalion commander now has one of his four rifle companies fully in the fight. For the other companies, there remains a few weeks in garrison at Hunter, two weeks of block leave, and a week of training away from Hunter for training simply known as Off Post Training (OPT), the last major block of training before deployment. The weeks in garrison are busy. At Hunter, there is equipment rehab, the preparation and staging of equipment that will be taken on deployment, and range training at Fort Stewart. The time at Stewart is yet another round of train-

ing and proficiency with grenades, grenade launchers, heavy machine guns, and rockets. And there's the St. Patrick's Day parade.
St. Paddy's Day in Savannah is the biggest holiday of the year, and
1/75 marches in the parade when they are not deployed. Sergeant
Major Michael Hall, author of the preface to this work, began his
Ranger career as a young private at 1/75 and rose through the ranks
to become the 1st Battalion Command Sergeant Major and the Regimental Command Sergeant Major. He has marched in this parade
sixteen times.

The Off Post Training period is when each company conducts its
own training independently. It's a time when the company commander, company first sergeant, and the senior platoon leadership
assess where they are in their combat preparation and readiness.
They also decide where they may have shortcomings and what might
be done in the time remaining to correct those deficiencies. The
companies are given great latitude in what training needs to be
addressed and where. Alpha Company will go to Fort Bragg; Bravo
Company to Fort Knox. I will follow Delta Company to Fort Benning. Just who goes where is a combination of timing, training-range
availability, and the connections each company first sergeant may
have with his opposite numbers at these host Army bases. This, like
a great deal of Army business, is facilitated by these first-sergeant-
to-first-sergeant liaisons.

"It's a time for us to put the finishing touches on our TTPs [tac-
tics, techniques, and procedures]," the D-Co first sergeant says of
the company's Fort Benning OPT, "and to smooth out any wrinkles,
both our planning and execution. And to do what we can in the time
remaining to better integrate our new Rangers."

Just prior to the OPT block, the battalion received twenty-one
new Rangers from RASP 1 Class 03-11. Nine of these new men are
assigned to Delta Company, three of them to my 2nd Platoon. All
are Eleven Bravo infantrymen. In Two-Delta, Sergeant Del Prather
assigns a single new Ranger to each of his three rifle squads. Two are

assigned as assistant gunners and one as his squad's grenadier. Technically, the AGs are with the weapons squad, but at this stage of the predeployment work-up and while on deployment, the weapons-squad gun teams are embedded with the rifle squads. The newest Rangers will have only the OPT and the remaining time in garrison to prepare for their first combat deployment.

"They'll complete the work-up and learn what they can before we deploy," the company first sergeant says of the new men, "and their learning will continue en route and on deployment. Initially, they'll go on missions in designated support roles. But even then, they'll not take an active combat role outside the wire until their platoon sergeants tell me they're ready."

"My squad leaders are all capable combat leaders," Sergeant Prather says in reference to his new Rangers. "I leave it to them to bring the new guys along. These are individual Rangers. Their current skill level, as well as how quickly they can integrate with their fire teams, will vary. Some will come on line quickly; for others, it will take a while. My squad leaders and fire-team leaders will tell me when they're good to go."

D-Co parachutes onto Fort Benning's Fryer Drop Zone Sunday afternoon, 3 April. After assembling on the DZ, they are bused across Fort Benning to the Shelby Range site. Shelby is one of the urban-training sites on Fort Benning and, while not as big as the complex at Fort Campbell, it is still a formidable facility. It's a small town with sixteen buildings, including residences (walled and unwalled), a police station, a government house, a gas station, a townhome complex with five units, and an office building. Each building is fitted out with TV cameras and sound systems to support the training. The three-story office building alone has thirty-six TV cameras. An integrated urban training site like this one at the Shelby range can support a variety of training from internal room and multistory building clearance to multisquad tactical movement from building to building. The D-Co Rangers bivouac in the woods near the training site in platoon patrol bases. Hot morning and evening chow is brought to the Shelby site from one of the Fort Benning DFACs. If training takes them away from the site during this meal service, there's always MREs.

Two-Delta begins the OPT midmorning the next day on a nearby 40-millimeter grenade range, where Sergeant Prather and his squad leaders set up a stress course for grenade training. This is not just for the designated grenadiers, but for all platoon Rangers. With the M320 grenade launchers, the Rangers are made to run in full kit across the range and engage targets at various distances, stationary and on the run. This is proficiency training for the grenadiers who carry the 320 as their primary weapon, but cross training as well for the riflemen and SAW gunners. The M320 is a relatively new weapon to the Regiment, so it's a chance for everyone to get some 40-millimeter rounds down range.

Midafternoon, the platoon is back at the urban site for full-mission-profile training. This training is very similar to the FMP training conducted at Fort Campbell, but at a different facility with a different set of target buildings. Prior to the formal training, the fire-team leaders have their men out practicing room and building clearance. Then the squad leaders run fire-and-movement drills with their two fire teams bounding from building to building. You can always tell a Ranger squad moving on an urban-training exercise; there's always at least one ladder per squad. They walk, then run, through the mechanics of infiltration, containment, assault and seizure, isolation, site search and exploitation, and exfiltration. There are twists and variations, and different assault and support packages, but it's basically the same battle drill, over and over.

Late afternoon, Two-Delta gets its first training mission, and the platoon leadership quickly works through the mission planning and develops an operational order. The planning is quick and many aspects are addressed briefly or made notional, as the focus is on tactical execution. Following a brief operations order, the platoon mounts a twilight attack on two of the MOUT-site buildings. One of the company's supply-section Rangers is captured and taken off target as the platoon exfils. After a brief AAR, there is another mission tasking, another mission-planning session, and a mission execution—this time with NVDs and blank fire. Shortly after midnight, Two-Delta begins to plan its third FMP. The company supply team serves as scenario role players, both as opposing forces and noncombatants. These final FPMs are conducted under the watchful eyes of the Delta Company commander and the company first sergeant. The final AAR is completed just before 0300. I find one of Two-Delta's squad leaders and ask him how his brand-new Ranger is doing—brand new from Class 03-11, rather than recently new, like his single Ranger from Class 09-10.

"My newbie is doing great and the others, from what I've heard, are also doing well," he tells me. "He makes the usual mistakes, but for the most part he's catching on quickly. The new guys we now get from RASP are a quick study and are eager to learn. In some ways, getting a new guy is good for us, as a squad and as a fire team. It forces us to slow down and go through everything by the numbers, which isn't all bad. You know what they say about pros and amateurs, don't you?" I don't, so he tells me. "Amateurs do it over until they get it right. Professionals do it over and over until they can't get it wrong. The new guys just make us all work harder and become a little better. It's battle drill, and even with the basics, you can never do it too many times. All this repetition will pay off when we get in combat."

On Tuesday morning, Two-Delta is on the shooting range, this time at the Homeland Security range on Fort Benning. This is a modern range, including several bermed shooting lanes with individual, tailored shooting venues. There is the ability to "shoot steel" on this range, which is to say that there are racks of steel targets on elevated stands, including silhouettes and other presentations, that tip when hit and reset by gravity. These are not the static metal silhouettes that the RASP classes engage at a distance, but close-in targets that ping and tip when hit. Special frangible training ammunition is required to engage these steel targets at close range.

The shooting day begins midmorning with the obligatory range-safety briefing and a review of training-casualty procedures. The three new Rangers begin by zeroing in their weapons for the first time, and several of the veterans check their sights on the zero range. Then it's battle drill. On three separate ranges, the squad leaders put their Rangers through shooting exercises that are not unlike those of RASP—shooting while moving left, moving right, advancing, retreating; barricade shooting; shooting strong hand and off hand. There are El Presidente and modified El Presidente drills and mini-stress-shooting routines. All are done in full kit, and all drills are team-centric combat shooting. Most of the shooting is with M4s, but there are also drills with the M9 Beretta and transition drills from M4 to M9 and back. After many hours of daylight shooting, the drills are run again at night. Each shooter gets close to a thousand rounds through his weapons systems. It's a long day and evening for the Two-Delta Rangers; they're back at the Shelby urban-training site by 0100.

On Wednesday, Two-Delta splits into two groups for training. The gun teams go to a machine-gun range, where they get extensive work with their M240s and the shorter, lighter, and more mobile MK48s. The current version of the venerable M240 medium machine gun is the Lima model, which, with its titanium-alloy construct, is lighter than previous models. The two new assistant gunners, under the careful instruction of the weapons squad leader and his gun-team leaders, get a great deal of attention. Aside from the running tactical movement, gun setup, shooting, gun breakdown, and more tactical movement—all in full kit—the new Rangers make dozens of new barrel changes with the M240. Such are the drills that by the end of the day, they can change gun barrels blindfolded, which is close to what they'll soon be doing in combat.

Across Fort Benning, the three Two-Delta rifle squads, less their gun teams, work at the Farnsworth Range shoot house. This two-story facility is but a block from the 75th Regimental Headquarters and the 3rd Ranger Battalion. The battalion is on deployment, but Two-Delta shares the Farnsworth Range complex with RASP Class 04-11. It's a large class of some sixty Ranger candidates. A good many of these Phase Two RASP candidates will be assigned to 3/75 on graduation. They will be joining the 3rd Battalion after it returns from its postdeployment block leave and begin training for operational deployment in midsummer of 2011. The cycle continues.

The Farnsworth shoot house serves much the same function as the one used by the 1-75 Rangers at Fort Stewart. This one, unlike the Stewart shoot house, does not have a wall around it to simulate an enclosed courtyard, but it's a two-story facility that allows the assault teams to clear stairwells as well as rooms. Small explosive breaching charges can be used, but the facility is not certified for breaching shotguns, nor is there a catwalk above the rooms for observation and critique. The squad leaders will observe their fire teams from inside the rooms during the blank-fire training iterations and follow along behind the fire teams during the live-fire training. The drills themselves are as they were at Fort Stewart—daylight walk-throughs without kit, daylight assaults with kit, daylight assaults with kit and blanks, and, finally, daylight assaults with kit, live rounds, and live breaching charges. Then they'll do the same thing all over again at night. Throughout the drills, especially the early drills, the action is halted, talked through, then walked through again—and then gone through again on the run. And always, an after-action review follows each iteration. Then the fire teams move from the shoot house to a grassy area nearby, running drills on a floor plan of the shoot house laid out with duct tape.

The gun teams return from the machine-gun range by late afternoon and join their rifle squads for the last of the daylight iterations. After a quick MRE dinner, the Two-Delta Rangers don their NVDs and begin their nocturnal battle drills in the Farnsworth shoot house.

Since this is the first and last time they'll be able to train with live rounds while clearing a stairwell, the squad and fire-team leaders spend a great deal of time in the two stairwells of this shoot house. Since only one fire team can be hot with live rounds at one time, the training goes well into the night. It's not until after 0400 that Two-Delta gets back to their patrol base for a few hours of sleep.

Thursday features a long walk and a long bus ride. The D-Co Rangers walk a land-navigation course in full kit that is more of a physical-endurance exercise than a drill with map and compass. Later that afternoon, they board buses for the five-hour ride back to Hunter Army Airfield. Friday morning, they are in early to clean weapons, overhaul and secure equipment, and prepare for a final parachute jump that afternoon. But this jump is a little different; it's a water jump into the Atlantic Ocean just off Tybee Island. Tybee is a nearby barrier island that's a five-minute ride out from Hunter by an MH-47 and a forty-minute bus ride back.

With the completion of the OPT and the Tybee Island water jump, the predeployment preparation of the 1st Battalion of the 75th Ranger Regiment is largely over. There will be some isolated daily training events interspersed with the extensive preparation for battalion deployment. I ask one of the Two-Delta rifle squad leaders about his squad in general and his new guys in particular.

"We're good to go. I feel better about this squad than any of my previous squads. This is my third rotation as a squad leader and my ninth overall. I've got two very capable fire-team leaders and some solid veterans. The new guys are coming along well. I have a single new man in one of my fire teams, but he's been with us for the entire predeployment work-up. He's ready. The Ranger who just got here is an AG with my assigned gun team, and he's making good progress. We'll continue to work with him in the time remaining and believe me, he'll be doing gun drills in his sleep before we leave."

"You've got block leave beginning in a week or so. What advice do you give your guys for when they're on leave?"

"I tell them to kick back, have some fun, and spend time with their families. Family time is important before a man goes to war. The only thing that I ask workwise is that they work out at least every other day. They know that when they return from block leave that a killer PT session awaits them, so they better not slack off. I also tell them not to do anything stupid and to be responsible with their drinking. We all count on each other, and to do something dumb and take yourself out of deployment rotation means you're letting your buddies down. My Rangers have their heads on right; I don't expect any problems there."

During and between these formatted, scheduled training periods, like the just completed OPT, as well as the scheduled garrison training, there is a great deal of unscheduled training—training between the training. This took place during the Hunter MLAT and the Fort Campbell TFT, as well as at the various company OPT sites. Squad leaders and fire-team leaders seem to take every opportunity to drill their Rangers before, after, and even during training exercises. They make use of every opportunity to use a room, a building, or a compound for assault drill and room-clearing practice. If there isn't the time or conditions to lay down duct tape for makeshift room-clearing drills, they use traffic cones. Gun teams, when their M240s are not needed for part of an exercise, are practicing clearing jams and doing barrel changes, usually blindfolded. If there is a stand of woods nearby, the fire teams are practicing bounding drills for fire-and-movement. No one tells these subordinate Ranger leaders to do this; no one has to. They've all been to the fight, and they know what it takes to win the fight. As they perceive issues or deficiencies in their teams and squads, new Rangers and veterans alike, they take every opportunity to address them. There's an occasional soldierlike grumbling, especially on those mornings where they've been out training for most of the previous night, but I saw very little of this. When a squad leader says, "Grab your kit, we're going outside for some drill," the squad Rangers do just that. Underlying all of this extracurricular drill was a willingness to get it right and do it right.

As I watch the Rangers from 1/75 complete their preparations for the battlespace, I can't help but wonder what the Afghan Taliban fighters might be doing. Are they also running battle drills for the fight this summer—the summer of 2011? Are they conducting fire-and-movement and support-by-fire exercises? Do they even have the spare ammunition to become proficient on their shooting ranges? With the coming of spring, the snow in the mountain passes between Afghanistan and their safe havens in Pakistan is melting. As the 1/75 Rangers prepare their equipment for loading and transport to Kandahar, just how many bands of Taliban fighters are bundling their meager possessions for their trek over and down from the Hindu Kush to begin the summer fighting season? I admire their courage and determination, but I don't envy the task they have in front of them. The Rangers they will have to contend with are indeed a formidable and well-prepared force. One might argue that there's a God on both sides of this fight, but the Rangers have battle drill on their side. Advantage, Rangers.

While my time at 1/75 was with Alpha, Bravo, and Delta Companies, Charlie Company's predeployment work-up paralleled those of its brother rifle companies. The preparation of these four rifle companies as they made ready for war was made possible by the Fifth Ranger company at 1/75—Echo Company. Echo Company is organized along the same lines as the rifle companies. The mission of this hardworking company is to support the rifle companies during training and in the battlespace. When the rifle-company Rangers arrived at Fort Campbell for Task Force Training, there were tents, cots, briefing facilities, and computers in place to support the training. There were ample supplies of blank and live-fire training ammunition at the ranges. There were Strykers and MRAPs prepositioned and ready for training. Each rifle company has a small, integral supply staff, but the heavy lifting of training support is provided by the Rangers of Echo Company. They arrived at Fort Campbell ahead of the rifle-company Rangers, and they remained behind to break down the training-support infrastructure. Elements of Echo Company helped with the setup and support at the company Off Post Training sites. They supported squad and platoon training at Fort Stewart. The truck drivers, mechanics, parachute riggers, fuelers, and supply clerks are found in Echo Company. And the cooks. At Fort Campbell, there was a large mess tent that provided hot meals delivered around scheduled range-training exercises. Behind the steaming chow tables, I noticed a single E-5 Ranger sergeant on patrol, checking that the food containers were full and that the table service was in order. This was clearly *his* chow hall.

"There are several DFACs here at Fort Campbell that have been closed down due to post consolidations," he informed me as the Rangers filed through his chow line. "We found one that hadn't been down for too long and put it back into operation. Now we can prepare food and have it ready to meet the needs of our training schedule. These guys work hard on the training ranges. Our job is to see that they get good chow and that it's delivered hot—here in the mess tent or out to the ranges or wherever." It was obvious this mess sergeant took a great deal of pride in his work, but then he was also a Tabbed Ranger as well as a Ranger cook.

Echo Company at 1/75 is commanded by a logistics officer, and the first sergeant is a chemical-weapons specialist. The company's Rangers come by way of RASP 1 and RASP 2, and roughly a third of them are Tabbed Rangers. Several are at Ranger School, and many more will attend after the next deployment. Nearly all but the riggers will deploy in support of the battalion in Afghanistan. In the battlespace, their duties will shift from training support to combat support. Depending on mission sets and type of mission, a few of them will find themselves on target with the rifle-company Rangers.

In this chapter, I've tried to present an overview of the activity that takes place when a Ranger battalion prepares for combat rotation, and, more specifically, what takes place in the life of a new Ranger on the eve of battle. There is a great deal of moving parts to a battalion work-up, and a great deal of time and effort goes into the planning and execution of this predeployment training—far more than I've touched on in these few pages. Each predeployment period builds on the lessons learned during the last deployment and the last predeployment training period. As in any long war, the body of combat knowledge grows, as does the level of experience and the tactical muscle memory of the platoons, squads, and fire teams. Yet it still comes down to the individual Rangers who have to carry the fight to the enemy. While the collective body of knowledge and experience within the 75th Ranger Regiment is extensive, it varies widely. There are individual Rangers who are going into combat for the first time and Rangers who are going back for the fourteenth time—all at the operational squad and platoon level.

Who are these individual Rangers, and what is their life like outside their operational family? How do they balance their military and nonmilitary responsibilities? How do they resolve the culture they know in this tight-knit regiment and the culture of modern America? They are, after all, as comfortable behind the gun as they are texting on their iPhones. How does an individual Ranger go back on his third deployment? On his thirteenth deployment? What do these men think of this operational treadmill that seems to stretch on with no end in sight? How do they reconcile their political perspective on this war with the reality they see on the battlefield? We'll touch on the political, big-picture issues in the epilogue, but first, the immediate and the personal.

To explore this, it might be helpful to first categorize these Rangers. One way to do this is to consider Rangers who are single and Rangers who are married or who may be in a committed relationship. First, the single Rangers. Most of these are junior enlisted Rangers. This is not to say that there are not senior NCOs who are single by way of having never married or, more commonly, by way of divorce. And there are certainly junior Rangers who are both young and have started a family. Yet perhaps half of the Rangers in the Regiment are junior and single—mostly privates, specialists, and a few corporals.

The mechanics of being a single Ranger are far simpler than for the married men. All single Rangers, up to and including E-5 sergeants, *must* live in the barracks if there is room for them there. At 1-75, they have the room in the barracks. And for you soldiers, sailors, marines, and airmen who are of my vintage, "barracks" today are not what you might envision. Every 1-75 Ranger has his own room with very adequate storage and closet space, a private shower, and a small, modern kitchen he shares with another Ranger. His vehicle, which is usually a pickup truck, an SUV, or a sports sedan, is conveniently parked in a lot adjacent to the barracks complex. Of course, a single Ranger may choose to live off post, but he will receive no housing allowance, which generally confines the single men to life in the barracks. But life *is* simple. A single Ranger, or any single enlisted soldier, is perhaps the most socialized of Americans. His housing, utilities, health care, meals (on post in the DFAC), military/work clothing, and extensive recreation and workout facilities are all part of his benefits package. There are modern laundry facilities in the barracks; only the seldom-worn work dress uniform or inspection-formation ACU needs the attention of the post cleaners. The company area and the squad cage that are his place of work are but a short walk from the barracks. A young private can blow his entire monthly pay in a single day and not have to worry about where he will sleep or where his next meal is coming from.

"It's a great life," Private First Class Garth Palco from Class 09-10 told me. "I'm kind of a neat freak, and so is the guy I share the kitchenette with, so it works fine. Sometimes I cook in, but mostly a bunch of us go out, especially on the weekends. I'm getting pretty creative with snacks in the microwave. And there's always the DFAC. It's a two-minute walk from the barracks, and if I don't want to eat there, I carry a meal back to my room. There's more storage here than I need, as I really don't have that many civilian clothes. I have my stereo, a laptop, and a small flat-screen TV. It's home inasmuch as we're here on post. I'm a little worried about my car when I go on deployment. I bought it new when I graduated from high school. I may cover it and leave it in the barrack's parking lot, or I may leave it with my parents—park it in their driveway."

"And what about the rest of your stuff—the stuff in your room when you deploy?"

"It's too easy. We just lock everything up and go. It's secure, and it'll be here when I get back. All I have to do is focus on the deployment, and right now, that's all I'm thinking about."

The married, more-senior Rangers live a very different life. "I remember when I was a private," a senior squad leader told me, "and it was a very simple life. Now I have a wife and three kids, and it's a lot different. But being a private and around the same guys all the time had its pluses and minuses. You really start to get tired of each other on deployment. I remember saying, 'When I get back, I'm not going to have anything to do with you guys.' But when you get back, you do. Who else are you going to hang out with? The only people who understand you are your Ranger buddies—the guys from your squad and platoon. So when you come back from end-of-tour block leave, there they are and there you are—in the barracks or in the squad cage. The first weekend back, you all pile into a van and head for the beach to drink beer and chase girls, or just hang out. It's like the first day of high school. Then we're all back out on the ranges, getting our work guns zeroed in and getting ready to go back to the fight."

"You miss those days?" I ask.

This gives him pause. "In a way and on a certain level, yes. But it was a point in time, and it's hard to compare the Ranger I was then and the Ranger I am now. When you're a private or even a gun-team leader and you're single, you have only yourself and your gun to get to the fight. It's just about you and your Ranger buddies. Now I have eight or ten Rangers to train up for combat. I have junior leaders that need my time and attention. They're all still my Ranger buddies, but the relationship is different. I have to worry about their training, their well-being, and their personal lives. If they're married, then their families are my concern as well. If one of them gets hurt or, God forbid, has a DUI, then I'm a man down and I may have to go to war with a fire team that's a man short. So yes, I miss the simplicity. Staying in shape, keeping up with my responsibilities, and training my Rangers is a full-time job and then some. It's a business that breeds a workaholic. And I still have to be a husband and father. When I'm at home, I think a lot about the job, and when I'm here [we're in the company area], I'm wondering when I can get off and get home to the family. If it weren't for the block-leave periods, none of us could stay married or get to know our kids."

I asked several of these veterans how they balance their leadership responsibilities and family duties.

"I have a good marriage," another squad leader told me, "but I confess it's had its moments. I'm like a lot of the guys who got married after a couple of rotations. Things went well during that first rotation—for me and my wife. That first homecoming was like a second honeymoon. Then there was the baby and another rotation—and another baby and another rotation. I think we just grew into it; it was about learning our roles. In some ways, I'm a guest in my home, a guy who has certain privileges and defined responsibilities. But I don't run the house. My wife runs the house, and she does it well. She's also the alpha parent, and my role at home is to support her."

"What about the next rotation—the next separation?"

"This one will be number eight. My enlistment's up next summer, and then we have a decision to make. I'd like to finish college and maybe look at an officer program. I like what I'm doing, but it's no longer just about me. There are a lot of guys in my situation who are staying in, so there's a good deal of competition for the E-7 [sergeant first class] slots. We'll take a look at it when I get back from this trip."

A veteran platoon sergeant put it this way: "I've been in the Army for thirteen years, and I'm headed for twenty—maybe more. This will be my thirteenth rotation. I've already had a tour at Regiment, so I'm here in battalion rotation for the duration. Like a lot of the married guys, my wife and I have settled into this life. She and the other wives talk a lot about what they'll do if their husbands ever come home every night, like for a whole year or so. We had a taste of that while I was on the regimental staff, and it was an adjustment. Now I'm back in overseas rotation, and we've settled into the home-again, gone-again routine. I know she's very glad to see me when I get home from deployment. I also know that about the end of the predeployment block-leave period, she's ready to have me out from underfoot. It's the kids that are the hardest. When they get older, they understand, but the younger ones just wonder where Dad is. Then when I get back, they wonder who this stranger is."

It seemed to me that both the single and married Rangers have had to, by necessity, evolve into the routine and demands of the combat deployment rotation. They've done this rotation by rotation, enlistment by enlistment. No one, it seemed, planned on the war lasting this long, nor the OPTEMPO being this active. Few looked beyond Iraq when that country was the focus of the conflict. When most veterans were new to the Regiment, and this now includes the current newcomers from RASP, they wanted to get on deployment before the war ended. They were worried the fighting would be over before they got there. Now the veterans of this veteran regiment have resigned themselves to a war without end. They've evolved to a life built around continuous combat rotation. But it does take its toll.

"My marriage lasted through three rotations," a fire-team leader told me. Like many of the veteran Rangers, they talk in terms of rotations, not years. "I was twenty and she was nineteen. Neither of us knew what we were in for; I guess neither of us handled the separations very well. I don't blame her for wanting out. I did, but I don't now. We're still friends; we have to be. We have a three-year-old daughter."

"Without the time away, do you think it might have been different?" I ask.

He gives me a quizzical smile. "I don't really know, but I doubt it. Some women can be Army wives and some can't. My leaving the Army might have changed things. Probably not. Now I'm just a Ranger fire-team leader when I'm on deployment and a part-time dad when I'm not. That's my focus, and I'm okay with that."

A company first sergeant tells me about the nine-lives concern. "Those of us who have been around a while have seen a lot of friends hurt and more than a few friends killed. Along about the sixth or eighth rotation, you start to wonder when your number might be up. It happens too often for you to kid yourself into thinking it can't happen to you. We're like cats with nine lives, but how many of those nine have you used as the combat rotations add up?"

Rangers, married or single, will make two key decisions about their service careers and their life as a Ranger in the Regiment. There are many variations to this, but this is the normal path that surfaced as I talked with these men. A young Ranger will typically make two combat rotations, go to Ranger School, get his Tab, and return to the fight for his third rotation, all during his first enlistment. By now he's a combat veteran, a Tabbed Ranger, and possibly a fire-team leader with three or four Rangers on his team for whom he's responsible. He may have just been promoted to E-5 sergeant. At this point in time, he knows this life, and he knows what's expected of him in garrison and in combat. He may say he's had enough and choose to leave the Regiment. At this juncture, our Ranger might look to an officer or aviation program, but most likely he will either stay in the Regiment or leave the Army. If he stays, he will re-up on another enlistement contract. Ahead of him is advancement to sergeant if he's not already one, another tour or more as a fire-team leader, then perhaps promotion to staff sergeant and squad leader—and more combat rotations.

This brings our Ranger to the second inflection point of his career, at about ten years of service. He's now a squad leader and a staff sergeant. If he signs another enlistment contract, he will do so looking for advancement to sergeant first class and to becoming a platoon sergeant. But the sluggish economy has caused a great many Rangers to think about the Army as a career, at least a twenty-year career, and the pay and benefits that go with putting in their twenty.

In making the decision to get out or to re-up, a war without end might seem as a *disincentive* for these Rangers to stay in uniform, but this is not always the case. These men are of a different breed. The challenge and "rush" of combat is a compelling one for them; it can be a narcotic. They may not do well without this periodic combat fix. For a good many others, it's an issue of patriotism. They will stay in the fight as long as their nation needs them. And there's the issue of professionalism; they take a great deal of pride in doing a difficult and dangerous job well.

Past the ten-year point and their third enlistment, a Ranger is usually in for the duration, which is to serve their twenty years. Close to or past the twenty-year mark, there may or may not be openings in the senior echelons of responsibility that go with being a master sergeant, a company first sergeant, or a sergeant major. The key career and leadership role in the Regiment for an enlisted Ranger, as has been mentioned earlier and often, is that of platoon sergeant. But for an Eleven Bravo infantryman, there are but fiftysome rifle-platoon-sergeant positions in the regiment. With a good many talented Ranger staff sergeants choosing to stay in uniform, that number may not be enough to absorb all that talent and all that combat experience at the squad-leader position. Later on, we'll address these issues of seniority and the retention of this unprecedented level of combat experience that is now present in the Ranger ranks.

As for the officers in the Regiment, nearly all of them are career Army officers. They were selected for the Regiment because they were proven leaders, and the regular Army will be glad to receive these officers back into the conventional ranks. For the Eleven Alpha platoon leaders, they may or may not return for another tour in the Regiment. A few will migrate to Army Special Forces for a career in unconventional warfare. But for most, their career and path to senior command will be with the regular Army, where most will continue to serve and excel. An Army career in-regiment is an enlisted man's career path. As one captain told me, "I always wanted to be in the Army, and I wanted to be a leader. So I became an officer. Had I known about the role and life of an NCO in the Regiment, I might have made a different decision." I heard that from more than one officer platoon leader.

In keeping with the selection and retention of senior Rangers is the selection and confirmation of leadership at the company, platoon, and squad level. It was my impression that leadership in the battalion, at least from what I saw at 1/75, is merit based and that combat leadership is carefully scrutinized. Time in grade and experience are factors, but combat leaders are selected for their proven ability to lead. I clearly recall Sergeant Tad Crosby's comments to the wives, parents, and families of Class 09-10 following their graduation. He told them, "I want you to know that in the Regiment, we put a great premium on leadership. Please know that the finest leaders in the United States Army will be leading and caring for your Rangers in the months ahead."

While I was with 1/75, there were leadership changes. Two platoon leaders were relieved of their responsibilities, as was one platoon sergeant. There were changes with the squad and fire-team leadership positions as well. It is rare, but company commanders have been relieved for inattention to duty or because there was simply a better option available to the senior battalion leadership. Would this be different, or has it been different, in times of peace? Probably. But this is war, and it was my perception that the quality of leaders, especially at the platoon and squad level, is carefully scrutinized. Personal or individual career issues take a backseat to having the best available talent in combat leadership positions. This is not civil service or education, where there is union protection or tenure that affords a measure of job security. Lives and mission success are on the line, and only the very best are chosen and allowed to lead.

In the 75th Ranger Regiment, job security is performance dependent and standards dependent. In nearly all branches of the Armed Forces, the relief, the reassignment, or the dismissal of service personnel is a procedural matter. Except for violations of the Uniform Code of Military Justice, there has to be warnings and counseling before a service member can be kicked out. The Ranger regiment is one of the few service units that has independent release authority. If a Ranger at whatever level is not performing up to standard, he can be summarily released from the regiment. It's the standards thing again. Each year, *several hundred* Rangers are sent packing. It's called Released for Standard, or RFSed. A Ranger may be RFSed for a single failing, like a drunk-driving incident, or for a series of minor infractions from insubordination to failing the RPFT to a poor attitude. I'm aware of Rangers who are given a second chance—probation, if you will—and moved from one company platoon to another, but bottom line, they have to perform to standard. Or they are made to leave. A Ranger who is Released for Standard or misconduct of a minor nature may be posted somewhere else in the Army. Serious conduct offenses can lead to Article 15 separation from the Army under less-than-honorable conditions.

Finally, a few parting comments about the young Rangers from RASP 1 Class 09-10. Regarding those from what I've come to think of as "my class," they are doing well and are well received by the veteran 1/75 Rangers. I cannot imagine it being different in the other battalions. They are still new to the game, so they are still learning their craft, but with each block of training—each iteration of a training lane—I watch them gain professional skill and confidence. And maturity. Some progress more quickly than others, and all are, to varying degrees, anxious about their first combat. It all comes down to doing what they've been trained to do, but doing it in combat—when the targets are human and the targets shoot back. Veteran Rangers say that it makes little difference; you train like you fight and fight like you train. The creativity and thought that go into Ranger training in battalion make it very close to the real thing. I think the new Rangers understand this, but they'll not totally believe it until they've been in a few firefights.

I have also watched these new 1/75 Rangers break out as individuals. The RASP process had a tendency to suppress personalities and promote introversion. Life in the battalion, and more specifically within their platoons and squads, while demanding and central, has allowed them to reemerge as individuals. They're people again; they occasionally have free time on the weekends. This newly reclaimed freedom is spent in the gym, biking, clubbing, reading, or just hanging out with their Ranger buddies. I've even noticed a few new tattoos. Some are quiet and serious, others gregarious and outgoing—as they were before they enlisted in the Army. To a man, they're proud and happy to be where they are. There's understandably a certain amount of satisfaction that comes from the restoration of freedoms that were denied them through basic training, airborne training, and RASP. They're also Rangers; they wear the Tan Beret. They are accepted into this brotherhood, even though they are still apprentice warriors. It's a new belonging, and that, too, is intoxicating. I hear a lot of "The guys in my squad are really great—the best," or "There's so much to learn, but everyone is so patient and helpful." The veteran Rangers extend this brotherhood to those in Class 09-10 so long as they work hard and perform to standard. The veterans also have a vested interest in these new men; they will soon trust their lives with these new Rangers in combat. When I chat with them during a training break or on the weekends, they're all variously excited about the prospect of deployment. Yet they are all aware and even sobered by what they see as their duty to measure up to the expectations of the veteran Rangers. The learning never stops, and these men know they must earn their Scroll every day.

Along with the release of the rigidity they've known in RASP and relative normalcy of garrison life, there descends a certain reality: They're in the Army. There is the difference between being a *student* soldier, as they have been during Basic Combat Training, OSUT, Airborne School, and RASP, and being a soldier. While in the student-soldier role, they've been focused on learning tasks and demonstrating proficiency. They've been tested, graded, and ranked; they've been focused on getting there rather than being there. Now they are there. They're still rookies, and they understand there's still much to learn, but they are Regimental Rangers—unblooded, but still Rangers. Yet, again, they are still in the Army. For most, this regimentation is still new and novel, and a part of the life they've chosen. For others, especially some of the older, more mature new Rangers, this means dealing with all those irritations and inconveniences that go with Army life, from the seemingly petty rules and regulations to having some corporal who may be five years your junior telling you what to do.

In April 2011, ten 1/75 Rangers from RASP Class 09-10 leave Hunter Army Airfield for predeployment block leave before going to war. Two with B-Co are already at war. All I spoke with are going home for block leave. All I spoke with have been well counseled by their squad and fire-team leaders about conduct on leave. The basic message: Stay in shape; spend time with your family; don't drink and drive. In short, your Ranger buddies need you back and ready for combat rotation. This is not about you, they are told; it's about your role in your fire team and about the job ahead. Block leave for them ends in early May, and in mid-May they will be airborne and headed for war.

While I finish this book, the Rangers of Class 09-10 are in the fight, returning from the fight, or preparing for the next fight—the next rotation. The killing of Osama bin Laden has changed little for them. Taliban insurgents and the remnants of al-Qaeda in Afghanistan are still being hunted, captured, and killed by Ranger assault teams. By the time this book is released, most will have come and gone to Afghanistan, and now proudly wear their battalion combat Scroll on their right shoulder. Those in Class 09-10 who went to 3/75 and immediately deployed are finishing their second combat rotation. Most of those few from 09-10 in 2/75 will have finished their first full tour. And the twelve in 1/75 are back in the battlespace on their second tour. The medics from Class 09-10 are in or just getting to the fight, but very soon they, too, will be combat veterans. All, in their own way and of their own accord, are a part of the 75th Ranger Regiment. It's been my singular honor to have shared a part of their journey.

THE WAY AHEAD

In my opinion, any future defense secretary who advises the president to again send a big American land army into Asia or into the Middle East or into Africa should 'have his head examined,' as General (Douglas) MacArthur so delicately put in." This statement was part of an address given by former Secretary of Defense Robert Gates to the Corps of Cadets at West Point on February 25, 2011. He went on to tell these future Army officers that while their service would be valued and needed, the prospects for their leading soldiers in continuous combat with the support of an escalating military budget would most certainly not be as it had been for previous West Point graduates. Secretary Gates made those remarks well before our involvement in Libya and the attendant force commitment and expense of that military action.

While our SOF ground components will in all probability be the last forces to disengage from direct combat in Afghanistan, it would seem that in the not too distant future, our Ranger Regiment will no longer have rifle-squad leaders with eight continuous combat rotations or platoon sergeants with a dozen or more combat deployments. They may be the last out the door in the active theaters and the first in the door during some future conflict/crisis, but I doubt that the sustained and intense OPTEMPO the Regiment has known for the last decade will continue. This Regiment could and would continue in this manner if asked to do so, but the mood of the country is shifting away from these foreign military adventures. With the killing of Osama bin Laden, there's also a mood for closure in these campaigns. And the cost to a standing military force so deployed is prohibitive. The Rangers from Class 09-10 will probably not have to endure a war without end that was the operational life of their platoon sergeants and company first sergeants. That said, what's next for our military, our ground-combat forces, and this fine Ranger Regiment?

The Iraq and Afghan campaigns constitute the first long war for our all-volunteer military. Our withdrawal from those conflicts will be the first sustained combat to relative peacetime transition for this force. With this transition, what will be the character and posture of this postconflict force? How will the force internalize these changes? If Vietnam is to serve as an example, and notwithstanding our national budget deficits, there is sure to be substantial cuts in military spending. Given the character of modern war and what many see as a cost-benefit approach, there may be a focus on technology and a shift away from personnel-intensive programs—more drones and fewer troops. Generally speaking, Iraq and Afghanistan have been both insurgent and counterinsurgent conflicts. That is to say, we have opposed existing power bases during the invasion phase and supported existing power bases in the occupation phase. Insurgency warfare is lengthy, personnel intensive, and expensive. It involves nation-building and opposition to low-tech but zealous insurgent forces. And it's hard business. Just as antibiotics have led to the evolution of some virulent and resistant strains of disease, our advancing military technology has spawned some very insidious, relentless, and capable enemies. Al-Qaeda, the Taliban, and related extremist splinter groups that we might lump together under the heading of terrorists are considerably better than they were a decade ago. They've had to be to survive. I think it's safe to assume they will still be around after we withdraw from Iraq and Afghanistan. These enemies could well reinfect the nations we've tried to help or contaminate others.

In a perfect world, even one not so fiscally constrained, it would be nice to tailor the force to meet the threat. But the world is imperfect. There are political powers that will fight for the defense dollars in their districts and states, often irrespective of the threat. Their rationale will be their perception of national security requirements, but it's really more about local jobs and local economies. Within the armed forces, there will continue to be a competition for defense dollars: The Navy will want ships and submarines; the Air Force, stealth fighters and bombers; and the Army, its combat divisions. The U.S. Special Operations Command will want to maintain and support its SEALs, Special Forces, SOF Marines, special operations aviators, and Rangers. There are competing political and parochial interests at work here. As one might imagine, I have an admitted SOF bias. Yet I believe the last decade of fighting should buy our SOF components a good seat at the table for the budgetary food fights ahead. Quite often, political and interservice wrangling produces deadlocks that are resolved by across-the-board cuts. I'd prefer not to see this. It will inevitably shortchange our SOF components, those who arguably have carried more than their share of the load since 9/11 and will most likely be asked to do more of the same in the future.

Looking past the Iraq and Afghanistan campaigns, there will probably be no shortage of need for American military muscle. The attack on Muammar Gadhafi's forces in Libya was a nonstarter without our involvement. Furthermore, those Libyans who opposed Gadhafi didn't cry, "Where's the coalition?" They cried, "Where are the Americans?" We may have led from behind, but were it not for American military technology, staff experience, and weaponry, Gadhafi would still be in power. If all the capability and experience gained by our armed forces in the last ten years could be carried into the future, it would certainly give our policy makers a freer hand. A great many of us would like to think there will be political constraints and better judgment in the future use of force, but if the past two decades are a guide, that may not be the case. Even with budgetary constraints, the services may be asked to do more with less. Yet there will come a time when the perceived need simply exceeds our force-projection capabilities.

The service chiefs—Army, Navy, Air Force, and Marine Corps— will make their funding appeals to Congress, as will those representatives from the Coast Guard and Homeland Security. So will the U.S. Special Operations Command. The standing components of the Special Operations Command can and will make strong arguments for their allotment of SOF funding, as will the Joint Special Operations Command in support of its now-well-publicized special mission units. All have SOF responsibilities and need funding to carry out those duties and taskings. So decisions will have to be made within SOF as to who gets the money and how much. With the possible exception of the JSOC special mission units, I can think of no SOF component that has a stronger claim to future military utility, and future funding, than the 75th Ranger Regiment.

Our special operations forces are diverse and flexible. They all have specific roles in which they excel, and they are an agile and adaptive force as well. Yet only the Rangers are light infantry. In addition to the squad- and platoon-sized small-unit assault tactics they have perfected in Iraq and Afghanistan, they are the only SOF component capable of company-, battalion-, and, if needed, multiple-battalion-sized operations. One might offer that an airborne company/battalion assault is within the capacity of our conventional airborne components, but no one does it better than the 75th Rangers. I believe that a reliable, capable, flexible, and rapidly deployable direct-action-raid-force capability will be an option that future policy makers will want and need. It's also a deterrent to those who may want to seize an American embassy or set up a terrorist training camp next to a hospital and presume *The Americans won't come; it's too far,* or *It's too risky for an air strike,* or *They can't get here that quickly.*

I think all of us want American military power to be used more judiciously than it has been in the past. But the future is very uncertain. Robert Gates, the former secretary of defense, who I think rendered yeomanlike service to his nation and two administrations, made this candid admission during the Libyan crisis: "I think we should be alert to the fact that outcomes are not predetermined, and that it's not necessarily the case that everything has a happy ending. We are in dark territory and nobody knows what the outcome will be." Past the political and the parochial that will attend any future force restructuring, we want our future policy makers to choose carefully in the use of American military might. Yet when it comes to military intervention, we want them to have the best tools at hand to exercise those choices. So we simply *must* fund and use our military more wisely in the future than we have in the past.

So what might be ahead for the 75th Ranger Regiment? If not the intermittent years of peacetime stand-down they knew in the 1980s and 1990s, then certainly a period of reduced OPTEMPO. There may well be an end to the combat rotations as these Rangers have come to know them. Overseas time could be a few weeks, engaged in military exercises with old Cold War allies or new regional partners. A year, perhaps two or three, may go by with Rangers never firing a shot in anger. Prior to 9/11, there were regimental Rangers cooling their heels in garrison, wondering if their number would ever be called for real. Now there's every prospect of returning to those days. Few Rangers in the Regiment remember what it was like before 9/11; few of them have ever known service without war. Going from current deployment schedules to a noncombat rotation, with continuous garrison-based training and annual joint special operations exercises, will be quite an adjustment. In the 1990s, the 75th Ranger Regiment trained for war and was ready when war came. But it has not trained for peace. This may not require training per se, but it will need accommodation.

The end of active-combat rotations is sure to be a dual-edged sword. The good news is an end to long family separations, the ongoing casualties, and the wear and tear on the individual Rangers. Professionally, it will allow the Regiment to refocus on their role as an on-call, rapid-response raiding force. It was my impression during the multilateral airborne training and company live-fire exercises that the platoon sergeants and squad leaders did all that they could to relate this training to small-unit tactics and the real-world requirements of their upcoming deployment. There will come a time when the MLATs and LFXs will be conducted with a different focus and attention to mission expectation. On the other edge of this sword are the effects of *not* being in continuous combat. Currently, the level of combat experience in the Regiment has never been higher— as in never in the active history of the Regiment. This will degrade over time, as will the precision with which these current Rangers conduct platoon-centric assault in support of counterinsurgency operations. Perhaps the greatest loss in capability is that individual, situational awareness of an honest-to-goodness firefight, at night, with opposition that shoots back. That is very hard to replicate in training. There will simply be fewer Rangers who have that kind of muscle memory or instinctively know what to do when the bullets are flying, whether it's a reaction to contact or fire and movement. There are many other individual skills that can't help but suffer, from the Ranger medics who have been up to their elbows in human blood saving real lives to the Ranger dog/dog-handler teams chasing enemy squirters as they break from a compound containment to the JTACs bringing air-delivered ordnance in close but not too close. While the combat leadership experience at the NCO level will dissolve slowly over time, it will all but evaporate for the officer platoon leaders. The conventional units will in all probability precede the withdrawal of SOF from the active theaters. The loss of these fine Infantry Branch first lieutenants and captains with combat experience will be felt immediately.

It will be necessary for the leadership, from the individual squad leaders up through the Regimental Commander and Command Sergeant Major, to carefully and professionally orchestrate this transition. They are the ones who must help the veteran Rangers understand that the annual MLAT or some joint special operations training exercise with the Egyptians is now as important as their last combat engagement in Helmond Province. They must also ensure that the new Rangers stay focused and learn their trade *without* the prospect of immediate and certain combat. Leadership, especially at the platoon NCO level, will be critical in this transition. If the Ranger veterans transition well and they accept the new training paradigms and mission requirements, then the Regiment will be fine. They will move from a serious in-the-fight force to a serious on-call force. It's my guess that the professionalism and adherence-to-standard mentality of the Regiment will win the day. Yet it's a dramatic change that has to be carefully managed.

It's been my experience that few combat units, and that includes our ground-combat units across the board, are immune from what I call the Been-There-Done-That Syndrome. This is where a warrior, after a period of continuous combat, comes to believe in and thrive on an elevated self-importance simply because he's been in the fight. He may have even acquitted himself well in combat. This can lead to issues when there is no fight, and the prospects of the next fight are uncertain. For some, combat is a good repository for aggression.

For those who drink too much in garrison, a deployment to Iraq or Afghanistan is a chance to dry out. And there are those few who are simply unsuited for civilian life or even Army life without the adrenaline high of a firefight. The latitude that may have been afforded these soldiers, because they are good in combat, may make them unsuitable for soldiering in garrison. This is but another leadership challenge. It's difficult for me to imagine the Regiment not dealing with this on some level, but I also cannot see it becoming an issue. Regimental Rangers have been too well schooled in standards and professional attention to duty for the Been-There-Done-That Syndrome to gain much traction.

I believe these issues of transition are critical to the future of the Regiment. I also have few concerns that the Regiment will make this transition well. That certainty is based on the leadership and professional attention to duty I witnessed while in the company of platoon sergeants like Sergeant First Class Jon Jackson and Sergeant First Class Seth Kline and Staff Sergeant Del Prather. These accomplished leaders will seamlessly apply their skill and experience to the new requirements—the new mission sets. They will see that the Ranger combat veterans continue to perform to standard and exceed standard. They will also serve as a lens to focus these veterans on the job ahead, and to remember the past but not to live in it. They will help the new Rangers understand what is standard, and that both they *and* that standard are the future of the Regiment. Nothing less is acceptable for this breed of noncommissioned officer.

Finally, and for a moment, let's look if we can into the heart of a Ranger. In keeping with the text of *Sua Sponte*, what do the SOF boots on the ground think about the war they've been asked to fight this past decade and what they may be asked to do in the future? And, by extension, how do America's special operators see their past and future service? It's chancy business for me to represent the other SOF components, but I do have a good sampling of what the Rangers of the 75th Ranger Regiment think about this. It's my guess that the attitudes of the SEALs, the Green Berets, the SOF Marines, the SOF aircrews, and the SOF combatant-boat crews are not dissimilar.

It is no easy thing to represent the thinking and opinions of a group of individuals, even a group as homogenous as the 75th Ranger Regiment. A good many young Rangers I speak with have interests and lives, apart from their regimental duties, that are not unlike their twentysomething civilian contemporaries. Some follow politics and national security affairs closely, others not at all. Yet when it comes to their professional and service life, they are all about duty. They care about their Ranger buddies, their squad, their platoon, their battalion, and their regiment, pretty much in that order. They care about their brotherhood and their ethos—as warriors and specifically as American Ranger warriors. They are not above the normal grumbling in ranks about the decisions and directives from higher, but they tend to think they are well led at the tactical level. And they are content to leave theater strategy to the politicians and generals. It's not that they don't care; they just have other priorities. "Our job," one fire-team leader told me, "is to professionally get on target, bring the pain to those who deserve it, protect those from harm who deserve our protection, and get off target as quickly as possible. We do this well because it's the focus of our battle drill and our operational lives. We do other things, but that is job one. Not much else really matters."

I believe the Rangers of the 75th are able to sustain these multiple combat deployments for the simple reason that they look inward—as a culture and as a warrior class. They seem largely indifferent to the locals and noncombatants, most recently Afghan noncombatants, but keep in mind that they are not counterinsurgency warriors. They are not in the hearts-and-minds business; they are an assault force. They have a smoldering antipathy for the Taliban, both as a tactical adversary and for the callous and brutal treatment they've seen in how they treat other Afghans. They feel that their side is "good" and those they oppose are "evil," or at least "bad." But these are side issues when compared to the loyalty these men have for one another and their Regiment, and what they see as their patriotic duty. Their work does not allow for shades of gray, or that any grayness must be personally compartmented. These warriors engage in mortal combat. That they can do it well and in the company of their Ranger brothers is enough. There are those who may suggest there should be more—some higher belief in a values-driven agenda or in making a difference in the world. That's not what I observed. They do what they do for the guy next to them and for their brotherhood. Taking into account current Greatest Generation texts to the contrary, I suspect it was little different for the soldiers who fought their way across Europe and across the Pacific in what many see as our last good war. I know it was the same for the SEALs in my platoon in Vietnam. We had some notion that we were on the right side of things and of some nobility in our cause, but it was secondary to killing Vietcong and getting everyone home in one piece. Regarding my assessment of these Rangers, some may find this businesslike approach to war callous or shallow or even self-serving. I find it worthy, refreshing, and honest. Above all, it's professional, which is perhaps the best a wealthy nation can expect when they exempt their citizens from a military draft and seek paid volunteers to do their fighting.

In closing, I would recommend that the parent commands of the 75th Ranger Regiment, the U.S. Special Operations Command, and the U.S. Army Special Operations Command do all in their power to preserve and husband the capability and experience of this unique SOF component. These are gifted soldiers who have any number of options outside the military—economic conditions aside. So far, the professional pay and reenlistment incentives afforded the Regiment have not kept pace with other SOF components. The rank structures and manning allowances that permit higher rates of promotion within the Regiment need to be addressed, as they have for the SEALs and the Green Berets. It's the only certain way to retain this rare level of NCO talent and special warrior ethos that only they can pass along to the new Rangers of this fine Regiment.

A LOOK BACK

RANGER ASSESSMENT AND SELECTION PROGRAM,
LEVEL ONE, CLASS 09-10–AN OVERVIEW AND A
PERSONAL NOTE FROM THE AUTHOR

Class Numbers:

> Soldiers originally assigned to RASP 1, Class 09-10 as of
> 0800, September, 6, 2010: 159

> Soldiers in Class 09-10 on transfer from Holdover to Phase
> One on September 9: 143

> In-Service Soldiers reporting late for Class 09-10: 4

> Official "Class-up" number for RASP 1, Phase One for
> Class 09-10: 147

> Soldiers in Class 09-10 who began the week of Cole Range
> training, September 20: 91

Soldiers in Class 09-10 the Monday following Cole Range training, September 27: 52

Soldiers in Class 09-10 who successfully completed Phase One training: 44

Rollback Soldiers joining Class 09-10 for Phase Two: 4

Soldiers in Class 09-10 who began Phase Two training: 48

Solders graduating with RASP 1, Class 09-10 on November 5, 2010: 39

Class Profiles:
During the course of the Class 09-10's RASP training, I spent a few moments with selected individual Ranger trainees. This is the disposition of those soldiers at the time this work went to press:

PVT Bill Mann. Private Bill Mann graduated with RASP 1 Class 01-11. He has completed one combat rotation with the 1st Ranger Battalion and is now on his second rotation.

PVT Jeffery Jennings. Due to medical complications, Private Jeffery Jennings was unable to complete RASP I and is now serving in another unit of the U.S. Army.

SGT Mark Ikenboch. Sergeant Mark Ikenboch has completed two combat rotations with the 3rd Ranger Battalion and is preparing for his third rotation on this enlistment.

PFC Salvador Santos. Private First Class Salvador Santos was unable to complete RASP 1 and has returned to civilian life.

PFC Brendan O'Connor. Private First Class Brendan O'Connor is on his first combat rotation with the 1st Ranger Battalion.

PFC Garth Palco. Private First Class Garth Palco has completed one combat rotation with the 1st Ranger Battalion and is now on his second rotation.

PFC John Zeaman. Private First Class John Zeaman completed his training as a Special Operations Combat Medic and is assigned to the Ranger Special Troops Battalion. He just completed his first combat rotation.

PFC Eldon Northridge. Private First Class Eldon Northridge graduated with RASP I Class 02-11. Following his completion of the Special Operations Combat Medic course, he is assigned to the 1st Ranger Battalion and on his first combat rotation.

SPC Jon Edson. Specialist Jon Edson completed one combat rotation with the 3rd Ranger Battalion and is preparing for his second.

PVT Kevin Seiple. Private Kevin Seiple is assigned to the 1st Ranger Battalion and is preparing for his second combat rotation. He recently completed Ranger School and is a Tabbed Ranger.

PFC Alex Hammond. Private First Class Alex Hammond has completed two combat rotations with the 2nd Ranger Battalion and is preparing for this third.

SPC James Neuman. Specialist James Neuman completed one combat rotation with the 1st Ranger Battalion and is on his second.

At this point in time, none of the Rangers from Class 09-10 has been reported as wounded in action or killed in action.

A Personal Note from the Author

Since my time with the 75th Ranger Regiment and the 1st Ranger Battalion, much has happened. We tracked down Osama bin Laden and killed him. We have removed our combat troops from Iraq. In Afghanistan, we have reduced troop levels with deployed military personnel dipping well below the 100,000 level. Yet for the 75th Rangers, they remain in combat rotation with a battalion-plus continuously committed to the fight. That may change at some future date, but not in the immediate future. For the Rangers of the 75th, it's still about the next combat rotation; it's still a war without end. But there is one Ranger who will not be returning to the fight. Sergeant First Class Kristoffer B. Domeij will not be with the 2nd Ranger Battalion on their next combat rotation.

On October, 22, 2011, Sergeant Domeij was killed in action in Kandahar, Afghanistan. Kris Domeij was twenty-nine years old, and on his *fourteenth combat rotation*. Sergeant Domeij joined the Army just before 9/11, entered the Regiment after basic training and airborne school, and was on continuous combat rotation for more than a decade. He is survived by his wife and two daughters. Other than the accolades from his battalion leaders and his brother Rangers, we know little about this Ranger—this warrior patriot; Sergeant Domeij left instructions with his family and his command that should he fall in battle, he wanted no publicity or notoriety. Indeed, he was the essence of the quiet professional.

In this book I've tried to focus on the assessment, selection, training, and deployment of Rangers in the 75th Ranger Regiment. I've also made it a point to sidestep political issues and issues that may be parochial within our military or our Special Operations Forces. And admittedly, I've grown close to these fine soldiers. Yet, I would be remiss if I did not at least make this observation: Our country and our political leaders had better make damn sure that there are *serious* matters of national security and national interest at stake for us to send one of our warriors back on their fourteenth combat rotation. Or, for that matter, even their first.

In deference to Sergeant Domeij's wishes, I'll say no more about him personally. Yet his life, his service, and yes, his death cry out for some acknowledgment of his passing. Does this nation realize how well they were served by this fine Ranger? By his brother Rangers, now and in the future? Do any of us for that matter? So in memory of Sergeant Kris Domeij and the many fallen of the 75th Ranger Regiment, I'm asking you to visit this website: http://www.rangers scholarshipfund.org/. This is the site for the Ranger Scholarship Fund, a 503(c)(3) nonprofit established to support the education of, among others, the children of those Rangers who died for their country. Support this organization; it's the least we can do for all they have done, and continue to do, for all of us.

INDEX